D1439116

MIKE SUMMERBEE

THE AUTOBIOGRAPHY

MIKE SUMMERBEE

THE AUTOBIOGRAPHY

C

Century · London

Published by Century 2008

4 6 8 10 9 7 5 3

First published in Great Britain in 2008 by
Century
Random House, 20 Vauxhall Bridge Road,
London SW1V 2SA
www.randomhouse.co.uk

Addresses for companies within The Random House Group Limited can be
found at:
www.randomhouse.co.uk

The Random House Group Limited Reg. No. 954009
A CIP catalogue record for this book is available from the British Library

ISBN 9781846054938

The Random House Group Limited supports The Forest Stewardship Council
(FSC), the leading international forest certification organisation. All our titles
that are printed on Greenpeace approved FSC certified paper carry the FSC
logo. Our paper procurement policy can be found at
www.rbooks.co.uk/environment

Mixed Sources
Product group from well-managed
forests and other controlled sources
www.fsc.org Cert no. TT-COC-2139
© 1996 Forest Stewardship Council
FSC

Typeset by SX Composing DTP, Rayleigh, Essex
Printed and bound in Great Britain by
Clays Ltd, St Ives PLC

'The credit belongs to the man who is actually in the arena, whose face is marred by dust and sweat and blood, who strives valiantly, who errs and comes up short again and again, because there is no effort without error or shortcoming, but who knows the great enthusiasms, the great devotions, who spends himself for a worthy cause; who, at the best, knows, in the end, the triumph of high achievement, and who, at the worst, if he fails, at least he fails while daring greatly, so that his place shall never be with those cold and timid souls who knew neither victory nor defeat.'

Theodore Roosevelt

'To my wife, Christine Elizabeth Summerbee.
"It started with a kiss . . ."'

ACKNOWLEDGEMENTS

Thanks to Jim for his patience and understanding of my life and all the ways he has helped in the writing of this book.

Thanks to my children, Nicholas and Rachel, and thanks also to my grandchildren: Harley, Samuel, Jessica, Leah and Millie.

Thanks also to the Roman Way Hotel in Cannock, and especially to Gemma Park for looking after us so well.

CONTENTS

1

THE BEST DAY OF MY LIFE

The crowd were shaking their fists at us in the streets as we sped through every red traffic light in Glasgow, and the closer we came to Hampden Park the more hostile they were and the more intense my exhilaration became. I loved the way the police motorcycle outriders took us racing through the city, and I was almost overwhelmed by the fact that here I was sitting next to Bobby Moore on the England team bus and on the way to make my international debut. Then the silence was broken by the voice of Sir Alf Ramsey. 'Look at them Scottish barrrrstards!' he said, and I had a massive rush of adrenalin such as I'd never known before and never will again.

It was the moment it sank in that I was going to play for my country, to play centre forward for the reigning world champions – and I thought it must be how Sir Edmund Hilary and Sherpa Tenzing felt when they had conquered Mount Everest and were standing on top of the world.

It was the best day of my life.

To tell the truth, the match against Scotland went so quickly it more or less passed me by. I can barely recollect any of the action on the field. What I do remember so vividly is the build-up to the game – sitting on the team bus and thinking that it was an amazing decision by Sir Alf to throw an untried youngster like me into such a game in preference to great strikers like World Cup-winner Roger Hunt and the incomparable Jimmy Greaves. I thought it was astonishing in itself, and even more so when you knew that this classic old rivalry was also doubling up as a qualifying group showdown to reach the quarter-finals of the 1968 European Nations Cup.

Yet Sir Alf had done it – and although I never had the natural self-belief of many other footballers, I knew that day I must be a reasonable player. You had to be if the manager of the world champions picked you. He didn't give out cheap caps.

I remember the great thrill, as well, of walking into the dressing room and seeing the pristine white No. 9 shirt waiting for me on the peg, three lions on the chest. I could hardly believe it was mine. The other thing I noticed immediately was a huge stack of telegrams on the wooden bench directly below it. There were so many of them and I read through them greedily. They were from people like Joe Mercer and Malcolm Allison, who had created my fabulous club team at Manchester City; from Francis Lee and Colin Bell, the other two members of our famous City trio; from Tommy Lawton and Stan Mortensen, two of the greatest England centre forwards; from Stan Ogden of *Coronation Street*; from my youthful pal at my first professional club, Ernie Hunt; and from Cecil Green, the director of Swindon Town who had spotted me playing for the Baker Street YMCA team in Cheltenham and given me the lucky break I needed to make a life in football.

All the telegrams meant so much to me. They were a symbol of the fact that what I had achieved had also given pleasure to so many other people. Football is nothing without fun and friendship, in my view, and the telegrams were very important. I wasn't married then, my family weren't at the game, so really I was on my own. But the telegrams suggested I wasn't. There they were, piled up below my No. 9 shirt, and I still have them at home in a scrapbook. There was a bit of banter from the other players in the England team, all the world champions, and I did feel a bit embarrassed as they remarked, 'We never get any of them, do we?' But it reminded them of when they had played their first match and the messages had been piled high for them, too. They knew exactly what I was feeling.

Another telegram was from George Best, my closest friend in those days in the 1960s in Manchester when life overflowed with fun: 'I SUPPOSE I CAN'T SPEAK TO YOU NOW. GOOD LUCK. GEORGE' it read. I was delighted, and I remembered how the pair of us had gone together to watch the World Cup Final at Wembley on 30 July 1966, to see the glory of Gordon Banks and Martin Peters and Geoff Hurst and all the other heroes I was now about to play alongside. George had driven us down from the North in his flash white Jaguar and had been stopped for speeding on what was then the new M1 motorway. The policeman booked the most famous footballer in the land without showing the faintest glimmer of recognition. I'm sure he knew, but he was playing it straight. It was probably the most anonymous day of George's life. The crowd at Wembley wouldn't have recognised me, but even George was left alone, both at the game and when we went into London that evening to a club in Shaftesbury Avenue.

George was in a different world from me. He was an established star, and it's funny to think that I was watching the World Cup Final with the man who was probably the best player in the world at the time. We were sat down at ground level by the halfway line on the opposite side to the Royal Box, and my thoughts during the match were not only that I was not good enough to be an England player, but also how difficult the game was, full stop. I was also deeply envious of Alan Ball and the others, of course, because every footballer wants to play for his country.

We were fully into the match as fans, jumping up and down with the rest of the crowd. George never got to a World Cup tournament, so you could imagine what was going through his mind. It should have been *the* stage for him. It would have been wonderful to see George against the Brazilians, for example. I would think there was more than a little envy on his part that day. We'd both have loved to have been a part of it. It was bedlam after the final whistle, and the players came round near us with the trophy and Nobby Stiles was dancing that jig.

They wouldn't have seen us. I was just another face in the crowd admiring their talent and dedication. They'd climbed to the very top.

Watching it spurred me on, however. I wanted to do what they'd done – and the feeling I had when I made my debut for England was that my dedication had enabled me to reach the summit of football.

George was also there the day I was selected for the England squad. What did he do? He took me for a champagne lunch at a pub on the Oxford Road in Manchester, of course – along with Frank Clough, one of the top sportswriters of the time. I was shocked to have been called up, but George said, 'No, you deserve it, you're playing well.'

When I joined up with England they roomed me with Bobby Moore. It was a good move, not only because it settled my nerves but because Bobby and I had been pals for a number of years since we'd met at a pre-season friendly when Swindon played West Ham. I was only sixteen but pushing for a first-team place, while Bobby was eighteen and already making a name for himself. You could sense his aura even then. We got beat 2-0 at an empty Upton Park and afterwards Bobby came into our dressing room for a chat. We started talking and just seemed to gel, and we kept in contact and over the years became very close friends. Sir Alf probably knew to put us together, and it certainly helped me.

On the day before the Scotland game Sir Alf had pulled me to one side after training and said, in that clipped way of his, 'Michael, congratulations. I have selected you to play against Scotland. Good luck.' I kept a straight face, but I already knew I was in the side because Bobby Moore had told me the night before. 'Look surprised when Alf tells you,' said Bobby, and I just about managed it.

Sir Alf was wonderful before the kick-off, talking quietly in the dressing room and boosting my morale. The other players were great, too. But nothing anyone says can prepare you for the wall of noise as you stride out on to the pitch at Hampden Park when Scotland play England. You can't hear anything from the dressing room, and that only makes the effect even more dramatic. I remember looking at the great bank of fans on the Hampden terraces and thinking that the faces of the spectators seemed to go all the way up to the clouds. The sound of 134,000 people was phenomenal. I also remember how the fans near the tunnel threw cups full of piss at me and the rest of the England team. A couple of them struck me on the shoulder. I'll never forget that.

It was a bitterly cold day and when we lined up for the national anthems Princess Alexandra came out to meet us. She was wearing a full-length mink coat, and she stopped in front of me and said, 'Is this your first game?' Somebody had kindly informed her. I told her it was my debut and she wished me well.

But I wasn't thinking about the match. As the princess stepped away I looked up to the sky and thought about my late father, George Summerbee, who'd been a professional footballer himself but had been treated very badly by the game. I hoped he was looking down on me from the heavens, and the one thing on my mind then amid the Hampden din was the first day I'd ever played a representative football match – for the Cheltenham Boys' team against Stroud Boys when I was twelve.

That match was at Whaddon Road, the home of Cheltenham Town, where my father had been the manager for a few years in the early 1950s and where I had spent many happy hours as a young child helping to paint the stands and sell programmes on match days. Playing for the town boys was a big thing, a real step up. It was a similar feeling to being picked for England. It was so exciting. A letter had been sent to my school and it went home to the house, so my father knew that I'd been picked and he was pleased. He'd never seen me play a football match in my young life – not once, not even down on the Rec in our endless kickabouts. Why not? It was partly, I suppose, because he'd been so busy working in the game, a player at Preston, Chester and Barrow. I think some of it was also due to the fact that my elder brother John was the apple of his eye and he hadn't had much time for me. There was also the fact he was seriously ill towards the end of his life with Addison's disease.

The doctors had sent him to stay with his brother in Bournemouth for a spell of convalescence by the sea, but I knew he was due home for the day of my game and I was desperate for him to see me play for Cheltenham Boys. I kept looking for him throughout the match. It was important to me because football was the one thing I was good at. They'd put me in a special class for children with learning difficulties, and I was always doing things wrong. I was late learning to ride a bike and I couldn't tie my shoelaces. I wanted to prove something to my dad that day. This was my opportunity. I knew he was coming back but I didn't know how gravely ill he was, or how depressed he was because of his hard times in football.

I kept looking and looking, but I never saw him. He didn't turn up. We won the game and I played pretty well. I went home, and in the early hours my mother left the house to see my father who'd had to halt his journey at Cirencester because he was too ill to carry on travelling. Only later did I find out that he'd started to come back because he knew he was dying. My brother and I went back to sleep and in the morning my mother told us that Dad had died. The opportunity of him seeing me play had gone.

What I wanted more than anything in my life was for him to watch me in a game and say, 'Yes, son, you've got a chance.' That never happened. It was a major factor in my life. I would have loved him to see me in the early days, all the progress I was making. The day never came. When I was picked for Swindon's first team at the age of seventeen, he never saw it. When I was transferred to Manchester City for £35,000 and played in the big stadiums, he never saw it. When I wore the white shirt of

England, with all the emotions involved, he never saw it. And when I won things, the League title and the FA Cup, he never saw it. I still shed tears to this day when I think of it.

We rarely even talked about football together. The only time I sat with him at home to watch a match was when the family bought a television especially for the 1953 FA Cup Final – the Matthews final – and the Coronation. It was a beautiful day and we drew the curtains and watched the great comeback by Blackpool to beat Bolton 4-3. Dad once took me to a live game, to watch Kidderminster Harriers when he was scouting for Bristol City and they were thinking of signing somebody. There was a particular centre forward playing and I said to my father, 'He's like a donkey.' It was Gerry Hitchens, who went on to play for Aston Villa and Inter Milan and for England in the 1962 World Cup quarter-finals. I was never taken again.

What I didn't know, and hardly even sensed as a young boy, was the great sadness of my father's life. He was a very good player, a robust and clever wing half, but he spent eleven years at Preston North End hardly being picked for the first team and was never given a proper chance or allowed to try his luck somewhere else while he was in his prime. There were some fine players at Preston then, and for a time Bill Shankly was the first choice wing half. Even when Preston reached the 1938 FA Cup Final my father was only twelfth man. When I went to Deepdale for Sir Tom Finney's testimonial I looked at all the photographs from that Cup Final on the walls, and my father's face was on none of the pictures taken that day. Not a single one. My dad was always on the verge of making it in professional football but it didn't happen. There were happier times when he became manager of Cheltenham after his playing days had finished, but even there it ended brutally with him being pushed out as his health declined.

By the time he died football had done nothing for my father. I think he was a man who was shattered by the way the game treated him. Football has made my life – but it broke Dad's heart. Yet what happened to him made me all the more determined to be successful. I put everything I had into playing football.

Would my father have wanted me to be a professional footballer? I've often asked myself the question, and the answer is: I don't think he would have been too keen. But what happened to him really drove me on throughout my career. It gave me an inner strength and I told myself that what had happened to him wasn't going to happen to me – and I could not have been more proud standing there in the England line-up alongside all the world champions as the national anthems sounded out at Hampden Park on that freezing Saturday afternoon in February and I looked up to the sky and thought, 'I hope you're watching now, Dad.'

Moments later the match kicked off and the noise was deafening. The Hampden Roar they called it, and what a coup it would have been for the Scots to knock England out of the European Nations Cup. They had already won 3-2 at Wembley in that qualifying group the previous April, but the other results had all been in our favour. A draw was enough for us. It was an awe-inspiring occasion and I didn't want to let anyone down. For a few moments I did think, 'What am I doing in this company, what am I doing here?' But I wasn't afraid of crowds or of playing, and the hostile atmosphere held no terrors for me.

The snowy weather had made it a difficult surface. The ground was very hard underneath but it had started to melt and there was a layer of mud on the top. The first thing was to get a good touch on the ball, control it, and get it back to a team-mate. I did that all right. After that I didn't get too much of the ball, although there were plenty of kicks from Ronnie McKinnon and Billy McNeill, the Scotland centre half who'd captained Celtic to their European Cup glory in May 1967. The Scots were tough defenders, and they didn't take any prisoners, but they also played the game as it should be played. Anyway, I always performed better when people were kicking me. Against West Ham, where they didn't, I always struggled.

As a professional footballer you always puff your chest out and try to give the impression on the field that you're full of confidence. And that's what people seem to remember most about my career in the game – the showmanship, the bravado and the tricks I used to pull, like the day against Burnley when someone threw a paper cup at me as I was about to take a corner. I picked it up and balanced it on the ball. Then I took a couple of steps back, sent over the cross and nonchalantly caught the cup as it flew up in the air. It was a spontaneous thing, for a bit of fun. And we nearly scored from the cross, too.

When you get picked for your country, though, it's serious. I loved the banter with the crowd in club games with Manchester City, but this was different. I suddenly realised I was a small fish in a great big pool of players. I always felt at the centre of the action in the First Division, but this match was passing by in a flash and there seemed to be nothing I could do about it. The other players weren't attuned to my game like club colleagues were, and I wasn't in tune with them.

I only wish I could remember more about it. Martin Peters gave us the lead in the twentieth minute, and John Hughes equalised a few minutes before half-time. One goal apiece was the right scoreline for us, and in the dressing room Sir Alf came over and said, 'Well done, keep going.' I went for a leak and Bobby Charlton was also there. 'You're doing very well,' he told me and that gave me a big lift. If Bobby Charlton said so, it had to be true, hadn't it? There were no more goals in the second half and we had qualified to face Spain in the European Nations Cup quarter-finals.

My overwhelming feeling was a sense of relief just to get through the match. I knew I hadn't done that well overall on my England debut. Professional footballers are prone to be kidded by fans into thinking they have played better than they actually have, but I knew I could have made more of an impression than I did. Yes, I contributed to an important result, but I hadn't set the world alight. Doubts filled my mind as I stuffed my white No. 9 shirt into my bag with all the telegrams, and I wondered what Sir Alf would say now that the game was over. He'd taken such a risk in picking me.

'You had a good game, Michael,' he said. 'You've helped us qualify and I look forward to seeing you again in the future.' My heart lifted to the skies. I'd done it. I'd played for England, and I might do so again.

2

A BOY CALLED TICH

England against Scotland was the first football match I played in. It was down on the Rec at Christmas time when the professionals from Preston North End visited my father, their former team-mate, who was home from his new club, Barrow, for a couple of days. They were famous players – Andy Beattie, George Mutch, Bill Shankly, all Scottish internationals – and they came and had a kickabout with all the boys from the street. It had to be England v. Scotland, of course, and I remember wearing the new boots I'd been given for Christmas and sprinting as hard as I could to get past these laughing men. I was only five years old, and I didn't know they were famous heroes of football. Sport was in my blood, it was in my body, and kicking a ball and chasing after it was the most natural thing in the world for me to do. We'd play against anybody down on the Rec, and if my dad's pals wanted a game of football that was perfect. Who didn't want to play against Scotland?

They were innocent times just after the Second World War,

when my elder brother John and I made our own entertainment in the streets and fields in Penwortham, the area of Preston where we lived. In the summertime we'd go building dens – sometimes in the roofs of bombed houses, sometimes digging out a pit in a field and putting a corrugated iron sheet on top. We'd climb down into our hideaway and light a fire and feel as if we hadn't a care in the world.

My earliest memory is of air-raid sirens sounding towards the end of the war, and the blackouts that came afterwards. I hated not being able to see a thing. I also remember going on holiday to my Uncle Bunt's home in Bournemouth just after the war ended and seeing the German prisoners of war clearing away barbed wire from the beaches. They weren't easy times for anyone. In my mind's eye I can still picture the ration books we took to the shops on Liverpool Road, and the fact that there was no such thing as an egg. To make an omelette you poured water on to powdered egg. I remember as well going out to scrounge coal and wood in the freezing winter of 1947 to help keep us warm. Today, in the twenty-first century, it sounds like that was an impossible life, but that's just how it was, and it went on for a long time.

But I don't want to give the impression we had it really tough. Although football treated my father very badly, his professional player's wage was still a good one compared to many, and we lived in a good home with nice food. My father George had high standards, and he made sure we were well dressed and comfortable even though he was living away in Barrow for most of my early years. I wasn't aware then that my dad was struggling with his life in football.

In truth, my father was a stranger to us. He was away for the whole football season apart from a Christmas visit, and we brothers lived alone with my mother, Dulcie. Only once did she take us to watch Dad play for Barrow. It was by far the best time of his career; he played 120 games for the club, but that day he got himself sent off. He had a streak in him – and I had the same one – always of looking after himself on a football field – and that's a good thing. But it had to happen that he was sent off the one day we watched him. I never saw him play again.

Tom Finney has told me that my father was a good player, but that he was unlucky to be at Preston in the late 1930s when all the great Scottish internationals were there. Bill Shankly was a very close friend of my dad's, and he transferred that relationship to me when I played for Manchester City many years later. When we went to Liverpool he always used to stand there assessing the opposition as you walked into Anfield. He used to see me and say, 'Hello, son, how's Dulcie?'

I'd say she was fine, and Shankly would say, 'She's a fine woman, your mother.'

I'd be cheeky and reply, 'See you later, Dad,' and his voice boomed out, 'I'll have you, son. I'll see you in the boot room!' And I used to go to the boot room – and it was very rare for a player to do that – but he allowed me to go. Shanks was lovely.

Such moments told me that my father must have been a good footballer. He grew up in Winchester, and both he and his brother Gordon (my Uncle Bunt) were taken on by Aldershot Town as nineteen-year-olds. Both were wing halves, and soon enough they were being monitored by scouts from First Division clubs like Arsenal, Huddersfield and Blackpool. But it was Preston who made a bid of £650 for my father and it must have seemed like a wonderful move when he was transferred to Deepdale in 1935. He wasn't to know it would turn into a nightmare, with all the international players in his position blocking his path to the first team. I've already mentioned that he was twelfth man when Preston reached the 1938 FA Cup Final. He also played 186 games for Portsmouth in the war years, but when they reached the wartime Cup Final it was another regular Pompey player who came back to play in the most prestigious match of the season.

I only learned all this much later, but the heartbreak he'd suffered through his career gave me an inner strength and determination. Another lesson it taught me was never to look down on people in football. I know how rough the game can be on people's lives.

After the war Preston finally allowed George Summerbee to leave, and he went to Chester City. His bitter experiences had made him an active believer in the value of the players' union, the Professional Footballers' Association. But when he tried to organise the players at Chester into union membership the club suspended him for six weeks without pay. I was too young to understand the trauma it brought to our family but I'm told money was so scarce that my parents had to raid our piggy banks for extra coppers to buy food.

It must have been a horrendous time for my mother. She went through hell with Dad's mood changes because he could be a difficult man. I can remember there being arguments in the house, and quite a lot of friction and tension. I'm sure some of that was caused by me. With my learning difficulties, Dad put enormous pressure on me. Even when I had learned to tell the time, I fell apart when he asked me what it was – and more than a few times there were a lot of tears. My mother backed me up, and she always favoured me. I'm sure that I wasn't a planned baby when I was born in December 1942. I was a shot in the dark, and I'm not sure my father was very happy when I came along. He was always more interested in John.

One of those Scottish internationals I mentioned, Andy Beattie, gave my dad the best years of his playing life. In 1947, at the age of thirty-three, he was transferred to Barrow, where Beattie had become the manager. Three full seasons of football, albeit at a lower level, restored some of the pride and dignity that had been savaged by his time at Preston. Whatever his faults, it must have been a crushing experience for a man who had travelled north with dreams of finding glory and fame in football. All the disillusionment, though, didn't stop him responding to an advertisement by Southern League club Cheltenham Town in 1950, when his professional playing days were over. They needed a player-manager, and George Summerbee fitted the bill, so off the family went on a huge new adventure. It was a mighty upheaval in all our lives.

We made the long journey by coach and I was upset to be leaving all my friends in the terraced houses of our street, West End. The contrast between a northern working-class mill town like Preston and the Regency promenades of a plush spa town like Cheltenham hit me straight away. At the age of seven I was old enough to know this was a serious change in life, and I found out how serious it was very quickly.

At Penwortham Infants School I had thought I was a normal-sized lad, but I was actually tiny, and as soon as I arrived in Cheltenham everyone called me Tich. I hated that, but even worse was the fact that nobody seemed able to understand my broad Lancashire accent. I had always been a bit slow at schoolwork but here at Naunton Park Junior they put me straight into a special class down the road from the main building for children with learning difficulties. I hated that even more, and I felt incredibly lonely and out of place. My life had been turned upside down, and for a lad who already had an inferiority complex it was a miserable time.

But the school was right: I needed to be in the special class, and it helped me so much. I gradually found some confidence and although I failed my eleven-plus exam with flying colours it put me on the right road. So did my natural football ability. John and I played on the Rec (everywhere in England had a recreation ground in those days) and the lads who called me Tich could see that I was a useful player to have around. You'd never be without friends if you could race down the wing and cross a football on to the head of a centre forward. I just played on the wing naturally. It was a pure thrill to run past the defender and get to the dead-ball line and clip over an inch-perfect cross. My thrill was in being able to make things happen. Here was something I was definitely good at.

We played mostly with a tennis ball, but sometimes a lad had a proper old laced leather ball. I remember we used to nick a ball from the St Mark's youth centre football club as well. The small tennis balls helped you develop your skills because they were harder to control. Playing with them made you smart on your feet. You didn't think about it at the time, though, you just played. But, looking back, I can see that I was self-taught as a footballer by those endless kickabouts.

Football was where I overcame the inferiority complex I suffered from so badly. There was self-doubt in my mind all the time. When I first tried to ride a bike they had to put blocks on the pedals because my feet didn't reach them. I had a nervous habit of plucking wool off my sweaters. I don't know why. I did that throughout my professional football career and only stopped when I was about fifty. Why? I've thought about what prompted it, and it was probably because my grandma Lillian came to live with us in Cheltenham and if we didn't do things properly she would hit you with a dog lead. Once she broke a bowl over John's head. I think the plucking also developed from my general feeling of uncertainty about myself.

And being called Tich didn't help at all.

The name stuck, though. I didn't start growing until I was fourteen and because I was good at football I always played with older boys, which only made me seem even tinier. Tich it was and Tich it stayed. Even among those telegrams that arrived at Hampden Park on my England debut there was one addressed to 'Tich' – with congratulations from St Mark's youth centre football club.

At least in Cheltenham I saw more of my father and got to know him a little better. We lived in a club house in Oaklands Avenue about a mile and a half from Cheltenham's Whaddon Road ground. One day I nearly came a cropper coming home from Whaddon Road. John and I were cycling down a street and I caught my brother's pedal on his bike and I slipped as a lorry was coming straight towards us on the other side of the road. Luckily it was only my bike that skidded under the lorry while I happened to fall away clear. They were happy days, though. I could see that my dad was someone of standing and I remember talking to players like Roy Shiner and Peter Rushworth, both of whom would later be sold to First Division clubs.

Football dominated my life. There was nothing else I wanted to do. Thankfully, I had some wonderful teachers at Naunton Park Secondary Modern School who realised that and did everything they could to help me. Within six months of arriving I was made the captain of Drake house because of my talent for football and the fact that I helped the school team to win matches. That was the first organised side I played for, with the sports master Eddie Whittaker in charge. We played in an all-yellow strip, without numbers, but I was always outside right. Mr Whittaker stressed that this was a real match, not like the slapdash games on the Rec, and I loved the responsibility of trying to create goals. There were other brilliant sports masters, too, like Arnold Wills and a Mr Parry. The headmaster, Mr Wilson, also went out of his way to help me through my school days. I used to worry about mental arithmetic. I was always bottom of the class. But Mr Wilson would overlook it, and even a fearsome lady teacher called Mrs Holdenhurst, who was very strict, understood that I was struggling and never picked on me. It all slowly helped to boost my confidence.

By the end, after my father had died, I often didn't go to school at all. I would kid my mother I was going by putting on my school uniform, but when she'd gone to work I went home and did some housework and peeled the potatoes. Before she came back I would put on my school uniform again. Eventually, the headmaster found out; he didn't tell my mother but instead called me into his study. He told me to carry on so long as I always came back for football and cricket. He knew I wasn't going to be an intellectual person, but he still supported and helped me. So I went to school, but not all the time, and the arrangement suited everyone – so long as I didn't tell anyone about the secret deal.

I learned a few lessons at school, though. One of the biggest concerned my first ever girlfriend, a lovely lass called Christine Slater.

We'd have a kiss and a cuddle in the back of the bus. Then, one day, the girls were skipping in the yard and I pulled the rope as a joke and Christine fell and broke her ankle. Naturally, she wouldn't have anything to do with me again. It upset me hugely, but I learned a valuable lesson about respecting other people. A few years ago I was invited to give a speech in Plymouth and when I was there a fella said there was a lady coming who wanted to meet me. It was Christine. She was married with two children, and we had a chat about those school days. Amazing.

The other avenue for playing football came through the Baker Street YMCA, a club for local youngsters that had a thriving team. We'd train once a week in their gym and then play in league matches against teams from Pershore, Winchcombe and all over the area. We played in an all-blue strip but we didn't have a proper manager or coach. The team seemed to be automatically picked, probably by the captain, Bobby Skeen. I was always in the side, and we mostly won our games easily. Once we had only eight players but we still beat the other lot 6-0. We ran them off the park, and I scored a couple of goals. The YMCA had its own pitch on the Rec and I remember we used to have to clear the dogshit off the grass before we could play. I started as a twelve-year-old there, and was straight away up against sixteen-year-olds. I was Tich Summerbee to everyone, and Bobby Skeen used to protect me when people tried to kick lumps out of his fast little right-winger.

Bobby and his brother Kenny were big pals of mine. They were among a group of us who used to take the train to First Division matches in the Midlands on a Saturday afternoon – me and John and a lad called David Shakespeare. We went to see the four big clubs, Aston Villa, Wolves, Birmingham and West Bromwich Albion. It was a great education in football. We learned by watching how the pros played. Outside Birmingham we needed to go on the Licky Banker – where one train was pulling and another pushing the carriages up a slope outside the city. Outside the station we'd buy baked potatoes and roast chestnuts and then go to a sports shop owned by a former Villa player, Harry Parks, where we'd buy a rosette. We'd already have been reading *Charles Buchan's Football Monthly* on the train and we'd go early to whichever ground it was, and stand by the players' tunnel to get autographs. You'd stand there and dream of playing at Villa Park one day yourself. We saw some great players like Ronnie Allen at West Brom and Dave Hickson, who was centre forward for the Villa. The adrenalin shot through me as I watched, and I wanted it for myself. I loved Molineux, too. Wolves were the best team in the country along with the Busby Babes of Manchester United, and I saw them play on one of those Saturday afternoons, and again just after the Munich Air Disaster when Stan Pearson had joined them. On the way back we'd read the *Green 'Un* newspaper that gave you all the other results and a blow-by-blow account of the match you'd just watched. We'd be home by seven o'clock and my mother never seemed to worry.

Even though my father was a player and then a manager, my football education didn't come from him at all. It came from watching these players, and learning for myself on the Rec. If I had a particular hero it was Tom Finney, the Preston winger, and I loved to watch his speed on the run and close control.

Kenny Skeen and David Shakespeare were also involved in an incident I've never forgotten. We cycled to a hamlet on the River Severn called Wainlows to go fishing for trout, and we camped out behind the Black Widow pub on the riverbank. It's where the Avon and Severn meet and a dangerous spot with currents. We were used to going camping in an orchard close by in Cheltenham and my mother said it was okay to go further afield for a few days. A Primus stove we had caught fire and the flames took hold of Kenny's trousers and burned his legs. My mother found out because it was in the local paper and she came rushing over and went berserk. I think she came with my dad; we were never allowed to go again.

I don't have too many memories of my dad. When he was manager of Cheltenham we'd sometimes go on the coach to games. I remember when he got floodlights at the ground and I helped with putting telegraph poles up. Stan Cullis brought Wolves down for a friendly under the lights and it generated a lot of money for the club. I thought it was another indication of my dad's good name among the football professionals that Cullis would bring a team to Whaddon Road.

My mother used to do the sandwiches at half-time and I would sell programmes on match days. I would have been eight then. We also used to go and watch the cricket festival at Cheltenham and my dad became very friendly with Tom Graveney, of Worcestershire and England. They used to play golf together and I would be the caddie. That was a wonderful time. You could play on the hills all round Cheltenham; they were the happiest days for John and myself.

Then our happy life suddenly fell to pieces in the spring and summer of 1952. Well, it seemed sudden to me. All the good players at Cheltenham like Roy Shiner were sold off to make money for the club and the team began losing badly. As ever in football, the manager was the man who carried the can for the club's troubles. The official reason given by Cheltenham was that my father resigned through ill health, and he was certainly not as well as he had been. But there had been a power struggle in the boardroom at Whaddon Road, and the truth is that he was sacked as a convenient scapegoat. Football had crushed him once more.

My mother was simply relieved, although fearful about what it meant financially for the family as we had just planned to move to a new house in Pennsylvania Avenue in Cheltenham. She had seen what football had done to Dad and she was glad it was at an end. The club wanted to kick us straight out of the house in Oaklands Avenue and it took a court order to keep us there for a while. Football was a harsh world in those days.

As a former manager of the town's football club my father was well known. He was soon offered a job as a warehouse storeman at Dowty Equipment Ltd, a company willing to give him time off to accommodate another offer of help from his old friend Pat Beasley, who had become manager of Bristol City. My dad accepted the chance to stay in the game as a scout for City, going to watch matches and assess potential transfer buys. He used to take John to matches all the time, but I went only once. That was the time I told my dad, in earshot of all the VIPs in the directors' box, that Gerry Hitchens wasn't much good at playing centre forward.

The final couple of years of my father's life were wracked with pain. I didn't really understand it until one bright summer's day when I was sitting on the edge of the settee by the front room window looking out into the street. It was a habit of mine to watch the world going by from this vantage point, and that day I saw my dad come round the corner on his way back from Dowty's. He was struggling to walk; he looked as if he was drunk, as if he had lost all power in his legs. He lifted one leg up slowly then pushed the other one forward. Finally, he gave up and just sat down on the pavement. For a twelve-year-old boy it was a terrible sight.

We went out and brought him in, and he couldn't move. Although it was a hot day, he felt freezing cold, as cold as ice. There were yellow and brown patches on his skin and his eyes were more sunken in their sockets than ever. I remember everyone being very emotional; we had no idea what it was. The doctor was called and he said it was just nerves. You take the word of a doctor, but he had no idea either. An hour or so afterwards some of the feeling came back into Dad's legs and he was okay. The anxiety quickly returned, though. My mother woke us at two o'clock that morning and said that my father was struggling again and could we come and help to rub his legs to get some circulation back into them. John did one leg and I did the other. We knew it was serious then. It was horrible to see someone in that situation. Eventually he went to sleep. The next morning he decided to go to Bournemouth to convalesce by the seaside where his brother lived. Uncle Bunt came to pick him up.

A letter had arrived a few days earlier saying that I'd played so well for the school team that I'd been picked for the Cheltenham Boys' side. The game would be at Whaddon Road and my father thought it was fantastic. So did I – to be playing at the ground where I'd helped out so much when he was manager. He told me he would come and watch; it would be the first time he'd ever seen me play. Then he went away but I was sure he'd come back.

The kit was a white top with blue shorts, and it was like a tent on Tich Summerbee. I was given the No. 7 shirt – the first time I'd worn a number in a game – and my mother had to stitch the shirt into the shorts so that I could play. Most of the 7 was hidden inside the shorts, and they had to be rolled up as well. John was there to watch and the lads from the YMCA, but although I kept looking for him my dad didn't arrive. I thought perhaps he had stayed away because he was the former manager of Cheltenham Town and shouldn't be there, but that was just a daft boy's thinking. After that game I knew I had the ability to be a professional footballer. There was nothing else I was ever going to be good at. I kept the shirt with pride after the game and my mother looked after it.

I didn't know then that my father had tried to come back to Cheltenham. He was desperately ill and had lost consciousness in the car and been taken to hospital in Cirencester. He died that evening, killed by Addison's disease, an extremely rare illness that he may have contracted on one of the foreign tours he went on with Preston. It attacked fewer than one in a million people in those days. Just before he died the hospital had done blood tests and finally discovered the reason for his poor health.

Addison's disease causes weight loss, skin discolouration, severe fatigue and pain in the legs, among other symptoms. Today it is treated effectively with cortisone. American President John F. Kennedy was treated that way, but cortisone only came into general use a couple of years after my father died. In the summer of 1955 the disease was incurable.

My mother went to hospital in the middle of the night but my father died forty-five minutes before she arrived. By morning she was back home and I will always remember her standing there in front of us and saying: 'Your father has died.' It was very traumatic. John went to pieces. It was worse for him because he knew Dad better than I did. It affected him so much that he gave up on football and cricket even though he was exceptionally talented, a better player at both sports than I was.

I couldn't understand my brother. He was such a good player but the influence my father had on him must have been tremendous. He saw that football had destroyed his dad and he wanted no part of the game. I wish I'd known my father better, but, if I had, would it have put me off a career in football as well?

On the day of the funeral so many people came to the house – Andy Beattie and Jackie Fairbrother among them from the Preston days. My father was a popular man and it revealed the great camaraderie in the game. My mother didn't think we should go to the service so we were sent to play on the Rec. Dad was cremated and a plaque was placed at Prestbury cemetery and we went along to see it and thought about him, about all the great expectations that had turned to dust in Preston and all the heartache he suffered from a life in football. You can imagine my mother's apprehension at knowing that I wanted to follow the same path.

How she kept everything going I will never know. It must have been incredibly tough, but she was an amazing woman, my mother, and she tried to make sure that as little changed for us as possible. She had several jobs: working in the perfume department at the Cavendish House department store, then at a chemist on the High Street. Later she became an inspector at the Goddard factory. Money was tight, and I remember that when we couldn't afford a Sunday newspaper one would be delivered by Kenny or Bobby Skeen, who did rounds. We'd get a paper that should have gone somewhere else, because they were trying to look after us.

John left school soon afterwards and became a carpenter, but we still played together, and I remember us watching England against Australia in the 1956 Ashes series on television. John

Arlott was the commentator and he said in that wonderful voice of his 'I do believe there is a ray of sunshine and we will get some play.' It was the famous match at Old Trafford where, on a sticky wicket, Jim Laker took all ten wickets in an innings as England won the Test. I remember it so clearly.

While John gave up on playing, I continued to progress on the football field. Doing well for Cheltenham Boys brought an invitation to play another step up for the Gloucestershire County Boys' team. That was a really big thing and there might be 100 or 150 spectators watching these matches. For a tiny lad like me it felt like a 100,000 crowd. I thought, 'I'll have a bit of this.' I was still called Tich, I still suffered feelings of insecurity and inferiority in life, but out on the pitch my confidence rose once I discovered I could cope with the improved opposition. I started to believe in myself through football.

The county games were all organised very professionally, but my mother still had to stitch my shirt into my shorts every time. It wasn't until I was fourteen, when I started to grow, that the No. 7 could be seen properly on my back. Another boost came in school assemblies when Mr Wilson would read out 'Congratulations to Michael Summerbee for his sporting exploits'. They also came in cricket, where I played for Cheltenham Boys and then the Gloucestershire County Boys' side as a budding fast bowler. I loved cricket, and I still do, but I knew I wasn't good enough to be a professional in the summer game.

At the age of fifteen I was going to leave school, or as much of it as I still attended. By this time I'm sure my mother knew about the 'secret', and she was more concerned with my life ahead. She knew how much I wanted to be a footballer, and probably against her own better judgement she spoke on the phone to Pat Beasley, the Bristol City manager, about my prospects. It was time to find out if I was good enough, and she found a willing accomplice in Beasley. He might have seen me play for the YMCA side, or had reports, but I doubt it.

I'm sure he gave me a place on the ground staff out of a sense of loyalty to my father. There was no contract to sign, for a start, and no contact with anyone from the club before I left home to go to Bristol. Beasley had kept in touch with my mother and I think he thought he was looking after me and trying to do me a favour. But it was only a favour and therefore I felt it unreal.

I went to Bristol, of course; I went on the train, and it was only years later I learned that John had cried his eyes out when the train left the station. I enjoyed the football side of being with a professional club. I relished all the jobs: cleaning the boots and sweeping the terraces, the afternoon training, such as it was, and the weekend matches for the B team. Everything else was pretty much a nightmare. I was lonely and I'd just wander round the streets or go to the pictures on my own. They put me in some digs in Ashton, not far from the City ground, and that was a complete contrast to my neat and tidy home. The landlord worked at a sewage plant and he would come, sit down for the evening meal, and his hands were still black from his job; he hadn't even bothered to wash them properly. It disgusted me. The house was also freezing; there was no central heating, of course, so I used to sleep in a duffel coat my mother had bought me. It was damp, too, and I never had any dry clothes, and it didn't help me to feel wanted.

The end came within a month, on a wet day in the Forest of Dean, where I'd been taken to watch the A team play. It was a tough game in a mining area and I saw a player suffer the most horrific compound fracture of his leg in a collision just a few yards in front of me. I'd never seen anyone break a leg before and he was screaming and I just thought I couldn't face up to anything like that.

The incident really put me off. It scared me. I can understand people pulling out of tackles when you see a situation like that – and I made my mind up immediately that I was going home and having nothing to do with this any more.

I returned to the ground and picked up my gear and went to see Pat Beasley and said I was homesick and wasn't going to settle. He didn't try to persuade me to stay and I think he was thankful that I wanted out. He'd done the favour he felt he had to do, and he probably didn't think I was going to make it anyway. Everything was against me: I was skinny, not very tall, and too young to cope with being thrown into a man's football life with no help. My heart wasn't in it, to be honest. It was an opportunity – but I let it go by. That wasn't on purpose, but I missed home, and it seemed a false thing all round.

My mother was relieved . She thought I wasn't going to be a footballer and that I would be spared the traumas it could only bring. She told me to get a job and I joined Dowty's as an office boy in the section where they did stress drawings for the mining equipment they manufactured. They offered me an apprentice-ship but I didn't take it. I didn't think I'd be good enough for that. I didn't think I'd be good enough for anything, and I was just so disillusioned because I thought my chance in football was gone. But all I wanted was to be a professional player.

I was back at my vantage point on the settee in the front window of our house, No. 6 Pennsylvania Avenue, being a nosy parker, when my dreams of a life in football started to come true. It was a summer evening, just getting dark, and John was out courting – he had found out that girls were not just for kissing. I saw this big car come slowly down the street, looking at all the numbers for the house it wanted. It was a Mark 10 Jaguar, racing green, the most beautiful car I'd ever seen, and it stopped outside ours. A gentleman got out, a tall, handsome man, and I watched him come through the garden gate and knock on the door. He said he was Cecil Green from Swindon Town Football Club, and he asked my mother if it was possible to talk to her son.

'Which one?' she asked.

'We've had very good reports about Michael Summerbee,' I heard him say, 'and our manager, Mr Bert Head, would be very interested in him coming to play in our B team.'

My heart started thumping madly as he spoke and I knew I had another chance, a real chance this time, because they had seen me play and had been impressed and they wanted me. He said they had been watching me for a long time, and thought I was good enough for the Swindon B team that played on Saturday afternoons.

My mother was horrified; I knew that. She'd thought she was rid of the curse of football, and she ummed and aahed as Mr Green stood there in our front room. John came back, and he immediately stuck up for me, but it was only when I said to Mum that I could still play for Baker Street YMCA in the mornings and then catch a bus to Swindon to turn out again for them in the afternoon, that she relented. It wasn't hard to go against the wishes of my mother because I wanted it so much. The door had opened an inch for me, and now it was my job to work hard and make my ambitions come true.

It only took a few minutes, but those minutes changed my life. Mr Green's wife had stayed in the car and by the time he left the house it was surrounded by a gaggle of kids. I knew well enough that football could be harsh and brutal, but I still believed in the dream represented by that glamorous racing-green Jaguar parked outside the front window.

3

ONE OF THE BABES

'You'll never be anything, Summerbee. They'll bury you under a football pitch.'

They were the last words I heard as I left school, the words of metalwork teacher Jimmy Crowe. I've never forgotten them. I've never forgotten their casual cruelty. I've never forgotten how they inspired a rage to prove him wrong.

The more that people told me I was going down the wrong lane with football the more determined I was to prove myself. I loved the day not so many months later when I returned, driving my own car, to Naunton Park Secondary Modern School as a first-team professional footballer with Swindon Town. That showed Jimmy Crowe, and he had the good grace to congratulate me, if not apologise.

It didn't happen overnight, of course, although the wonderful thing about Swindon in the late 1950s and early 1960s was that they were willing to put players in the first team at a very young age. That was a lucky break for me – not that I knew it on the first Saturday lunchtime I took the bus from Cheltenham to Swindon to play for the B team. I remember being so happy getting off the bus and joining other emerging talents like Ernie Hunt, John Trollope and Bobby Woodruff for these fixtures played on the pitch at the back of the County Ground.

They were an uncertain couple of months still working at Dowty's as an office boy, declining the option of going to night school, and concentrating all my efforts on Saturday morning matches for the Baker Street YMCA and then Swindon's B team in the afternoon following an hour's bus ride. Looking back it seems a mad schedule, but to me playing was just a natural thing to do, and the more games the better. Soon enough youngsters like Ernie, John, Bobby and myself were being asked to play for the A team, a sure sign of progress, and a great sense of camaraderie grew up between us. It was a total contrast to the Bristol City experience, but I still had that sense of doubt and inferiority, I was still as skinny as a rake, and I still didn't know if I was going to make it.

I nearly didn't.

Bert Head was the manager of Swindon, and when the time came to make a decision about whether to take me on to the ground staff he wasn't too keen. He thought I was too small and too slight, a traditional worry for managers with young players. Alan Ball was told just the same before he got his chance. My good fortune was that Cecil Green and the Swindon secretary, Bert Davis, stood up for me in the decisive meeting. They both said I was a good prospect and must be kept on; they said that Swindon would be missing out badly if I was shown the door. I had one more chance, a reserve match against Devizes in the Wiltshire Cup, and I had an outstanding game. That was enough to make Bert Head change his mind.

Throughout my life I've had many people to be grateful to. If it wasn't for Cecil Green and Bert Davis I'd have gone into oblivion.

That was one battle won. But there was another to contend with – the opposition of my mother, who was still set against me becoming a professional footballer. Cecil Green's diplomacy and persuasion were required again, and he offered to give me lodgings that would help me acclimatise and avoid the intense homesickness I'd suffered in Bristol. And so I joined my great pal Ernie Hunt on the ground staff and left home to live with Mr and Mrs Green, who looked after me like a son. Cecil Green became a second father to me. I was just sixteen.

My confidence had already begun to grow at Swindon among so many like-minded lads. We shot up together into the reserves where we were now playing with hardened professionals as well as cleaning their boots and scrubbing out the dressing rooms. The fixture list took us to the big grounds in London, and the special one for me was going to Highbury for the first time. It was empty, but to my mind it was full of 60,000 people. The stadium had an aura; the changing-room floors were heated and the marble entrance hall was magnificent. I thought, 'I want a bit of this' as I came down the very narrow tunnel on to the pitch and felt that my dreams were starting to be realised. It was the most fantastic feeling, and I remember thinking, 'Yeah, this is what it's about, this is what my father loved.'

We were all young then, so the results didn't always go our way, but the experience was there and it encouraged us. If we got past one player, or made a good pass, it felt as if we'd scored a goal. It was the same at Upton Park and Stamford Bridge and Craven Cottage, where I played against Johnny Haynes who was coming back from an injury. Our team was full of sixteen- and seventeen-year-olds and to us these were all massive matches. The only downside was that we got beat heavily quite often. But, as we progressed, the 5-0s became 3-0s and 3-2s and the day we won a match against one of the big teams was like winning a cup final. The education I had at Swindon was second to none because of the environment I was in and the belief the manager had in us.

People always talk about the Busby Babes of that time, and quite rightly so, but there were also Bert's Babes down at Swindon, and they never get a mention. Yet, Bert Head was so successful, and so many of his young players went on to play for bigger clubs. We had a couple of fantastic runs in the Youth Cup. In my first season of 1958–9 we beat Chelsea in front of a 16,000 crowd and then Bristol City, who were renowned for being a good side. We were eventually beaten in the semi-finals, and then the next year Swindon ended up in the final playing Manchester United over two legs. At Old Trafford the crowd was 45,000 and George Best was in their side.

Bert Head was a tough guy. He used to come on the training pitch wearing his shoes and do sliding tackles and things like that. I think he'd have been a general if he'd been in the army, and he told us how he'd been in the Home Guard during the war. We'd train pre-season down at Weymouth, and sleep in tents close to the beach. He also took us every year into a prison so we could play a match against the Borstal boys. The smell of the bad food was a real lesson to me. That made me appreciate my own freedom.

Ground staff duties were still our first job. I had to lay out the kit for the first team in the dressing room on match day, and did that for a while even when I was playing in the side myself. After the game the first-teamers took their boots off and we had to stack them away and get the dressing room sorted out before we could have our own bath. We were still in our playing kit from the match, and we could only have our bath when all the others had their suits on. By then the bath water was black.

The older pros would try their tricks as well. One day they nailed my training boots to the duckboards. I went to pick them up and was done good and proper. At other times we made ourselves look right fools. Ernie and I were down at the training ground, and we'd been told to cut the grass. It must have been one of the first mowers you could sit on, and we were down there on our own mowing the grass and we started messing around. The nets were up for the season and we were bowling along on this mower when the *Red Dragon* Cardiff to London express went flying past. We looked at the train, forgot where we were, and suddenly found ourselves mowing straight into the middle of the goal with the nets and goalposts falling on top of us. Luckily, the trainer saw the funny side.

Ernie and I were becoming inseparable, and, after a spell living with Mr and Mrs Green, and then in digs with a couple of senior pros, I moved in with Ernie and his family in Redcliffe Street. It was a terraced street with the factory wall behind and a pub on the corner, as traditional working class as you can get. There was no bathroom but his dad, Ernest, used to have a wash in the big basins they had in those days. I hadn't had a home life for a long time and to become part of a family was wonderful. Ernie's mum, Hilda, took me in like a second son and that was a vitally important part of my life. It has helped me to be the person I am. I'd never lose my station; I'm a working-class lad and I'll always be that way. I always try to make time for people; if I can help somebody I will do. Ern and I became very close.

His real name was Roger so I'd call him Rodge and he'd call me George – my middle name.

We made progress on the field together as well, and a vital moment in my football career came in the summer of 1959 when Bert Head decided to have a public practice match before the start of the new season. He played the Possibles against the Probables, which meant all the youngsters against the experienced pros. We were all sixteen, seventeen, eighteen and we beat the first team 5-0. Bert had another practice match to make sure, and we beat them 4-0. That's when he decided to put his very young Swindon team together, although he was sensible enough not to start playing us all at once.

I was still only sixteen, but I felt an increasing confidence that I would make it in football. I did well in the reserves and was playing centre forward as well as outside right. Ernie got picked for the first team, and I was so envious, but I knew my chance would come. When, though? Bert Head never told us himself and each week you'd look at the team sheet he stuck on the wall of the first team changing room to see who was playing. It was always in the first team room and we would see it while doing all our ground staff jobs. Suddenly, one day, there was my name: Summerbee – No. 9. I was playing centre forward at home to Bournemouth on Boxing Day. I had turned seventeen only a couple of weeks earlier. There had been an inkling of it during the week because the regular centre forward, David 'Bronco' Layne, was suspended for being sent off, but I hardly dared believe it was true. And it was quite eerie that it came against Bournemouth, for whom my Uncle Bunt had played and the club where he was now chief scout. I was nervous before the start but Swindon controlled the match and I played well in a 2-0 victory. I knew I had, and the reports in the local paper were complimentary. I was on my way. After the game I spoke to my uncle; it was the first time I'd seen him since my father died because there had been a confrontation between him and my mother and the family had split apart. It was a decision taken by my mother and my brother and I respected that. What I didn't know was that Uncle Bunt had tried to persuade Bournemouth to sign me up for their ground staff. So he sat in the stand and watched my Football League debut with satisfaction and told me how proud my father would have been and how proud he was. The words lifted my heart.

My performance kept me in the side for the next few games. That was one message of hope at the start of my football career. Another swiftly received message was how hard the game was physically. There was no hiding place for a skinny teenager in this brutal man's world. I had been on the ground staff for a year learning my trade, but the lesson about the raw courage required could only be delivered out on the pitch. There was one match against Derby where I chased after a through ball and their goalkeeper hit me with everything. I felt like I was dying; I wanted the ground to open up. I couldn't suck air in at all. That was an education. It said, 'Right, son, you're here now. It's a man's game.' You learned quickly and if you didn't you were finished. These fellas were not like Sunday League players who just kick you; they could do serious damage. They could put you out of the game for ever.

Another lesson came against Notts County. I'd seen well enough back at Bristol City what could happen, and in this match I pulled out of two tackles against their centre half. Afterwards, Bert Head raged at me in the dressing room: 'Just shut your eyes and go in,' he said in the middle of a stream of insults. I did just that in the next match and came out with the ball and I understood what he meant. You had to be able to look after yourself; once you showed that you could the respect followed from opponents. That helped you, however frail you might look. I learned how to use the top half of my body, too. I was the strong, wiry type and I realised that the edges on my body were dangerous. People who are thin can be more dangerous to tackle because they are bony. I used that advantage, just as Denis Law and George Best did. It was about survival.

There were still injuries, of course. I remember a game against West Ham when my thigh was smashed up. Their goalkeeper, Lawrie Leslie, came out to the near post and caught me with his knee. I was in agony; the thigh just blew up, and the medical treatment was rudimentary at best. The only way I could get the swelling down was to put a towel round my leg, sit in the bath, and pour a kettle of boiling water on it to let the heat soak through. Goodness knows what today's physios would make of that. I couldn't bend the leg for a week, but as soon as I could Bert Head put me back in the team to face Barnsley. I thought I was okay but I took a corner near the end and completely tore the muscle from the kneecap right up to the top of the thigh. I had never known such pain. I was out for ages after that and there is still a lump on my thigh to this day. Looking back, you could say that Bert Head was wrong to pick me so quickly, but it didn't feel that way at the time. I was young and every game I missed made me feel terrible. I frequently played when I shouldn't have done with stitches in the back of my legs. I'd have played with a broken leg if they asked me to.

The atmosphere at Swindon was ideal for a young player starting out. It was a working town with big factories and a huge railway industry and they loved watching football when the hooter went for the end of the working week. I always remember the first time I played for the reserves on a Wednesday afternoon and there were maybe 3,000 people in the ground to watch us. Even for these games it was a big thing to come striding down the tunnel and hear the noise of the crowd as you ran on to the pitch. You felt important but then the fans' comments quickly brought you down to earth if you made a poor pass. The crowd for my League debut was about 10,000 and that seemed huge. Each step up the football ladder felt like a giant leap. I ran out thinking about the No. 9 shirt, and all the good players who'd worn it before me. It was exactly the same at Manchester City and England, and you suddenly think, 'Oh, God'. For me those nerves were vital to playing well.

There was something about Swindon Town Football Club. You knew that 50,000 people were coming out of the factories and although not everyone went to the games they were looking forward to the weekend to see what the Hunts and the Woodruffs and the Summerbees could do for the town team. You'd be walking down the street and people would say hello to you. When you were riding your bike people were always waving at you. Once we were in the first team you'd go into a coffee bar and the girls would be looking at you. We liked that all right.

It may be hard to believe these days, when every young professional footballer seems to have a fancy sports car, but Ernie and I used to ride to the ground on match days on a tandem bicycle. I'd usually be in the front because Ern didn't like his hair getting messed up in the wind. We'd have our boots and gear on our backs in a bag and we'd ride the two and a half miles to the County Ground on a Saturday lunchtime, waving to all the fans who were coming to watch us play. Glamorous? You wouldn't think so now, but we thought it was great fun and the supporters seemed to like it as we parked our bike outside the ground and walked in.

We'd be back on the bike on a Monday morning, the time for cleaning boots and sweeping the terraces, because we were still on the ground staff. You could end up getting a few quid extra because fans had dropped coins on the terraces. I was earning £5 a week when I made my debut, so it was a tidy sum.

Looking back now, I think Swindon was the most important part of my football life, probably even more than Manchester City. I guess that will surprise those people aware of my association with City. It was fantastic to win all the trophies we won at Maine Road but none of that could have happened for me without my football education at Swindon as one of Bert's Babes.

They gave me the opportunity. They made me a professional footballer on the princely wages of £15 a week. That day came not long after my debut, and both Ernie Hunt and myself signed on as seventeen-year-olds. Much to our amazement we signed live on the local television channel as the hot properties of football in the area. It was the same night that Denis Law signed for Manchester United in a £100,000 transfer from Italian club Torino. I'd come a long way, but there were many mountains ahead to climb.

4

THE LIKELY LADS

I'm not a man to harbour regrets, but sometimes you do think back and wonder, what if?

What if Bert Head had accepted an offer from Tottenham manager Bill Nicholson to buy his seventeen-year-old right-winger for £10,000 in the summer of 1960? What if I had been allowed to join Spurs just as Nicholson was in the process of creating his historic team that would win the Double nine months later? What if?

Professional football is full of speculation and newspaper transfer rumours that don't amount to anything. But there was substance to all the talk about a possible move to White Hart Lane. Mr Nicholson did come in person to watch Ernie Hunt and myself play a number of times. He did make at least two direct transfer bids for me that were publicly rejected by Swindon. And I was invited to play in a testimonial match at Reading alongside most of what would be the Tottenham Double side. It may have been an informal trial, maybe not.

Nothing official was said to me, neither by Spurs nor by Swindon. At the time I thought I was in with a shout of going to Tottenham and I thought my style of wing play would suit their team. If it had happened I know I would have forced my way into the first team; I wouldn't have got stuck in the reserves.

What if I had been a Double-winner in the famous 1960–61 season?

But nothing happened. Nothing came of any of the newspaper talk that also linked me with moves to clubs like Newcastle, Leicester and Plymouth. I read it all and it did have a huge impact on me as a young player. You tend to believe what you read, even though sometimes it's true and more often it's not. Bert Head never said anything to me about transfers at any time. It was the club's business, not mine. You have to suppose that he didn't want me to leave and that he liked having a vibrant young team to play his way. You also have to suppose the transfer bids weren't big enough to tempt the club.

All the speculation was exciting, but it didn't make any difference to playing. We were young lads enjoying what we were doing. And the maximum wage of the time meant there wasn't any anger about the possibility of losing a fat salary elsewhere. We also knew that playing in the Third Division was better than being in the reserves at a big club. There were two Second Division players who made it into the England team at that time – John Atyeo of Bristol City and Geoff Bradford of Bristol Rovers – so you also felt that if you were good enough you could get picked for England from the lower leagues.

We were playing competitive football and you learned after a while not to give much heed to paper talk. It boosted your confidence to see your name linked with big clubs but the reality was that we were just starting to step up the ladder and very few young players had a transfer to the top flight at the age of seventeen and became stars. I remember reading in the paper that one transfer was a choice between a lad called Mickey Bennett from Watford and myself. I never did hear what happened to him.

It was another summer fundraising match that proved far more important to my life. Swindon played Aston Villa in a testimonial for trainer Harry Cousins and I scored two goals in a 4–3 victory. There was a certain irony, I suppose, that one of Villa's scorers was their centre forward Gerry Hitchens, the player I had scorned to my father's embarrassment. Joe Mercer was then the manager of Villa, a man I had admired from afar as one of the good guys of football. Mercer played for thirty minutes in the second half and I was just happy to be on the same pitch as such a legend of the game. I had no clue then that Joe would be the manager who would take me to Manchester City and to fame in football.

In the summer of 1960 Ernie Hunt and I were just another couple of young likely lads. We spent the summers at Swindon doing all sorts of jobs to earn some extra cash as we were only paid a basic salary by Swindon in the summer. One time we were employed to cut the grass verges for the Corporation. Years later I met the wife of Steve Bruce and she said the first time she saw me was cutting the grass outside her family's house in Swindon. Steve looked at me with sheer disbelief when he heard that story. But we had to do it to make ends meet. Another time it was painting and decorating near Oxford at an RAF base, and we also had a spell as window cleaners.

The strangest job was probably the time that Ernie and I had as gravediggers at the Randall Street cemetery in Swindon. They were always reopening jobs – when a family grave had to be dug up so someone else could be buried. We had to dig down to the coffins already there and put wooden supports in and we became pretty good at it. Sometimes I'd be working there on my own, cutting the grass around the graves and keeping things tidy and I'd be thinking about RIP, Rest In Peace. It could feel a bit eerie; I'd start to hear things, and Ernie used to come up behind me and drop the shovels and it gave me a terrible start.

There were some sad times. A hearse would drive up and a big black car behind, but with nobody in it because the person who'd died had been living on his own. So we used to end up attending the funeral service and then going outside to bury the poor soul.

Once we did a half-past-four burial on a Friday and we were supposed to clock off at five. We dressed the grave with fake grass because we were ready to get moving, but the mourners were people who knew us; they were Swindon supporters. While we were impatient, they couldn't believe it was two first team players digging the grave and they wanted to talk to us. We ended up signing autographs and getting away even later than normal. But it was all part and parcel of the life we led.

We played a small part in helping another likely lad join the club. He was Don Rogers, a year or two younger than ourselves and a winger Bert Head was very keen to secure. I remember that Bert phoned us up one day and said he was going to a match and did we want to come with him. So he drove Ernie and me down to Somerset where he was trying to sign up Rogers. He took us to talk to Don and told him how we'd moved very quickly into the first team at Swindon, and the same opportunity would come to him. We were living examples to show Don Rogers and he joined Swindon, and what a talent he proved. He was outstanding at beating players on the dribble, better than anyone save George Best. Don had so much ability and there was a good period when he was on the left wing with me on the right. Later on, Don was the inspiration behind Swindon's famous victory against Arsenal in the 1969 League Cup Final. He had so much more ability than I ever had, but he lacked a little bit of heart, a bit of devil. If he'd had that he would have been an England hero, I'm sure.

Bert's Babes gradually improved and became one of the best sides in the Third Division as we gained experience to complement our energy and talent. Some of the matches were rough, but we learned how to handle ourselves and we grew up quickly. Not so quickly, mind you, that I avoided the embarrassment of being the only player left on the pitch when a match away to Walsall was abandoned because of fog. I'd chased a pass up the right wing and went to take the throw. Nobody came calling for the ball, but it still took me a couple of minutes to realise there was nobody else left on the pitch. Visibility was down to fifteen yards, and by the time I got back to the dressing room the rest of the team were in the bath.

We'd do silly things off the pitch, too. We'd go tramping at night – walking round Swindon dressed as tramps, just for a bit of fun. On Sunday nights we'd go to the town hall where there was a dance on for a shilling and there were lots of girls around. It was a lovely environment to grow up in. In the week we would go training and then off to Notton's café on the road outside the ground. All the lads used to come in and we'd have a bit of lunch and talk football. The spirit on the pitch came from our closeness off it as well.

Ernie Hunt was a great guy. He did things on the field that no one else was doing and he was a tough player as well. I'd swing in corners and nine times out of ten he'd hit the target.

When the scouts and the managers came to watch Bert's Babes he was the number one attraction, and he made it into the England Under-23s before the rest of us. Ernie was never still. He'd been a hairdresser and he used to cut our hair, even Bert Head's. We grew up together, we had a few birds together and we got our first cars together.

Getting your own car was a big thing as a young footballer, even if we didn't mind riding tandem. Ernie got there first and when he passed his driving test we'd go to Wootton Bassett for a drink; there were twenty-odd pubs in the main street. There was a hole in the floor of his Vauxhall and Ernie had to wear a wellington boot on his right foot when it was raining. I remember the huge thrill I felt when I passed my test, and also the cautious words of my driving examiner: 'I'm passing you but I don't want you to go out on your own for six months.' Some chance. I bought a Hillman Minx with one of the old bench-front seats. You couldn't put your foot down; if you did it made no difference. A man on a bike could overtake you going uphill. It cost £75, and Cecil Green lent me the deposit and I paid the rest on hire purchase. At the end of the 1961–2 season I decided to drive down to see my mother, who had moved from Cheltenham to Slapton Sands in Devon after remarrying. Without a car I'd rarely been able to see her, and I was going to pick up my brother John on the way at Yeovil, where he now lived. Just as I got to the town there was an enormous bang and the big end went. Welcome to real life as a motorist. It was Cecil Green who came to the rescue. When I called him and said my car had broken down he said, 'Send me the bill.' It was £175, more than double what I'd paid for the car, yet he sorted it out instantly. I had a nice week down in Devon waiting for it to be repaired and then came back and started paying off the debt. It took the best part of two years.

The kindness of Cecil Green was vital in so many ways to my life. How vital? He was there right the way through, from spotting me at Baker Street YMCA, and one of the greatest joys of my career was helping his beloved Swindon to win promotion to the Second Division for the first time in the club's history.

I was still only nineteen when that 1962–3 season started, but I'd already played a hundred first team matches, and even though we were a young side we were one of the best in the division. We'd finished ninth the previous season and the optimism of the supporters was justified. It was now or never, it seemed, while Bert's Babes were still together. The season started well and we were in contention when the Big Freeze came that winter and disrupted everybody's lives. Bert Head had a solution for the few matches we played then; he made us play in basketball boots with thick rubber soles and he bought us yellow gloves to wear. And we won those games to keep up our momentum.

An FA Cup tie also helped us that season, even though we lost 5-1. It was against Everton in the fourth round; they were the First Division leaders at the time (and were eventually champions). A crowd of 25,000 crammed into the County Ground, and we played well enough despite the score line to take heart in the knowledge that we were a useful team. Our main rivals in the division turned out to be Peterborough, and we made it harder than it should have been by losing to them home and away in quick succession. Then they stumbled, and we won three out of four games to leave everything hingeing on the final match of the season, at home to Shrewsbury. Victory would take us up.

It was an evening match in front of another big, noisy crowd like the Everton game. The pitch was a dung heap as well, really bad, and the tension was horrible throughout the game. It took until the eighty-ninth minute for Roger Smart to score the only goal and then the whole town went mad with delight. I remember it was the most fantastic feeling when the final whistle blew. It was the furthest Swindon had ever gone in football, and I still have pictures in a scrapbook of the team going to the town hall amid wild scenes of celebration in the streets. That's what I felt most – that it was fantastic for a town I had come to love so much. Swindon was renowned for building trains and we had won it for all the people who worked in the factories during the week. We were heroes, local heroes, and we knew so many of the fans by name and sight. There was a spirit in the town as well as the football club, and although we were heroes we weren't bothered by people. They knew we were just lads trying our best and doing a job, like them. That was the amazing feeling for me. I hadn't scored many goals that season, only six in thirty-seven League games, but my job was to create them for others. We'd all pulled together to achieve something unique for Swindon.

In modern football there would be money swilling around after success like that. It was different back then. Ernie and I asked for a rise because we'd done well, but Bert Head wasn't having any of that. He used to give out the wages in cash every Friday in a brown envelope as if it was his own money, and his response to us was to take us down to the 'Thirty-bob' tailors and buy us a suit each. Ernie's was way too big, and my suit was too small. They were never worn. I rewarded myself by getting a different car, an MG sports car that was my pride and joy. I guess that's more like the modern player, but although I did like

my cars I only ever had one at a time. I wouldn't really criticise
players of today for having six different cars, because people
must have been saying the same about me.

Winning promotion didn't really sink in for a couple of days,
probably not until I drove down to have a holiday in Devon
with my mother. There was a sense of relief that I wasn't playing
football for two months and could spend time away from the
game. My mum had moved to Devon in 1961, a couple of years
after I joined Swindon, when she married a gentleman called
Cecil Smith. For a while my brother and I found it difficult to
come to terms with this. We were young and selfish and thought
about our father more than the life our mother had to rebuild
for herself. But the truth was she had done so much for John and
me, and now she had to do something for her own happiness. It
was a wonderful place she'd moved to, and I adored spending
summers down there.

Just as in Swindon I would do all kinds of jobs to earn money
through the summer. I worked the deckchairs on Tor Abbey
beach, which was ideal for getting to know girls. Another time
it was lifeboat duty, even though I couldn't swim. But nobody
asked me and I didn't see a problem. I got friendly with Robin
Stubbs, who played for Torquay United, and it helped that we
both drove around in MGs. We'd find out when the Swedish
girls were coming in and get to the railway station in our cars
with the tops down and ask them if they wanted a lift. We had
some fun in those blissful summers.

The dream continued into the start of the Second Division
season 1963–4. We were unknowns to all the bigger name teams
and we won our first six matches as Bert's Babes had their finest
hour. Bert Head had told the Swindon supporters that we were
heading for the First Division, and for a couple of months they

dared to believe it. The sixth match was at home to Manchester City, who had been relegated from the First Division and spent more than £200,000 on new players in the hope of winning promotion back immediately. We thrashed them 3-0, and I scored the first goal with a flying header in the third minute of a game watched by a crowd of more than 28,000 fans. I set up the second goal for Jack Smith and Ernie Hunt scored the third.

It was at about this time that I had a fateful meeting with Joe Mercer, who was then the manager at Aston Villa. I was coming out of the ground in the early afternoon following training and Joe was sat in his car, a racing-green Humber, in the car park with his wife. He saw me coming, wound down the window and introduced himself and said that he'd played with my father George at Aldershot during the war. I got into the back of his car and he asked me straight up, 'Do you fancy playing for Aston Villa?' Of course I did. If truth be known, Villa had always been my favourite club as a boy when we used to take the train up on Saturday afternoons from Cheltenham to watch the big teams in Birmingham. I'd loved the atmosphere of Villa Park. I was excited again, but once more it came to nothing. If there was a transfer bid I never heard about it, and not too long after Joe had a breakdown and left the club.

The FA Cup was exciting, too. We drew Manchester City at home in the third round, and beat them again, 2-1. After winning against Aldershot in the next match we were up against West Ham at home in the fifth round. This time we lost to Bobby Moore and company, and they went on to win the Cup. We'd missed Ernie Hunt through illness, and I always thought that made a real difference. The perfect start in the League season couldn't last, of course. We were being found out, although it was a huge thrill to play against teams like

Sunderland and Newcastle. To finish in fourteenth place was more than respectable, and the youth team reached the FA Youth Cup Final. What also happened, inevitably, was that some of the paper talk about Bert's Babes being snapped up by top teams finally came true. The first to go was Bobby Woodruff, who left for Wolves in a £35,000 transfer in March 1964, towards the end of that season. I was pleased for him, but also envious. I wondered if my turn would ever come.

Looking back, perhaps that was also the time the atmosphere started to change imperceptibly at Swindon. Earlier in the season we'd been filmed in a TV documentary called *Six Days to Saturday*, where they let the cameras on to the team bus and into the dressing room and every part of our lives for a week. They filmed Ernie and me playing football in the street with the kids, which is what we did anyway. It showed the way football was at the time – it was down-to-earth with no pretensions and you could see that the players were part of the town and the people. I have the documentary on DVD at home and I think it would be instructive for today's young footballers to watch it, to see what we did in those days. It would be an education. It must be difficult for managers like Sir Alex Ferguson, who have come from the same era as me, to deal with the attitudes of modern players. It was so different then. We'd travel on the Corporation buses, and walk into the ground with the fans on a Saturday afternoon. You didn't need bodyguards for protection. The mood in the documentary is so optimistic; you can see it in our faces and in the demeanour of Bert Head. But that had ebbed away by the end of the season, and the era of Bert's Babes was over.

The next season Swindon would be relegated to the Third Division. Reality had come back to haunt a little club with big ideas. We struggled from the start and won few matches. One of them was particularly memorable: the afternoon we went to Maine Road and beat Manchester City 2-1, when they had reached their lowest ebb. The crowd was only 8,015, the lowest in the history of Maine Road, and I scored one of the goals. Before the match I had walked out on to the pitch in more than a little wonder at this huge ground. I sat on a wall at the side of the pitch and talked to the groundsman, Stan Gibson, who was a real character for many years at City. I told him the pitch was beautiful, that it looked a fantastic surface to play on. He was happy to be flattered and told me I should come and play here, that I should sign for Manchester City. He said I was the type of player who'd do really well at the club. After the game it wasn't so friendly. The City fans staged a loud protest outside the ground, throwing bottles and bricks at the stadium walls and demanding changes. I sat in the dressing room listening to the commotion, not thinking I would soon be here trying to make these same supporters a happy bunch again.

Relegation only came for Swindon on the last day of the season. We were level on points with Portsmouth, but with a better goal average, so we had to match their result. We didn't. We played away to Southampton and lost 2-1, the goal that sent us down scored by Terry Paine. Meanwhile, Portsmouth drew at Northampton and they stayed up.

The consequences were inevitable. Bert Head was sacked despite everything he had done for the club and they brought in Danny Williams as the new manager. He was a northerner, from Rotherham, and never had any praise for me. He always seemed to be nitpicking and finding faults. The main problem was that he wasn't Bert Head. The team immediately began to break up. Ernie would soon enough be on his way to Wolves, where he joined Bobby Woodruff, and Cliff Jackson went to Crystal Palace.

It made me desperate to get away as well. I was twenty-two now, with two hundred first team matches behind me. Despite relegation, I had done well. I'd been voted player of the year at Swindon and been called up to play for the England Under-23s against Turkey, along with Ernie. I wanted to better myself, and I was sure I could if only I got the chance somewhere. I was fed up with hearing lots of rumours about my future and them all coming to nothing. I was very disillusioned, and began to wonder if I really was as good as I thought I was. I knew I had to leave. I went down to Devon to work on the deckchairs again and spent all summer hoping something would happen.

One of my pals there was John Benson, who'd been at Maine Road as an apprentice and then joined Torquay. Years later he would be manager of Manchester City, too. One day that summer we were doing the deckchairs and heard on the radio that Joe Mercer had joined City as manager with Malcolm Allison as his assistant. I knew Joe had been interested in me as a player and I'd met Malcolm once at Swindon and seen what a striking figure he was. In the back of my mind were also the words of City's groundsman, Stan Gibson, who had said Maine Road would be perfect for me. I thought to myself, why not ring Joe up and see if he has a space for me? I don't know what John Benson really thought, but he knew the club's number from his time at City, and when I got back to the house I rang them up. It was cheeky but I got through to Joe and made my pitch about wanting to play for City, knowing he had liked my football.

'Leave it with me,' said Joe, and put the phone down.

A fortnight went by with no news, but little did I know that

Joe had decided to go for me and travelled down to Swindon to talk terms. It was only when I got back to report for training, more desperate than ever about being stuck in the Third Division again, that I was told the clubs had agreed a £35,000 fee for me to join City. It was a week before the beginning of the season. There was still one final hurdle, however, as there always seems to be. As I was getting my stuff together to drive up to Manchester for the medical, someone at Swindon came up and said: 'Give us a hundred quid and you can go.' I don't know how it would be taken these days, but that's the way it was then. It seemed to be part and parcel of the game. If I hadn't gone to the bank and got out £100 I could well have lost my transfer.

You were on your own then as a player. There was no decision to make about his demand. I had to pay up. And I'd had to make the phone call myself to Joe Mercer that ensured I made progress in my football and in my life. Otherwise I would have stayed at Swindon and probably faded away, a journeyman pro that nobody much remembered.

And that was the fate that Swindon's new trainer, Bill Harvey, told me lay in wait. When I picked up my boots at the County Ground he confronted me with the words: 'The real players here are Ernie Hunt and Don Rogers. I don't know why you're leaving because you're just a Third Division player. You'll do nothing. You'll be nothing.'

I didn't say a word. I'd heard it all before. I'd spent my life proving people wrong and I'd do it again.

5

A FOOTBALL EDUCATION

The M6 motorway hadn't long been open when I drove north from Swindon full of excitement and apprehension at the prospect of joining Manchester City. I always remember passing Stoke and seeing workmen planting fir trees by the side of the carriageway. Those fir trees are still there today – and I always look at them when I go past. They remind me of growing up.

It was a huge step for me, and a huge risk. I had grown in confidence at Swindon, I knew I was the right standard there, and I had a comfortable life in football. After so many years when the paper talk had come to nothing it was a nervous moment to be on the way to a big club with a history of great players. I'd dreamed of this moment for a long time, but the reality brought all my old insecurities flooding back. Would I be good enough? How would a country boy cope with life in a big city?

I wasn't going back to Swindon. I couldn't do that. I knew it was now or never. But would it be never?

The journey seemed to take for ever. In those days the M6 only started at Penkridge, near Wolverhampton, but eventually I was on the dual carriageway driving in my MGB towards the centre of Manchester. Then I realised I actually had no idea where City's ground was. I kept driving but there were no signs for Maine Road, and when I finally pulled in and asked a fella he laughed and said I'd gone well past the turning. At least I hadn't done what some new players in a big city do and gone to the wrong ground.

Maine Road was buzzing when I turned up. There were so many people outside I thought there must be a match on, and I knew the excitement that had been stirred by the arrival of Joe Mercer and Malcolm Allison. I jumped out of my car and was astonished – and this is not false modesty – to discover they were all waiting for me. Many of them were journalists and photographers who had been tipped off that I was due to become the first signing of the Mercer–Allison era. It was truly unbelievable because nothing like that had ever happened to me before. I'm sure most of them had never heard of me, unless they had been among the few faithful City fans who'd been in that 8,000 crowd when I'd scored for Swindon in our last season in the Second Division.

The receptionist certainly hadn't heard of me. I walked into the lobby at Maine Road and said I'd come to see Mr Mercer; she had absolutely no idea who I was. She went away and came back with the message that I was to go over to the greasy spoon café across the road where Mr Mercer would join me. Joe walked in wearing his blue tracksuit and we had a cup of tea, and I knew straight away that I wasn't going to be cosseted at City. I'd come down to earth before we'd even talked terms. There were no agents in those days, and Joe must have known that my wages wouldn't be an issue because I'd been the one who'd made the phone call to him. I certainly had no intention of going back; it never crossed my mind.

'There's no money here,' said Joe. 'But things could start to happen at this club. You're earning £35 a week at Swindon. I can only give you £40 a week.'

On the drive up I'd thought of all the bargaining I could do, the money I might ask for.

'No problem,' I said in a flash.

And it wasn't a problem to me. I got £500 of the transfer fee, which was a helluva lot of money, and I was going to wear the famous blue shirt of Manchester City. I was going to pull that on and play at a fabulous stadium. Maybe it sounds naive, but I didn't care about the money, I really didn't. I had an opportunity and I walked back across the road and through the front door of Maine Road with a wonderful feeling in my heart.

I was at a great club with a great manager. Joe Mercer was one of the giants of football, a household name to rank with Jock Stein, Bill Shankly, Bill Nicholson and Matt Busby. He was the most famous of all of them as a footballer, the captain of England. But they were all club figureheads and people had so much respect for them. If Joe walked into a room you knew he was there. He could have told me to walk to the moon and I'd have tried to do it. Instead he told me to go back into the ground and into the dressing room.

I can't remember having a medical. I had that ruptured thigh but nobody took any notice. I signed on in the office and went to the changing rooms where there was a pile of kit in the dressing room, a mish-mash of different colours, not City blue. I put one on and laced up the boots I'd brought with me in the car.

Then Malcolm Allison was introduced to me as I walked down the tunnel. There was nothing warm about his greeting, just: 'Come on, we'll see what you're made of.' He took me out on the pitch alone; all the other players had gone home at lunchtime. I was fit, but I wasn't used to the type of training he was doing. It was the best part of an hour of fitness work, shuttles and so on. There was nothing with the ball, and he really put me through it. I enjoyed it and did okay, and he said: 'Well done, son', but I wasn't sure if he meant it. Malcolm was very dour that day. I think Joe wanted me more than Malcolm did at that time. I'm not sure Malcolm was enthusiastic about me at all.

A more pleasant welcome lay in store. City had arranged for me to stay at the Grand Hotel in Aytoun Street in the centre of Manchester, and it was that big it felt like driving into New York. I wasn't used to it. I'd only been to the centre of London twice in my life before then and the luxury of the hotel was overwhelming. But it quickly became a second home in the months I stayed there and it literally was a grand place to be. I was particularly friendly with Jim Barker, the head waiter in the restaurant and a big football lover, and I quickly got to know Sandra Cargill who worked on reception.

The next day was the start of the season and my debut for Manchester City would be away to Middlesbrough. I had barely met my new team-mates before I was running out on to the pitch with them at Ayresome Park. Malcolm Allison didn't make a fuss of me beforehand. It was captain Johnny Crossan who introduced me to the players. Then my heart was beating. They were senior pros like Roy Cheetham, Derek Kevan, Neil Young and former Wolves winger Jimmy Murray. There was also Ralph Brand who had come from Glasgow Rangers. I was among people who were way above me in football.

In the dressing room I put the pale blue shirt on, the white shorts, and felt like a king. I knew it was a great club. At Swindon I had played as a deep-lying winger, and Malcolm told me to play my normal game. That was easier said than done because I was up against Mick McNeil who was one of the best left backs in the country and had played eight times for England a couple of years earlier before Ray Wilson emerged. We were getting beat 1-0 for much of the match, but we ended up drawing one each. I crossed the ball for the equaliser by Jimmy Murray and it gave me immense satisfaction. I'd made a contribution, and that's what I always wanted to do in a football game. If you make a contribution in a team sport you've played a part.

As we were driving back down to Manchester on the bus Malcolm took me to one side and gave me the first of many lessons that turned me into an England international. He sat me down and said: 'Now listen, son, if I'd wanted to sign an extra full-back I'd have signed one. You're not a full-back; you're a winger. Don't come back into our half. You're not a defender. You're only trouble to us coming back to help defend. Just stay wide and take the full-back on when you get the ball. Try to get round the back and get a cross over. That's your job, okay.'

It wasn't a question. It was a mighty command.

That night I had my introduction to city nightlife. A couple of players, Harry Dowd and Matt Gray, along with sportswriter Peter Gardner from the *Manchester Evening News*, took me to the Corn Exchange where it was wall-to-wall girls in miniskirts. They were drinking Bacardis; I showed my naivety by insisting on a pint of Mackeson stout. Swindon would have closed down by eleven o'clock on a Saturday night; here it was just beginning to get lively. I was in heaven.

The next morning I had to drive back to Swindon to pick up all the clothes I'd left behind. I'd parked my car back at Maine Road, something the other players never did. I found out why soon enough. I got as far as Penkridge on the journey south when a wheel came off on the dual carriageway. Someone had tampered with the wheel at the ground, loosened the wheel nuts probably, and I crashed into a lorry and the car rolled over. The MGB was a write-off, but I was lucky: I only needed a few stitches above an eye and in one of my elbows.

City's secretary Walter Griffiths came and fetched the new player who looked like he was going to cause more trouble than he was worth. He'd seen all sorts come and go through Maine Road and this wasn't an encouraging start. No doubt Malcolm Allison was also wondering what the club had signed.

Maybe all the fuss about that accident is why I don't have a clear memory of my first home match for City, a 2-1 victory at home against Wolves, thanks to two own goals. I was stiff and sore, but there was no chance I was not going to play. That was my way; I always felt there was something special about putting on the pale blue shirt, and I guess that attitude helped me to win over both Malcolm and the City crowd.

I was lucky because the crowd took to me straight away. You need the crowd behind you and I won them over. I'm sure that's because they could see that I was always a tryer. They could see that I worked hard. If I'd been a ballplayer like Tony Currie, the kind who doesn't look as if he's working hard even when he is, it could have been different.

After a 0-0 draw at Bristol City, the fourth match of the season was a Tuesday night game away to Wolves again at their atmospheric old Molineux ground. We were already 2-0 up when the ball was played up the line. I went for it and Wolves defender Dave Woodfield hit me with all his force; the momentum of the challenge sent me crashing over the brick wall by the side of the pitch. I landed with my feet on seats where no one was sitting, but I slipped and caught my head on one of the metal stanchions. There was blood everywhere, and I mean *everywhere*. Apparently, a pregnant woman in the crowd was so traumatised by the sight that she lost her baby. I wasn't unconscious and was taken away on a stretcher back to the dressing room where they stitched me as best they could. I am told they were pulling the stitches through the top of my head with pliers, and I believed it because it was my old pal Ernie Hunt telling me. Ern was at the match because he was about to sign for Wolves from Swindon; they'd finally agreed to let him follow me out of the club, but only after a lot of ructions. He'd rushed down to the dressing room when he saw the accident. Another extraordinary twist was that the Wolves caretaker manager was Andy Beattie, my father's team-mate at Preston. The last time I'd seen him had been on the day of my dad's funeral.

So now I was a right old mess: four stitches in my elbow, three stitches above the eye, and eighteen on my head. And I still had to get down to Swindon to pick up my gear from my digs at the Hunt household in Redcliffe Street. Cecil Green had agreed to drive me down from Wolves in his Bentley because my MGB had been smashed up. What he didn't expect was a medical ward on the back seat with blood oozing out all over his leather interior. I took the train back from Swindon to Manchester.

Did I play in the next game against Coventry on the following Saturday? Of course I did. Malcolm asked me if I would play, and I said yes. There were no thoughts of X-rays of my skull or worrying about concussion. The only instruction was to the rest of the team – don't play the ball in the air to the winger with the bandage on his head. The first ball, naturally, came in the air and I headed it and started bleeding. But I played the whole game as we drew 3–3.

That night I was out on the town as well. Sandra, the receptionist, had invited me to a party and I wasn't staying in despite all the blood and stitches. I was having too good a time – and I think Malcolm approved. He loved the high life more than anyone.

I have to say that Malcolm Allison helped me more than anyone in my career. He was a flamboyant person and it rubbed off on me. You knew you weren't letting the side down by expressing your personality and confidence in the game. But Malcolm couldn't have done it without Joe Mercer. The great thing about City when I signed was the partnership of Mercer and Allison and the contribution they made together is impossible to exaggerate. Joe was so respected and he gave the club such status. When we arrived at Highbury to play Arsenal he was the only person anyone was interested in. Joe talked to you and quietly built up your self-belief as a player; he kept you ticking over with encouragement. We always played with a smile, too, because that's how he wanted the game to be played. After some difficult times as manager at Sheffield United and Aston Villa, he was so effective at City because Malcolm took much of the burden off his shoulders. Joe set the tone as manager and Malcolm did the tactics and the training. It was a perfect combination. Malcolm was the greatest coach English football has ever had, but he wasn't a good manager, and without Joe he would have been nothing.

Joe might say a few words to you, but it was Malcolm who

really worked on you. And as he got to know me, Malcolm worked me out. He is a very clever man, apart from being a brilliant coach, and he used psychology a lot. Sometimes Malcolm would speak to me and sometimes he wouldn't. That was psychological, making me wonder what I'd done, making me want to prove a point to him all the time. In the end he would say 'well done' but it was a hell of an effort to get those two words from him.

He made me as a winger. Instead of me standing with my back to goal and receiving the ball, he made me run and receive the ball as I was running. He gave me control. He told me: 'You've always got to use your assets, and one of yours is pace. Don't try to do something you can't do. Your asset is going past the full-back and crossing balls. You're the best crosser I've seen.' There were better crossers of a ball than me, but he was building up my confidence and I always needed that. I was back to square one at City – my confidence was low. I had to prove myself to Malcolm and I could only do that by doing exactly what he wanted me to do.

Malcolm always used to shout at me from the stands. 'Michael do this, Michael do that,' he would bellow. He never called me anything but Michael. Nobody else called me that at the time. He would always shout at me. He built up my confidence and that's what it's about. You can have all the ability in the world, but if you don't believe in yourself it's almost worthless.

I remember so vividly the match that really won him over. It was a home game against Portsmouth a couple of months into that first season in the Second Division. Pompey's left back was Ron Tindall, who had been a centre forward for Chelsea but was coming to the end of his career and filling out in defence. The instructions from Malcolm were crystal-clear. I was told to take him on all the time. In the first half I did it as best I could, but didn't have a go all the time. I was still finding my feet at City, and I didn't want to make a fool of myself.

At the break Malcolm said: 'What did I tell you to do? When you get the ball just take on your man and get round the back. That's it.'

This time the command sunk in. In the second half I did just that. Malcolm was on my touchline now and he kept hollering orders to me whenever I got the ball: 'Take him on, take him on, take him on.' I kept doing it, kept trying, and it was throw-in, corner, throw-in, corner, but no luck. Then it suddenly came good. I pushed the ball past Tindall, reached the byline, crossed it, and boom the ball was in the back of the net. I did it again – another goal. And again, a third goal, and we'd won 3-1. Malcolm came up to me afterwards and said: 'That's the best game of football you'll ever have in your life. Keep doing that and you'll satisfy me and you'll satisfy the club.' So that's how I played. I wasn't the trickiest winger but I had pace to get by people and I could cross a ball.

Malcolm knew me. Don't ask me how he knew, but he did. He could get that little bit more out of me. Sometimes he treated me like dirt. You don't have to tell a pro when he's playing well or badly. He knows. When he was trying to psych me out by ignoring me, I would be so angry and think, 'I'll show that big arrogant bastard what for.' Joe would let him do that. Then the boss would come round and just tap me on the head. It worked. Malcolm could get another 25 per cent out of me. He couldn't get 25 per cent extra in skill – I was already at the peak with skill – but he gave me confidence. And the club started to take off.

He lifted us all up. That side included players like Mike

Doyle, Alan Oakes, Glyn Pardoe and Neil Young, all of whom had come through the youth system but were being questioned by the supporters because they were in the side that had been relegated from the First Division. Malcolm made those players just as he made me – and one of the big factors was that he made us really fit.

At Swindon the training had been pretty basic, but at City we couldn't wait to get to the ground. Training started at ten o'clock but we were all in a café up the road by nine. Then we went into training. The surfaces weren't good but we couldn't get into the ground quick enough. When we trained we *really* trained. We worked through the week as athletes and played on Saturday as footballers. Our day off was playing football on a Saturday.

The change in mood that Malcolm Allison inspired happened almost instantly. You knew straight away that you were working with someone special. I knew that if I was to get anywhere I had to do exactly what this man said. He gave us all a bit of arrogance, but in a good way. He was arrogant and egotistical, a big, handsome bastard, but he was a lovely man, too, a well-read man.

Maine Road had never seen anything like it. The crowd were so used to City being in the doldrums and here, suddenly, was this bold new regime. Malcolm gave us an aura on and off the field. He deliberately walked around the pitch before a game looking so big and dominant. And when the match started the fans could hear his incessant shouting. You could hear it all round the stadium, in fact, and for Malcolm it just came naturally.

If Malcolm Allison could be a bastard as our coach, the truth was that he was also our mate. He socialised with us; we went out together and he would nick my girlfriends off me when I was single. Within a few weeks of my arrival in Manchester, Malcolm invited me to his house-warming party. All the single players at City and United went along. George Best, whom I'd already met, was there and so were Denis Law and Paddy Crerand and Noel Cantwell and so on. They all came and they all made me feel so welcome. Denis was a particular hero of mine at the time and I was astounded to be meeting him in the kitchen at such a convivial party. I knew about the camaraderie of team football, but now I was being introduced to the wider fellowship of those in the game. I was still a wide-eyed country boy then, but I was being treated as an equal by the great stars of the day.

It was, thanks to Malcolm, another small lesson in my football education.

6

THE GYMNASIUM TREATMENT

The day I knew I'd truly been taken to the hearts of the Manchester City fans was when they started singing a song for me. It came from a January 1966 hit by the Small Faces, a song called 'Sha-La-La-La-Lee'. Of course, it wasn't too hard to adapt the words to fit the name Summerbee, nor for opposition fans to add their own final line of 'Who the fucking hell is he?'

In the same spirit I can say: That-was-oh-so-great-for-me. The whole Kippax – the main stand – would be singing it and it gave me a huge lift. The crowd only sings for players who engage them, and I've always loved that tune. What I didn't know at the time is that it was co-written by comedian and singer Kenny Lynch, who would soon become one of my best pals.

I would talk to the crowd, home fans or away fans, and they would talk to me. You could do that in those days; today it would probably result in an immediate charge of bringing the game into disrepute. I don't think football has changed for the better in that respect. I talked to the supporters automatically because I played wide. And I liked talking; I'm a natural talker. People understood the way I was, and I have always felt the fans are the most important people in football. They pay their money to be entertained, and I always tried to give them a show.

Do you remember when people used to throw toilet rolls on to the pitch? It was a craze for a time. Well, I threw one back once and it knocked a policeman's helmet off. It wasn't deliberate, but the crowd loved it. Manchester City fans still remind me of that incident to this day. Another thing I used to do was join the Salvation Army band when they were playing before the match or at half-time. I'd also walk out on to the pitch a certain way for a bit of fun, taking the mickey out of something or somebody. Why not try to give the crowd a laugh or two as well as being deadly serious with the business of football?

Being a winger I got to know the people who stood by the touchline and the fans in wheelchairs, who used to sit beside the pitch at that time. As I was taking a corner I'd run the backs of their heads. The photographers were also part of my routine. I used to run into them after I'd crossed a ball and I'd ask them how long there was to go in the match.

We certainly gave the City crowd a proper show all that season with our football as well. Right from the start we were winning matches, and promotion back to the First Division looked a possibility early on. The more matches we won, the bigger the attendances became, so that by the end of the season our gates were actually higher than those of Manchester United in the First Division. It was an amazing transformation, and beyond all expectations.

Unbeknown to me, Malcolm Allison had had a bet with

United midfielder Pat Crerand at his house-warming party in the autumn. Malcolm boasted that City would have bigger crowds than United within two years, which seemed ridiculous when they had been down to as few as 8,000 a few months earlier and when United were a wonderfully attractive team, going well in the European Cup with superstars like George Best, Denis Law and Bobby Charlton. Of course, Crerand took up the challenge. He was a feisty character anyway, and that was a red rag to a bull. The bet was made. It took less than a season for Malcolm's prediction to come true.

Maine Road changed from a place like a morgue to a vibrant stadium packed with expectant fans. Blue scarves that had been hidden away in embarrassment for years were suddenly being worn with pride. We swiftly became an exciting, attacking side that the supporters loved to watch. I was lucky that I arrived at City when they were at their lowest ebb; the only way was up. I was lucky as well to play in every match that season when we romped to the Second Division title and won promotion. Those who doubted the appointment of Joe Mercer and Malcolm Allison quickly shut their mouths.

It was December 1965 and nearly 35,000 came to see a 0-0 draw against Norwich, and I scored my first goal for City in a 5-0 win at home to Leyton Orient the day before my twenty-third birthday. I don't remember it, so it was probably a tap-in. Most of the goals I scored were tap-ins. I was in the team to make goals more than to score them. And I always felt the game was about teamwork and team success rather than individual glory. You couldn't be a hero on your own in a winning team.

People ask me what made the real change at Manchester City in that season. The managerial and psychological work of Mercer and Allison was vitally important, but I believe the most significant factor of all was the punishing fitness regime that was introduced by Malcolm Allison. He brought in athletes like Olympic long jump gold medallist Mary Rand, and Derek Ibbotson, who had been the world mile record holder in the 1950s. There was also Danny Herman, a 100-metres sprinter, and marathon man Joe Lancaster. They would get us running on a cinder track in spikes, and the first time was so tough. It was complete chaos for us players who were supposed to be highly tuned professional sportsmen. We realised just how unfit we actually were compared to real athletes.

Ibbotson would lead us on interval training, running the three or four miles round Wythenshawe Park. He would be leading the way, talking merrily to us as he ran. We were trying to suck in air through our backsides we were such wrecks. It was slightly better with Mary Rand, but only because we enjoyed running behind her. Back on the running track we'd do abdominal work as well, and after a couple of weeks we had progressed enough to run wearing sweat bags under our tracksuits and against our skin. At the end you needed people to help you get the gear off. It had to be peeled off and the water just cascaded off you.

To start with we hated this physical torture, but after a month to six weeks the benefits began to show themselves on a Saturday afternoon. We'd never get tired, even on muddy pitches, and in the last twenty minutes Malcolm would shout 'second gear' and we'd step up the pace and destroy the opposition. Other teams just couldn't handle us. Saturday really was like a day off. It was easy playing ninety minutes compared to what we were doing during the week. We dreaded Monday mornings; they were hell. But once you were through it – fantastic. And we loved the advantage it gave us in matches.

We were doing things in 1965 that people think are unusual

today. We were wired up to running machines at Salford University to test us out, and we played training matches with special units on our backs that measured heart rate and so on. It was like playing carrying a baby on your back. It was a piece of cake for someone like Colin Bell, who was a natural athlete, but much harder for others. There were also countless recovery exercises in the gymnasium at Maine Road just off the tunnel that leads to the pitch. We learned about different kinds of fitness, too, from the legendary squash player Jonah Barrington, and we also had training sessions with the Salford rugby league players.

Once we were really fit it was great to play five-a-side against the athletes. Derek Ibbotson and Danny Herman would be left knackered at the end of those games. And one of the great things is that they all became part of the Manchester City family and would come to matches to cheer us on. They were an integral part of our success, and I'm certain that the players today in the twenty-first century are no fitter than we were.

We accepted it because we became an exceptional side with players that others had written off. And it was Malcolm's doing – the track work, the weights and all the work on match situations. He had us moving around the field, not always in the same position. It was a pleasure to play in that team because we were confident we could win every match. I always say that if you're a competent player and really fit you can become a good player. If you have ability and you're very, very fit you can become an exceptional player.

I think those days at City proved it. Our fitness enabled us to destroy opponents. You know, it annoys me that when people talk about the sides of the 1960s and 1970s they never mention Manchester City. We had a great side. We destroyed them all.

We won everything. I have a picture at home of the Charity Shield, League Championship Trophy and FA Cup all in one picture. Yet people hardly ever mention us. People don't speak the truth.

The gymnasium off the main tunnel had another use as well. During matches I would talk to Stan Gibson, who stood in the same place on the touchline throughout every game. When he died they put up a plaque where he stood to commemorate him. Stan was a wonderful man who used to look after me, and he'd been the first person to encourage me to join City. He was a big friend and I used to visit him at his house, and when I won the player of the year trophy. I used to let him keep it at his house. Most of the time during matches it was just idle chatter with Stan, but if there was any aggravation or problems in a game I'd tell him near the end of the ninety minutes to make sure the gymnasium door was open. It was halfway down the tunnel and Stan had the key.

He knew what was coming – the Gymnasium Treatment. That's how we referred to our method of dealing with anybody on the opposition team who'd been sneaky or cowardly in a game. At the final whistle we'd wait for him to go by and lob him into the gymnasium, lock the door behind us and give him a little smack. Today, with all the television cameras, such behaviour would be spotted, but in those days we'd just go in and do it. Stan would open the door and we'd sort it out.

It didn't happen very often but the possibility was always there.

I have to say that Terry Paine got the Gymnasium Treatment when Southampton came to play us. It was just a little reminder that you couldn't come to Maine Road and go round doing the sort of things that he got up to. Terry was a fantastic player, a part of England's 1966 World Cup squad, but he, at least in my view, could be a sneaky and dirty player. The one thing that footballers don't like in the game is people who are sneaky and cowardly. He wasn't my cup of tea. He may have been a very good player but he had that side of him which wasn't very nice.

When you're playing in a game you want people to be up front. The real tough guys of the game hit you head-on. Terry didn't, so he got the treatment – and he got the message all right. We told him it was better to do it in the gymnasium than out on the pitch where everyone could see it. We told him it was better because he might cry out there.

There was a code of conduct that existed in the game between players then. It wasn't written down anywhere, but it existed all right. Big Jack Charlton apparently had his little black book of players he took against. But there weren't too many names in that book. The people he was talking about were those who didn't play correctly. When you played against Jack you knew he was a tough man and he would try to soften you up a bit. It was the same with Dave Mackay, a wonderful player and a really hard man. You knew it was a legitimate tackle with Dave Mackay. And you'd feel it. The only way to survive in the game was to be able to take it, especially if you were a forward. If you were good enough you could dish it back a bit as well. I did.

I never came across anybody, however, who came up to me afterwards in a players' lounge and called me a dirty bastard. They might have thought it, but you had a drink after the match and got on with it. My leg was broken twice, but I never broke anyone's leg in football. I played it as hard as anyone – but I did it up front.

During that 1965–6 season our League form was pretty good

throughout. We were unbeaten in the League at home and lost only five matches on the road. An exciting run to the FA Cup quarter-finals also helped boost our confidence. In the third round we drew away at Blackpool when I scored an equaliser in the last minute. I'll always remember it because the heavyweight boxer Brian London was stood behind the net and said, 'I'll have you, Summerbee' when the ball went in. Of course, it was only a bit of fun. Then we beat them 3-1 at home in the replay.

In the fifth round we overcame Leicester City, then a First Division side, also in a replay. That game was played the same night that George Best put on a stunning performance against Benfica in the European Cup at the Stadium of Light in Lisbon. More of that later.

The quarter-final pitched us against Everton, who were a fine team. It went to two replays. We drew 0-0 at home in the first match and I was up against Everton's England defender Brian Labone. He never liked playing against me because I would rough him up a bit. I'd leave it in occasionally. Someone played a ball to me, I turned round, and Jimmy Gabriel just stuck his head into me. He was trying to protect Brian. The impact split my eyebrow open and there was also a gash on Jimmy's face. There was blood everywhere but neither of us would go off and we were soon laughing about the situation because we were both a mess. It was only at half-time that the pair of us got stitched up. I've always had skirmishes with players. In life you have to look after yourself. It was all down to Bert Head's bollocking that first time and to being brought up in the Third Division. You had to look after yourself. It was a learning process. I'll go to my grave still learning.

In the first replay at Goodison we played Everton off the park in front of a packed house, but we couldn't score. It was 0-0 again. The second replay was on neutral territory, at Molineux; I was back there with more stitches over my eye. Tactically, we were the better team again, but Fred Pickering scored a couple of goals and we were out despite dominating the matches. Everton went on to win the FA Cup that year, but the prize for us was the realisation that we were turning into a very good team who could compete with the best in the land, never mind our current opponents in the Second Division. We grew up in those clashes against Everton.

We were always near the top of the League that season, but any doubts that we might fade away were banished by the signing of Colin Bell for a fee of £45,000 from Bury, where Bert Head was now manager. This time it was Malcolm Allison who was certain he wanted the new young player and Joe Mercer who was worrying whether it was a good move or not. Colin came in and immediately started scoring goals and creating havoc in opposition midfields. He was instant dynamite, and it was Colin who scored the goal that clinched promotion with three matches to go.

It came in a match away to Rotherham, one of the better teams in the Second Division that year despite having a rubbish pitch at Millmoor and a bath so small that only one player could get in at a time. It was a windy day, and a legion of City fans made the journey knowing that victory would guarantee us going up. Colin's goal was enough in a 1-0 win and I remember how ecstatic the celebrations were afterwards, and thinking I'd been part of something quite special. We drove straight back to Manchester and had a party at Maine Road. People were dancing on the tables in the boardroom, even the fearsome Mrs Dabell who was in charge of the cleaning ladies. She lived next door to Stan Gibson and was very strict. That night she ended up blind drunk and we pushed her under one of the tables where she fell asleep. Mrs Dabell never lived it down.

Southampton finished second in the table and were promoted with us. I didn't mind that at all. It would be interesting to play against Terry Paine again the next season.

When we beat Rotherham the player I was most pleased for was Johnny Crossan, the Irish international who had done most as a player to help me settle at City. His career had been what you could call chequered, once being banned for receiving an under-the-counter payment and forced to play abroad at Standard Liège in Belgium. I'd played against him once for Swindon, when he was at Sunderland, and now he became a really close pal. He had a beautiful wife, Barbara, who looked after me with endless cups of tea and allowed me to be part of their family in Sale. Johnny made me feel at home in Manchester, and also helped me with my football, not least in acting as a protector on the field when things got a bit rough. There was one match against Sunderland where I had a skirmish and Johnny was straight in there, saying, 'Leave it to me, I'll sort it out.' And he did. He could be quite lethal when it came to that. He wasn't a big man but he used to do it. He taught me how to look after myself on the field. He'd played more than fifty times for the Republic of Ireland, he spoke fluent French and I loved talking to him about all his travels when we were out socialising in the evenings. He was a skilful player and a great example and good influence on me. Johnny didn't stay long after that Second Division title-winning season; he was transferred to Middlesbrough. But I have so much to thank him for.

I spent a lot of time at the Crossan household once I'd moved out of the Grand Hotel. It took me six months to do so, much to the disgust of Mr Griffiths. He kept encouraging me to move into digs because the hotel was costing the club so much money but it was too comfortable for me to want to leave. The head waiter, Jim Barker, kept saying I could have digs in his house, but I always said no. I knew I had to find somewhere eventually and it finally happened when Sandra Cargill, the receptionist, invited me to her twenty-first birthday party. Her mother and father were there and it came up in conversation that I was looking for digs. Tom Cargill said: 'Why don't you stay here? Sandra's in the hotel all week and we have a spare room.' So I ended up moving in with the Cargills and Sandra became like a sister to me. It was my home until I got married.

Another benefit of living with the Cargills in Sale is that it wasn't too far from the digs where my best buddy in Manchester lived. That was George Best, who lived with Mrs Fullaway in Chorlton. I met George only a few weeks after I arrived at City, and it was a friendship that remained strong until his death in November 2005. It certainly made life more interesting in Manchester when the Swinging Sixties were in full flow. I went from being a nonentity, a naive country boy, to messing around with a superstar. But George wasn't just good fun, he was also a special person, a quiet, intelligent and shy man. We just clicked as people, and with his real friendship I knew I had fallen on my feet.

7

A CHARMED LIFE

The Kardomah coffee shop wasn't the trendiest place in Manchester in the Swinging Sixties, hardly the place where you'd bump into George Best – or so you'd think now. But George was essentially a modest man and fame hadn't sunk its claws into him then. So the Kardomah was *exactly* the kind of place a lonely young footballer went for lunch when training was finished, whether he played for City or United. You had so much spare time on your hands and didn't know what to do with yourself.

It was only a few weeks after I arrived at Maine Road that I first bumped into George at the Kardomah. He was sitting alone, and because I knew he was another player I went over and introduced myself. There was an immediate chemistry between us and we chatted away happily, and I soon noticed that a very attractive young lady was sat on her own across the room having a coffee. I looked at her, but she wasn't looking at me. She had eyes only for George.

Soon enough she came over to join us. Her name was Georgina and she was wonderful. But I had no chance next to George, and they started going out. We called her Georgie, and very often I'd be out with them as well because it was a friendship rather than a big relationship. Georgie was wonderful, but there was also an element of sadness in her life. It turned out she was the daughter of Ruth Ellis – the last woman to be hanged for murder in this country. It had been a crime of passion, and today she might easily have been acquitted. But Ruth Ellis had gone to the gallows.

We did all sorts of things together. Those were the days when there was a TV show called *Top of the Pops*, which used to be filmed at a studio in Dickenson Road. We'd go there to see it and went to the Simon Dee television show as well. There was lots of glamour and we got to know many of the stars such as the Hollies, Wayne Fontana and Herman's Hermits. But we were also entranced by football. Every Friday night George and I would go and watch Stockport County; they always played on Friday rather than Saturday to ensure a better crowd. It was called 'Go-Go County' night and we'd go through the turnstiles and stand on the terraces, watch the game and leave just before the end so that we could be in bed by ten o'clock, ready for our own matches the next day. It stopped me sitting at home on Friday night thinking and worrying about who I would be playing against. It was a kind of relaxation; it took your mind off things and helped me sleep well. George went just for the fun of it – he was never bothered who he'd be facing the next afternoon. We went to Stockport for a long time, and the other spectators were never a problem. We weren't troubled apart from being asked to sign a few autographs, and we never minded that. That's what life's about. The bad day is when nobody wants your signature.

For a few months we remained reasonably anonymous in Manchester. Nobody really noticed a young Second Division player with a long nose, and George got more looks from the women because he was a very beautiful man rather than because he was 'famous'. We were still just footballers, and they had always been ordinary working men rather than superstars.

I suppose the change came when George was approached to do a newspaper column called 'The Best Set'. It was just a bit of fun, and I was involved, along with Georgina, because I was a good pal of his. We had to dress up in some amazing gear, like old-fashioned clothes from the Victorian age while pretending to play croquet. I still have some of the newspaper cuttings at home, and they look quite odd and quaint compared to the celebrity photoshoots of today. But we had a whale of a time doing it, usually on a Monday afternoon. The photographer had to take sixty snaps of me to get the right angle for his picture. George only needed one shot. Some of the top models in Manchester would also be involved, and I was hardly going to complain about that. For a country boy I was growing up very fast in the big city thanks to my friendship with George. I was getting a foothold on life and beginning to see the opportunities it could offer.

At the time I had no ideas about being a celebrity. I don't think George had either. We were just a couple of young lads having a good time. They were simple days, and yet they were the days when footballers were starting to become more than just sportsmen. There's no doubt that George was the first football celebrity; everything you see nowadays began with him.

If 'The Best Set' was a gradual beginning, the big transformation happened overnight. It was the night George played for Manchester United away to Benfica in the European Cup in the spring of 1966, playing so brilliantly that he won rave reviews all over the world and was dubbed 'El Beatle'. He came back wearing a sombrero and his face was on every front and back page, and all over the television news. His long hair made him look more like a pop star than a footballer and his dazzling genius with the ball at his feet also made him a uniquely exciting sportsman to watch. Our FA Cup fifth round replay against Leicester the same evening didn't get much attention anywhere but the sports pages of the *Manchester Evening News*.

The next time I saw George was on the Friday lunchtime after training, about thirty-six hours after his electrifying display in Portugal. We were walking down the street on the way to the Kardomah, just as we had done for many months, when I noticed that all the traffic had stopped. Everybody was gawping at George, those with cameras taking photographs. They all wanted to look at George, to be able to go home and say, 'I saw Georgie Best on the street in Manchester today.' It was an amazing reaction, unheard of then for anybody but the Beatles. Football had never seen anything like it. I know that was the day celebrity culture began in English football. That was the day George Best the superstar was born.

Today it's commonplace. I've seen it myself with Andrew Flintoff, the England cricketer, who is a good friend of mine now. We were eating outside at a restaurant in Alderley Edge during the Ashes summer of 2005 and hundreds of people stopped to stare at him and take pictures. We had to retreat inside.

For George it was the start of a commercial explosion. Until then there had been only Denis Compton, the legendary England cricketer and also a fine footballer for Arsenal, one of the first sportsmen to be used by big companies to advertise their products. George was in huge demand, and it rubbed off a little on me. *Charles Buchan's Football Monthly* started to pay me for articles and I thought that was great. I was also the subject of an interview by a young reporter called Lynda Lee-Potter, who later became a famous columnist with the *Daily Mail*. The article was all about how footballers were the 'new glamorous rich' who bought fifteen-guinea shirts six at a time and drove a Jaguar. How tame that seems now.

We were actually more concerned about selling shirts than buying them. One venture George and I tried together was setting up a trendy boutique in central Manchester called Edwardia. A businessman called Malcolm Mooney approached us with the idea, saying that boutiques were the new in-thing. We weren't the most business-minded of people – we had football and a social life; that was our world. George and I put in an equal amount of cash and we set up shop in Bridge Street, opposite the tax office and next door to the Phonograph discotheque. That wasn't a coincidence. Soon there were plenty of girls coming into the shop, which was great for George and me socially but not so good for trade because they hardly bought anything. We had the concession for Ravel shoes and sold only a few pairs. It was a young man's adventure, really, rather than a business. It became a meeting place rather than a shop. We did it for eighteen months, and then I pulled out because I was courting Tina, who would eventually become my wife. George carried on, though. He loved the fashion scene and he opened a second shop in Sale.

Increased publicity brought other benefits to our lives. We did publicity stuff helping out Selwyn Demmy, a local bookmaker, for example, by being photographed with beauty queens dressed up as Father Christmas. We called them Mother

Christmases and they were the best Santas I'd ever seen. We did that every winter and Selwyn raised lots of money for worthy causes. As time went by we accumulated some good contacts. One big bonus was being invited to judge beauty contests like Miss Great Britain and Miss United Kingdom. We also judged the Stripper of the Year in a pub in Hulme. The girls wore rosettes on their G-strings and I thought it looked so funny. I used to count the number of rosettes they were wearing … three, four, five.

We met up with some of the beauty queens afterwards. There were some great girls among them. My favourite was Jennifer Lowe, who became Miss UK, and I took her out a few times. George was fond of Jennifer Girley, who was Miss GB. That was mere coincidence; it wasn't only the Jennys who were gorgeous. It was so exciting and very carefree. Being in the public eye was an attraction and they were nice girls; and they weren't dumb, as some people imagine beauty queens to be. Jennifer Lowe was a very intelligent woman who eventually became a magistrate. These were light relationships, though, because that was the mood of the time. We drifted around, and at one stage George was going out with the American beauty Marjorie Wallace, who was Miss World. We took her to the Phonograph to meet Bobby Moore when he was in town. The fact was that women couldn't take their eyes off George.

Most of the drifting was done on a Saturday night. I would never go out on the town before a game, and nor did George at that time. We'd meet mid-evening after our respective matches and the first port of call was often a classy restaurant called Arturo's. The reason for that was because four other regular diners there were Joe Mercer and his wife, Norah, and Matt Busby and his wife, Jean. We used to get there for eight o'clock and have a meal, usually a steak. George loved Steak Diane. We'd deliberately be drinking orange juice or lemonade so that when the managers and their wives came in we looked like a couple of sober professionals. Mrs Mercer and Mrs Busby were always concerned about the pair of us, so we went through this little charade. At about half past nine we'd go over and say our goodbyes as we were leaving, and it must have gone through the ladies' minds that these two young players were looking after themselves. Then we'd walk out of the door, and go 'Yeeaahh!' as we jigged off down the street to start the real night out.

Yes, we enjoyed ourselves. You're always looking for girls when you're young, aren't you? You were going to meet someone in a club most probably. But it's a big fallacy that we had women with us all the time. They said it about George and they probably said it about me. But it wasn't like that. We went out to have a good time. If we didn't start at Arturo's that was probably because we were at the Mersey Hotel on Princess Parkway, where there was always a bit of cabaret. Then we drove into town because there were no breathalysers then. It wasn't anything ridiculous: just a couple of drinks.

In town we'd start in the flash clubs, the nice places, like Dino's, where a lot of other United and City players went with their wives. Then we'd drift off to Mr Smith's and there were always a lot of girls in there. George was always the centre of attention, and we'd stand next to the ladies' toilet because they all had to go in there and that's how we'd see who was in the club. We'd drift around everywhere, and we might bump into our friend Selwyn Demmy. We'd gradually work our way through the clubs, and we'd try to get into the Phonograph, which was the in place then. You had to be at the Phonograph before midnight – whoever you were, even the owner of the shop next door. If you came after that they wouldn't let you in, and you had to be dressed the right way, too. It was a really good place, like Tramps in London. You'd be guaranteed to get a lot of good-looking girls in there, and groups were often there, too, like Herman's Hermits. There were actors as well: Richard Beckinsale and Ian McShane, if he was in town. George and I would sit and watch mostly, especially in the early days. I still spoke like a yokel and George was shy.

Then we'd drift into Moss Side, to Phyllis's, a shebeen-type place run by the mother of Phil Lynott, the lead singer of the band Thin Lizzy. Licensed drinking finished at two in the morning, but Phyllis's stayed open through the night, and the velvet curtains were so thick and the mood so mellow that you lost track of time. Suddenly, someone would open the curtains and it would be half past ten in the morning and the sun was streaming in. Some of the croupiers went there and it was a lot of fun. But it wasn't all women, women, women, as people like to think – and we weren't walking round legless. It was just a relaxed way of life.

There was very little aggravation at that time when I was out with George, and certainly not at Phyllis's. I do remember us going to Bredbury Hall one night, a more upmarket place and one renowned for there being lots of women. We got talking to two girls and they turned out to be with boyfriends. We had to scarper or we'd have been in trouble. But that was unusual, not least the upmarket bit. We didn't often go to the best places; we liked the normal back-street pubs better.

On Sunday mornings we'd go home to our digs for a shower, me to Mrs Cargill and George to Mrs Fullaway, and then we'd meet again for breakfast in town at Stanilands or Mr Smith's. There were always a few young ladies there, but we never drank on a Sunday because we were training the next day. In the afternoon we might wander over to Selwyn Demmy's apartment in Northenden. That was somewhere you could have some peace and quiet, have a cup of tea and cakes and play cards. George was always playing cards. I preferred to read the Sunday papers. Selwyn was a great help to us. We could relax at his place and feel comfortable. People said he misled us. But he didn't – he helped us. He kept a rein on us. He gave us a sanctuary. The weekend would more often than not end back at the Phonograph on Sunday evening, but not that late. Monday morning training was hellish enough without being hungover.

It sounds like a charmed life – and it was. I have had a charmed life in many ways. George gave me a stepping stone in life, and his friendship was invaluable to me. I tell you what he did – being in his company gave me a lot of confidence as a person. I was meeting so many interesting and beautiful people, but it all seemed so natural. That was the way with George. Strange as it seems, football never came into the equation. It was just a friendship between two people who got on. There were never any competitive conversations about United or City. He always asked how a particular game had gone, but it lasted about five minutes and then we drifted into another world. And success never changed George's essential character. He always looked after people. He had a distinct aura. I also think that people respected the two of us; I think we brought Manchester together a bit. People today talk about Wayne Rooney carrying the boxer Ricky Hatton's belt into the ring, but that's just to sell newspapers.

Life was wonderful for me, and for George, I would think. We were both settled and happy. There was no responsibility except for playing football. We had a few bob in our pockets and we weren't tied down by courting. Although Saturday night was the big night out, we'd see each other occasionally in the week. Sometimes we'd meet for lunch at Fuller's, which was downstairs in King Street. It wasn't pedestrianised then. We called it poseurs' paradise because people used to drive up and down – all the modelling agencies were around there. In a big city you needed company. George had a few acquaintances, but very few people with whom he was close.

Once when I was suspended for being sent off and Manchester United were playing Liverpool at Anfield, George asked me if I would take his dad, Dickie, to the game. That was no problem and we went into a pub by Everton's ground beforehand and later sat among the supporters watching the match. Nobody knew it was George's dad. Afterwards, I met up with George and we drove back to Manchester, dropped his dad off where he was staying, and had a night out. I decided to drive back to my digs at six in the morning in the black Mini I then had. On the way the police stopped me.

'Where are you going, Mike?' one policeman asked.

'I'm trying to get home,' was my pretty weak reply.

'Move over,' he said. 'I'll drive.'

And he took me home. That was the relationship we had with the police then. It was a good time. And, as I say, it was a charmed life.

The problem of going back to the digs in the middle of the night or halfway through Sunday morning became ridiculous in the end. It was unfair on our landladies and it wasn't ideal if we met a girl because you couldn't go back to the digs in that case. So George and I decided to get a flat together that we could use at the weekends and as somewhere to escape to, somewhere we could relax a bit. Josie Cargill had never had anyone in digs before and she deserved more privacy, and I needed some breathing space. George and I kept thinking about different things, and talking to a man named Jack Simmonds one day he mentioned a ground-floor flat that was available in Crumpsall, a nice area of Manchester. It was a Victorian house and the ground floor had been made into an apartment with big bay windows, one big lounge and one bedroom. We liked it very much, started to rent it, and did it up.

It was ideal unless we'd both pulled girls, in which case you had to get back early if you were trying to get them into bed. The flat gave us a bit of freedom, a little bit of independence. We were still young in terms of looking after ourselves and we used it quite often. Nobody knew about it and we tried as much as possible to keep it that way because the football clubs wanted you to stay living in digs until you got married. So we kept it very quiet. When we used to go back in taxis from the city centre we'd try to stop the girls from seeing where they were going. George Best was the target, of course. We tried to use the same taxi all the time; we told the driver it would be a good idea to use blindfolds so the girls wouldn't see the route – but he said no to that. Instead, the cabbie would go round in circles rather than straight to the house, and then suddenly we were at the front door. The girls who came back with us were sensible. You could relax and have a few drinks there. After a while, though, the secret began to slip out and there would be one or two girls just hanging around waiting for us – for George mostly, of course, but if I was lucky one or two might be waiting for me.

We were lucky, too, that the sportswriters were only interested in what we did on the pitch. We got away with murder really in that period when the celebrity lifestyle was just starting to take off.

George became the first football superstar because he was a genius at the game. He didn't know it, but he was. He did things on a football field that no one else could do, and he was brave and bold and he scored goals. It was all so natural for him. He would still be outside the ground ten minutes before kick-off in a derby game between United and City, and then he'd walk in, get one set of clothes off and put another set on, his football kit. He'd still be tying his bootlaces as you came out on to the pitch. I could never have done that. I had to work very hard at my football. It all came to George as easily as walking down the street.

During my career I had a lot of tough personal duels on the pitch, but there were no confrontations with George. Before the start of a derby match he'd come over and say hello. I'd tell him not to come anywhere near me and put the ball through my legs to make me look stupid or we wouldn't be going out that night. Then I'd say: 'See you tonight, all the best.'

Friendship went out of the window on the pitch. The derbies had great atmosphere and most of the games flowed from end to end, often with lots of goals. It could hardly be anything else with two such attack-minded teams. I'd see George straight after the game, and when we were single we'd go out on the town straight from the ground.

People tell me that couldn't happen today, a United star and a City player leaving Old Trafford or Eastlands together. If that's true I think it's very sad. People had a different outlook in the 1960s. There were no replica shirts then and it wasn't red one end and blue at the other. People would sit together in the crowd. They went to a football match for pleasure. Now it's more tribal. Now it's like a war, it's like wearing a uniform, it's like the Sioux versus the cavalry. I think it's very sad. When all's said and done it's just a football match. When the football was being played I was never the most popular player to visit Old Trafford, and once somebody threw a coin at me. They sang songs about me all the time, especially about the size of my nose. But I enjoyed that, and I enjoyed the banter and the shouting from the fans. It inspired me to play better; it proved to me that United supporters respected my football talent.

I never understood the animosity. There was one time I remember when I was taking a girl out and someone said: 'You know she's a Jewish girl?'

I said: 'What do you mean? What's the problem? She's a very nice lady.'

The thing was that I looked Jewish, but I had no idea. People think I was the first Jewish winger to play for Manchester City. I wasn't. But so what? I had great Jewish friends then and I do now.

I had a great friend in the Manchester United team when I was a City player. So what? There were a couple of occasions when someone remarked to me about George: 'He's a red.'

I told them: 'It's irrelevant. I'm going out with a girl who's Jewish. So what. It's irrelevant. What's it to do with you anyway? We're not playing football now. I don't have to explain myself to you and I never will have to.'

Friendship is a precious gift in my view. In football you make acquaintances all the time because of who you are and what you're doing. At clubs like City and United you are in the public eye. It's irrelevant to me what people do. George was my pal. And the fact that we had a trade in common was by the by.

That was the same when I socialised with Malcolm Allison, another man made for the Swinging Sixties. Even though his playing career had been ended early by tuberculosis, and he'd had part of a lung removed, Malcolm remained full of vigour for the good things in life. He was married to Beth, but that didn't prevent him coming out on the town. One time remains imprinted on my memory, when we went to the casino when I was serving one of my suspensions. Malcolm met me for a few drinks, and there were two girls behind the bar – one very, very attractive and one just attractive. Of course, he clocks the very, very attractive one, and I'm talking to the other one, an Australian girl named Jeanette.

I saw her for a few weeks after that, and then one Sunday morning I went to the ground for a soak in the bath rather than going back to the digs. Malcolm was there and he asked me how I was getting on with the young lady. I told him Jeanette was fantastic, and thought nothing more of it until she phoned me a week later.

'Mike, I've got a problem,' she said. 'Malcolm Allison has sent a double bed round.'

'What for?'

'He's moving in,' she said.

And that was that. He'd nicked my girl. But it didn't cause any aggravation with me. She was an acquaintance. We didn't fall out over things like that. He saw Jeanette for a long time after that and she ended up becoming the manageress of the Hilton Hotel in Bangkok. It was all good fun. Malcolm was a handsome fella, he had a glint in his eye – and, like George Best, there was an aura about him that women loved.

A few scrapes were inevitable along the way, but we did seem to have a charmed existence.

I remember one particular situation when George and I had a lucky escape from trouble. There was a blonde lady called Vivienne Nicholson who won a fortune on the pools and went on a famous 'Spend, Spend, Spend' (later turned into a TV drama of the same name) spree. In the middle of that she decided to put on a show on a Sunday morning at the Arthur Fox Revue bar in Manchester. It was like a striptease show and we were invited to a small première of this one. We watched for a bit, and it was a fairly shocking show, not professional at all. Suddenly, there was a police raid and we were lying down on the floor and the police were taking names and arresting people. One policeman spotted us and quietly told us to get out into the toilet. We climbed out of the window and did a runner, and we were very fortunate because it ended up becoming a big controversy in the papers. It was an illegal show but we hadn't known that. Thankfully, nobody found out at the time that we'd been there. It was part of growing up, and that's how life was.

There were times when we decided to go out in Birmingham rather than Manchester. I'd become friendly with the heavyweight boxer Johnny Prestcott, a Manchester City fan, and one of the many people from other sports that Malcolm Allison brought in to train with us. Johnny lived in Birmingham with his mum and we'd drive down there and sleep on his floor. He was a useful man to have around if there was any aggravation. I did have a problem once in Birmingham after a game. We had played West Brom a few weeks before the FA Cup Final in 1969 and a lad called Hughie Curran came up. He used to play for Wolves. He'd had a few drinks and he approached me and told me that I'd played crap that afternoon. I told him it happened once in a while and he looked at me with scorn and said: 'International, huh?'

Johnny Prestcott heard this and he picked up Curran and said: 'If I see you here again that's the last time anyone will see you.'

A year later Curran had been transferred to Oxford, and we were playing them in the FA Cup. I saw Hughie before the game and said: 'Prestcott's in the stands, you know.' He looked very sheepish. We beat them 6-0.

Johnny was there when George and I went on holiday to Majorca at the end of that first year in Manchester when I'd won promotion with City and George had wowed the world at the Stadium of Light. We met at the old Manchester airport, Ringway, which was then two shacks in a field. We were flying on the inaugural Iberian Airways flight to Majorca and we were flush then – we had £50 each in our pocket to last a month. We booked into the Atlantic Hotel on Magaluf beach, at that time the only serious hotel there. We were rooming together and we did nothing but laze around and have a bit of fun. Neither of us could swim so we couldn't run down to the beach and dive into the waves to impress the women. Instead we walked down and had a paddle into the four-foot deep water and pretended we were swimming.

One day we were sat on the beach and there was Johnny Prestcott marching along. We went out for a bit of lunch and the bar ended up like Dodge City with everything going off. We made a hasty retreat and let the boxer sort it out ... Mostly the bars were full of fun and full of girls. One night we had literally to tie George to the bar because one girl was so insistent on taking him away. He thought it was so funny. Occasionally I had a girl drifting my way, but George was the centre of attention, as ever.

People don't understand about George. They always picture him with a drink in his hand, but he was never an excessive drinker when he was playing football, certainly not in those days. He was superbly fit and he'd have a really good opinion in conversation. He loved his cards, and horses and gambling, and the thing was that he never expected anything from anybody. Maybe he was too gentle and laid back for his own good.

The change from our carefree early days together to the end of his football career at Manchester United was a slow process. He loved the game so much, but I think the adulation he experienced was difficult for him to deal with. He became public property, and I'm glad that never happened to me, however much money might come your way as a result. The expectation of him was enormous, and for a time he was strong enough to carry the burden of that.

Our lives gradually began to lead us down different paths. I started to court Tina and George followed a road into the world of glamour and celebrity. I was socialising more and more with Tina and I didn't see him much. The day I realised how much his life was changing was when I went to the opening of a house he had built for himself. There were girls camped outside waiting for him and photographers everywhere looking for pictures. They call them the paparazzi nowadays.

I couldn't have lived that sort of life. And I always knew that. As much as I revelled in the freedom and fun of those charmed days in the Swinging Sixties, I knew that I'd settle down to family life in the end. In that scrapbook at home I looked at one of the articles I did with the *Sunday Mirror* when Arsenal made a big transfer bid for me in September 1967 and I was given a new contract by City. Part of it reads: 'This is what I want when my days at Maine Road come to an end:

1 – A comfortable home already paid for.

2 – A lovely wife.

3 – A couple of kids.

4 – A business that provides enough to keep the wolf from the door.'

And that is exactly how it worked out.

8

'BALLET ON ICE'

England had just won the World Cup and the nation was besotted with football. All eyes were on the Wembley heroes on a blazing hot afternoon in August 1966 when a new season started. Nobody noticed me, but it was a massive moment in my career – I was finally making my debut in the First Division after seven seasons playing in the lower leagues. Nobody could say I hadn't worked my apprenticeship. We were playing away to Southampton, the team that had been promoted with us, which meant another collision with Terry Paine and another duel with my least favourite full-back, Denis Hollywood.

A lot of players kicked me in my career, but nobody more than Hollywood. He kicked me all the time, even when the ball wasn't there. He was sent off quite a few times playing against me, and it was stupid of him. It just got me in the mood to play. One time I completely flummoxed him. I stopped dead in my tracks, took off my City shirt and offered it to him.

'Here have it,' I said. 'It's what you want. Have it, with my compliments.'

That only made him even more furious. It embarrassed him. I've never seen him since, although Southampton fans sometimes come up and say with a smile: 'Denis sends his regards.' I always reply, 'Oh, is that all?'

I got the better of him that day – as usual. It was a 1-1 draw and I scored City's first goal back in the First Division. That was a real morale booster for me. I had become more confident playing under the intense scrutiny of Malcolm Allison, but this was yet another hurdle to negotiate. As a team, though, we struggled in the early part of the season, winning only three of the opening twelve League games, suffering a 1-0 defeat at Manchester United.

The improvements came slowly, but we gradually began to compete on equal terms with most of our opponents. A 1-1 draw in January at home to United showed that. United won the title that year, with George Best, Bobby Charlton and Denis Law at the peak of their powers. By contrast, we were definitely a work in progress. One match I remember particularly was a tough 0-0 draw away to Chelsea, the kind of game that proved we were no pushovers. They had a number of assassins in their side – Ron Harris, Eddie McCreadie, Dave Webb, Marvin Hinton and Peter Osgood. It had been a rough match and near the end I decided to give their goalkeeper Peter Bonetti a reminder of who I was. The assassins immediately surrounded me and started making threats.

'Listen,' I said. 'If I'm going, I'm taking two of you bastards with me.'

They backed off – and it was another small step in establishing myself as a good winger and as a player who you couldn't intimidate and mess around with. That was very important if you wanted to survive in the big time.

As the season progressed we were sat comfortably just below mid-table. The match that changed our mood, the match that made us believe the team could really be going places, was an FA Cup quarter-final away to Leeds United. We played them off the park, and even though we eventually lost 1-0 the performance gave us so much confidence. Our side was almost complete as a unit. We had tough players, we had grafters, we had skilful and elegant players like Neil Young, and we had fine goalkeepers in Harry Dowd and Ken Mulhearn. One of the toughest in the team was Tony Coleman, who was signed from Doncaster for £13,000. He was a revelation, a player with pace and aggression and trickery.

We weren't afraid to go anywhere. The only thing we really lacked was a guaranteed top-class goalscorer. Joe Mercer and Malcolm Allison knew that, but they didn't have much money to spend, and they had to bide their time till the right man came along.

While money was tight, you also had to know your worth as a footballer. I'd been on £40 a week when I signed for City and after a year in which we'd won promotion I asked the boss if there was any chance of a pay rise. He asked what I was looking for and I said: 'Ten pounds would be nice.' Joe said he couldn't afford that, but then there was an article in the *News of the World*, just a snippet, saying that Matt Busby was interested in signing me for Manchester United. A week later I had that extra ten pounds.

Another year on it took a bit longer to get my first proper pay rise in professional football. It was clear that my relationship with Tina was serious and I was thinking for the first time about long-term responsibilities. If I wanted to get married and settle down I would need a better wage. I also knew from the grapevine that other players were being paid more than me, and I asked to double my money to £100 per week in the summer of 1967. I'd played well in my first year in the First Division, and there was the usual newspaper talk about other teams – this time it was Everton, Leeds and Arsenal.

This time the boss turned me down flat. I had a bit of a volatile temper, but when I responded by making an official transfer request it wasn't a hot-headed, on-the-spur-of-the-moment decision. I knew it was the only way that the club would know I was serious. I didn't want to leave Manchester City, but I did want to be paid what I felt was fair and just.

Nothing was sorted out by the start of the new season. There was stalemate between us on a new contract, and amid all these off-the-field distractions the team had a bad start to the season. We drew 0-0 at home to Liverpool on opening day and then lost to Southampton and Stoke City in successive matches – and Malcolm's fury was obvious to everyone. But if he lost his temper he never lost his focus on finding a solution to the problem. This time it was to switch me from outside right to centre forward. Joe Mercer wasn't too happy, and in Sir Matt Busby's book it says that he always liked Mike Summerbee on the wing. The rumours that Busby wanted to sign me came about because he wanted another winger. But Malcolm could see things that other coaches couldn't. He knew I'd played in a central position for Swindon, and he thought it might be a surprise for opposition defenders to have me causing trouble where they weren't expecting it.

I enjoyed the central role. I enjoyed holding the ball up and taking the kicks that inevitably came. I relished the physical battle that the position entailed. I could shield the ball and help the team to get movement off me. It worked really well, and did so because I was an unknown quantity. I would have played anywhere they picked me, and in a team with so much ability it was probably easier to get players to change positions. Looking back, I got away with murder, really. But I was making chances for people, and it started us off on a wonderful run of five successive victories that took us to joint top of the First Division. I scored a few goals, too – it was my best ever season in that regard. I ended up with eighteen goals in the League.

Malcolm was so clever at finding ways to use a player's natural ability. He didn't think in straight lines, and he was always trying to find a new trick. In training we did a huge amount of work on free-kicks and we'd attack with great variation. There weren't any square balls played; we tried to be very direct with good, accurate passes. The fact that we worked so ferociously in training continued to make it easier to play the game on a Saturday. We destroyed sides because we were so fit. We destroyed everybody, and I mean we *destroyed* them.

It was during this run of wins that I was finally given a new contract by the club. It was a huge relief. I didn't want to leave City just when it looked as if the team was really going places. Why leave a club that is joint top of the table?

What happened was that Arsenal had made a transfer bid of £120,000 to sign me. It meant City had to do something – and Joe Mercer and Malcolm Allison both came round to my digs in Sale to talk, which was unheard of. As soon as I saw them at the front door, I knew they were chasing me and thought that it would be all right. I didn't know how strong the interest was from any of the clubs like Arsenal, but I knew this visit was serious.

'Come on, Mike, let's get this sorted out once and for all,' said Joe. That sounded good and then he said: 'I will never allow you to leave Manchester City, you know.'

Oh, oh, I thought, here we go again. But Joe followed it up, saying: 'And we have a new proposition for you.'

It was a new two-year contract at £75 per week, and I agreed to sign next morning at Maine Road. Maybe I could have got a little more money elsewhere, and there were friends telling me I should go to a supposedly more glamorous club with a better chance of winning trophies. But I knew something they didn't: I knew that the Manchester City team that Joe and Malcolm were building was as good as any in the country, and maybe the best of them all. So I stayed at the club, which was what I'd wanted all along.

And within a few months we were the champions of England.

After the contract saga was finally over we then lost three matches in succession. One was at home to Manchester United. We were beaten 2-1, but we had dominated much of the game and been done by a couple of goals from Bobby Charlton in an electric match. Again, the feeling was that we were just lacking a real goalscorer.

Joe and Malcolm had the answer once again. This time they were in total agreement on the man to provide the final missing piece of the jigsaw that would complete the team. That player was Francis Lee, who was signed from Bolton Wanderers for £60,000 and became not only an immediate star with the City fans, but also one of my closest friends in football. The team simply took off when he arrived. He had an arrogance about him that lifted everyone, and he had such a powerful physique that he took the load of two players. He also scored tons of goals as we went on an eleven-match unbeaten run. As I said, we destroyed opponents. We swamped them with fast, attacking football and we overran them. One afternoon we thrashed Leicester 6-0 and the next weekend we won 3-2 away at West Ham, who had Bobby Moore, Martin Peters and Geoff Hurst, World Cup-winners all, in their prime. But the best match of all was a 4-1 victory at home to Tottenham in December.

It is perhaps the single most famous League match ever played by Manchester City. It went down in legend as the 'Ballet on Ice'.

The game was played despite blizzard conditions that hit Manchester. Heavy snow fell, and in today's safety-first culture there is no chance the match would have been allowed to go ahead. Back then you always tried to play if you could. So the pitch was cleared of the thick snow that had fallen and underneath the surface was a bit of a skating rink. But they marked out the lines and there was no hesitation from us about playing. It was probably a bit dangerous but the referee just said 'get on with it'.

I used to enjoy playing on ice. It was a balance thing. You could use your ability and it was a bit like skiing. You have to get your balance right. The thing is that I used to wear leather studs and the leather would sometimes break off and the nails would be sticking out. On the ice they acted like crampons. The day was freezing, and it was still snowing, but the match was fun. Tottenham were a good football team. Jimmy Greaves scored for them in the first few minutes after a free-kick by Terry Venables had been deflected. It encouraged Spurs to play a bit more than they had intended to, although they were still complaining all the way through to the referee that it was too icy and that the game should be called off. The ref took no notice, and it turned into a fabulous game – fabulous for us, that is.

You had to have the right attitude. There was no mood of 'be careful, lads, it's icy out there.' We had none of that, not even in the changing room before the game. We just passed the ball around and everything went to feet. It was an exceptional game and Kenneth Wolstenholme, who was commentating on it for the *Match of the Day* highlights on TV, said it was the best game he'd ever seen. It was later voted the match of the season and is still widely reckoned to be one of the great matches.

Colin Bell scored our equaliser and then I got the second with a header. I got up above everybody and beat Pat Jennings from about sixteen yards and I shouted: 'Hey, Pat, pick that one out then.'

He looked daggers at me. Pat was probably the best goalkeeper in the country at the time and he made several brave and brilliant saves that day to prevent the game turning into a massacre on ice. Everything we did came off – because we wanted it to come off. We were such a confident side, whatever the surface. We were always going to play football whether it was on mud, frost or ice. But there is something about an icy pitch. All you have to do is help the ball on. The passes have to be precise or the ball runs away from you. We made so many chances; we overwhelmed a wonderful Spurs team full of great players. Tony Coleman scored the third goal, tapping in after Bell had hit the post, and Neil Young finished them off with a fourth.

That game epitomised the attitude we had all season. It was a culmination of all the effort and understanding we had created. It ended up being a special match because we'd played so well in such difficult conditions and also because it was shown on *Match of the Day* that night to an audience of millions at home. Very few games were televised then. Only the FA Cup Final and a few England games were screened live and only one match from each Saturday afternoon was shown as recorded highlights later that evening. So they were lucky to get this match, and when you heard Wolstenholme say that Manchester City that day were one of the best sides this country had ever seen, and that you wouldn't see a game of football like it again, you knew it had been extra special. City fans always talk about the 'Ballet on Ice', and my memories of that game will never fade.

We were up to second place in the table now, but had a blip over Christmas, losing home and away to West Brom. The match at The Hawthorns was on Boxing Day and the police stopped me for speeding on the motorway on the way back home to Manchester afterwards. I didn't get a ticket, though.

'I don't know why you're bothering with me,' I told the cops. 'Malcolm Allison's just passed me doing over ninety and he's pissed out of his mind.' And off they raced, leaving me in the clear. I didn't have a clue, of course, where Malcolm was.

In the FA Cup third round we drew Reading from the Third Division. I was courting Tina then and it was the first match she came to see. It was rubbish, of course. We drew 0-0 and Tina hardly ever came to see a game after that. I was happy with that. Football was my workplace, not a social event.

The replay was very different. We won 7-0 at Elm Park and I scored a hat-trick, which was an incredibly rare occurrence. As we were coming off the pitch the man on the tannoy said: 'Ladies and gentlemen, you've just seen the best football side this country has had for years.' It was another sign that made us realise what a really good team we were becoming, and realise how all the hard work was paying off. In the next round we drew Leicester and lost 4-3 in a replay. It would be the FA Cup Final itself the following season.

Our belief was growing sky-high and confidence was rubbing off from one player on to another. It helped that we were a good-fun side. We enjoyed each other's company and would have a drink together at the Portland Lodge. Everybody came to the Christmas Party, too, even Stan Gibson. I've always felt that a sense of camaraderie is vital to a successful team.

We relied on a small group of players all season, and I only missed one match myself. I wasn't injured or dropped – the reason was that I'd been called up to make my England debut in that match at Hampden Park against Scotland. Club matches weren't cancelled for internationals in those days; in fact, they were often played on the same day as the First Division pro-gramme. That was the case here. While I went off to Glasgow, my Manchester City pals were facing Sunderland at home in the League. Thankfully, they won 1-0. The club didn't mind at all. They were delighted when a player received international recognition, and I was the first City man for about ten years to be selected by England. The club saw it as a privilege and an honour to have one of their men in the national team. The other side of the coin was that it showed me I wasn't indispensable to City, however well I had been playing at centre forward that season. It was always my rule to look at the team sheet when it was pinned up on the notice board. The moment you were complacent about being picked was certain to be the moment you were out on your ear.

It was one of the closest title races in history. We were competing with Matt Busby's Manchester United, Don Revie's Leeds and Bill Shankly's Liverpool – and that tells you just how fierce the competition was. There were several key matches, but I'm sure the most important was winning 3-1 away at Old Trafford at the start of April. That was a major pointer for us.

United were the reigning champions, they were the bookies' favourites and they were our deadly rivals. To win so comprehensively away to them was magnificent. I remember that Joe Mercer cried tears of joy afterwards and Malcolm Allison said it was the best we had ever played. The result was even better when you consider that George Best scored only thirty-eight seconds into the game. We came back to overwhelm United, and give ourselves a real chance of winning the League.

Another good match was a 1-0 home victory against the Chelsea assassins. And when United surprisingly lost to West Brom we were in a position where winning our last three matches of the season would guarantee the League Championship trophy coming to Maine Road. Even if United won all their games we would take the title on a superior goal difference – the system that was used in those days when clubs were equal on points. Our final home match was a 2-0 win against Everton, so two to go.

If you were picking a match to avoid with so much at stake, away to Tottenham would be one of them. Spurs were inconsistent, but they could be fabulous on their day, especially at home. In this game, the most vital factor was undoubtedly the tactical genius of Malcolm Allison. His idea was that we had to isolate the great Dave Mackay, who was a brilliant and fierce midfielder, but also beginning to slow down. Malcolm ordered Francis Lee and me to entice the other defenders away with angled runs so that Colin Bell could be released to go one on one against Mackay. That's what we did, and Colin destroyed him – so much so that Dave Mackay left the field afterwards and told Bill Nicholson he was finished as a top-flight footballer. Bill had just watched the demolition, and he agreed it was the end for Mackay. It wasn't, of course. Dave went off to Derby

County and won another title medal with them under Brian Clough. That day they simply misjudged things because of Colin Bell's dynamism and the tactical intelligence of Malcolm Allison. Colin scored two of our goals and I grabbed the third, slicing it home after being set up by Colin and Francis Lee.

The Lee–Bell–Summerbee combination was beginning to be talked about in the same way as Law–Best–Charlton. Manchester now had two great teams playing at the same time.

On the final day of the season the equation was very simple. If we beat Newcastle away at St James' Park it didn't matter what United did at home to Sunderland. The two teams were level on points but our goal average was much better. Nevertheless, the bookmakers still made United the slight favourites and the BBC took their *Match of the Day* cameras to Old Trafford. They expected us to fail as well.

In the build-up both Colin Bell and myself were struggling with injuries sustained in the victory against Tottenham. We both had to pull out of England's squad for a European Nations Cup quarter-final second leg away to Spain in Madrid. That was being played on Wednesday 8 May, just three days before the final round of League matches with the title still at stake. Playing for England meant everything to me, and Colin had yet to make his debut. That was a tough time for both of us; can you imagine what would be made of that scheduling of club and country fixtures today?

It was touch and go right up until Friday afternoon whether either of us would be fit to face Newcastle. We stayed behind for more treatment at Maine Road while the rest of the squad travelled up to the North East by train on the Friday morning. My problem was a severe ankle knock that I'd taken at Spurs, and Peter Blakey, the physio, put a lamp on it and worked all his magic. It was very sore, and if I'm honest now it was a bit dodgy that I played. I don't think players of today would have turned out with the injury I had. But neither Colin nor I was going to miss this match for anything. We just had to play, and we caught a late afternoon train, travelling up with my boxer pal Johnny Prestcott.

We were staying at the Five Bridges Hotel on the Gateshead side of the River Tyne. I was rooming with Tony Book, which was our usual pairing, and we got there just in time for the meal. Malcolm Allison had put some wine on the table, a few bottles of Blue Nun, I think. He felt that would help us relax a bit and help us get to sleep. Sometimes we'd take sleeping tablets if we were restless so that we got a good night's kip. After the meal, at about nine o'clock, we went next door to a bowling alley. It was just a distraction from the importance of the match. If we could win this game, we'd clinch City's first League title since 1936–7 and only the second in the club's history. It wasn't an easy evening. You could sense the tension, not least because it was United we were battling against.

The next morning I woke up at about eight o'clock to the roar of a crowd. For a moment I thought it was a dream. But the chanting was still there and when I opened the curtains it was to the sight of what seemed like 10,000 City fans outside the hotel. They'd travelled up early and the scene was unbelievable. Of course, we knew it was a huge game, but this was something else, seeing how much it meant to so many people. I remember that we had breakfast in our rooms and that we had to be down by midday. We were in our own suits; there was no club blazer. Then we all had a meal together. There wasn't a big meeting, just a quiet chat. I think Joe and Malcolm were trying to keep everything as normal as possible and not make out it was anything special. The boss said a few words and we got on the bus.

But it *was* special, very special. When the team bus pulled out into the streets we saw instantly just how special. It really hit us then. There was so much expectancy on the faces of the supporters, hoping beyond hope that we would win. It's a fans' game when all is said and done. It's about enjoyment and entertainment and giving value for money. The last thing City had won was the FA Cup in 1956, more than a decade earlier. The supporters knew this was a special time, a special era. We, the players, did as well.

Another set of people I wanted to win for was the board of directors. They had taken a lot of abuse in the lean years, and my first experience of Maine Road had been hearing some of the worst. The chairman was Albert Alexander and he was a wonderful man, seventy-six years old, who'd been a City fan since a boy and who'd been a scout and managed the A team in his younger days. We loved him. The other directors were good, too, and they came in before the game and wished us luck and then kept out of the way.

On the bus you could feel the emotion of the fans. We had a police escort to St James' Park and I always loved that. It's exciting – and if people say it isn't there is something wrong with them in my view. You really think you are somebody hearing the sirens go and rushing through red lights.

St James' Park is a magnificent ground. It was then and it is now. Back in 1968 there were open stands, one with a clock tower. Before the game we walked out and had a little look. It was a typical end–of–season pitch; it was bumpy, the goalmouths were bare and the centre circle was bare, too. It didn't look ideal, but we were confident we could play our football on any surface.

Most footballers are nervous in the hour before kick-off. I had a ritual to deal with my nerves. I got into the changing room, got out of my suit as fast as possible and put my playing gear on. Once I'd done that I felt satisfied, I felt at home. All the outward nerves disappeared then, but the adrenalin was shooting around inside. I'd put a bandage round my ankle, put my socks on, and the boots but with the laces undone. Then I'd put my shirt on and go and sit on the toilet and read a newspaper. I'd sit there and read, and the lads always knew because there was such a smell. That's the way I did it. Some players had a rubdown, but I never bothered much with that. The conversation was mostly normal, but Malcolm was a bit agitated because of the occasion. Joe came in fifteen minutes before kick-off and had a chat and a giggle. But he'd never put pressure on us; he just told us, 'Play your football – get out there and do it.' Finally, Malcolm gave specific instructions to everyone and we were walking out to win the League Championship title.

There was a bit of wind that day, which there normally is at Newcastle, and in the first half we were playing uphill on the slight slope there was at St James' Park in those days. Bobby Moncur and Frank Clark were playing and a fella called John McNamee at centre half, who was a big gorilla. Inside the first ten minutes we clashed hard, and the referee gave us a 'calm it down lads' lecture. As if that was possible on a day like this.

After ten minutes the ball went wide to Mike Doyle. He crossed it and the ball came through a ruck of players and I just flicked it into the top corner. So we were 1-0 up – a great start – and I was hardly feeling that ankle at all. They kicked off and, blow me down, Bryan 'Pop' Robson went straight down our end and equalised. 1-1. And I started to worry a bit. Another fifteen minutes went by and Neil Young scored with a brilliant shot from outside the box. 2-1. Kick-off again and, blow me down, Newcastle went straight down the other end and scored again, this time through Jackie Sinclair. Two each.

We came in at half-time and Malcolm Allison was immediately at us. 'What's it all about?' he ranted as he had a go at the defence. 'Get tight on people' was the big instruction, and in the second half we tightened up on Newcastle. The problem had been sheer nerves. We weren't being run apart, but a couple of nervous errors at the back had been costly. It's more difficult for defenders and goalkeepers. One small error can mean a goal conceded and everybody remembers it. A striker making a mistake is much more quickly forgotten.

All the nerves evaporated after the break. We took Newcastle apart in the second half. Neil Young scored another goal and then Francis Lee made it 4-2 after an hour, having already had one effort disallowed. The game was over and the title won. There were around 20,000 City fans in the ground and their excitement was amazing as the minutes ticked by. The supporters were allowed to come right down to the touchline and the atmosphere was just electric. At one point an over-exuberant fan ran on to the pitch and a policeman wanted to arrest him. I went over and pleaded with the cop to let him go. The fella had done no harm. McNamee scored late in the game to make it 4-3, and I always say we just let them have that goal to make it look respectable. There was never any danger that we'd concede another. And, as it happened, United surprisingly lost at home to Sunderland anyway. We'd won the League by two clear points – and I was £200 richer. Six weeks earlier I'd had a £10 bet at 20-1 that we'd win the title. I earned more money from that than from Manchester City for winning the bloomin' League.

It was wonderful in the dressing room. You could see the combination of elation and relief on the face of the boss. It was a great feeling to look at Joe Mercer and see his satisfaction. He had been through difficult times at Sheffield United and Aston Villa, and here was an important man in football winning his dues. I had a very close relationship with him, and I could see that he had become young again in that moment. He had become the captain of Arsenal again, a young man again.

What we did that day will stick in my mind for ever. It was a fantastic achievement, the best thing that happened to me apart from playing for my country. Malcolm was so delighted as well; it was the culmination of so much for him. For me, well, it was way beyond all the dreams I'd held starting out as a young professional footballer in the Third Division. I couldn't believe it sitting in the bath afterwards. None of us really could, I think.

The last thing I did in the dressing room was another ritual. I threw my boots away. I always threw them in the skip at the end of the season and started with a fresh pair next time. I wore Adidas and I had one pair of boots for a season. Then, after a few drinks in the players' lounge with the Newcastle lads, we went home by coach. It wasn't one of these luxury air-conditioned jobs with a toilet. It was an old banger, but it was a great journey. The fans were following us all the way, beeping their horns and shouting. We stopped at the Boroughbridge Hotel for a few drinks on the way, and photos were taken for the *Manchester Evening News*. I remember there was a feeling of complete contentment as we sat in that bar. Everything was right with the world. I'd won the title, I'd played a couple of times for England and I'd become engaged to a beautiful girl. And I had a few bob in my pocket. It didn't get any better.

We didn't get back to Manchester until well past midnight,

but the party was only just beginning. I had made arrangements, win or lose, and whoever had claimed the League title, that I would see George Best back at the Cabaret Club. It was one o'clock in the morning by the time I got there but George was waiting for me. That was the measure of the man, and I have never forgotten that. I wouldn't have blamed him if he'd given it a miss. He said, 'Well done', and then we were out on the town all night. We went to the Portland Lodge and the Piccadilly Club to play cards. Then we went to Phyllis's in Moss Side. I had been supposed to see my fiancée Tina, but I couldn't make a phone call and I didn't go to bed. On Sunday morning I went back to my digs, had a shower and then drove up to Stalybridge where she lived, stopping to buy flowers for her and her mother. Tina didn't know anything about football, but she was aware this had been a very special day for me. She could hardly escape it. The phone never stopped ringing that Sunday with messages of congratulations.

I never knew I had so many friends. I never knew there were so many Manchester City supporters. And my greatest pleasure was for the fans. It was a huge relief for them that City had arrived at the top again. They had been downtrodden for so many years and it was a pleasure to see people proudly wearing their blue and white scarves round the city. Nobody had really expected it to happen so quickly, if at all. There was a picture I saw in one football magazine of Albert Alexander and the directors celebrating at Newcastle. That meant so much to the players. The directors had been through tough times and it takes a while to turn a football club around. We only won the League Championship because we were a unit on and off the field at Maine Road. It was an immense team effort, and the result of bloody hard work. It was also an exciting team to play for. Big crowds came to watch us everywhere, even if the TV cameras didn't too often. We were recognised as a top side, and that team was as good as you will get – the team of Joe Mercer and Malcolm Allison.

A few weeks afterwards I returned the compliment to George Best. I went to watch him playing for Manchester United in the European Cup Final at Wembley against Benfica. I was there with the England squad, who were just about to fly off to Europe for some friendly matches before the semi-final of the European Nations Cup against Yugoslavia.

Some people say, 'Oh, City won the League but Manchester United did something a little better by winning the European Cup.' I didn't see it that way. I was so pleased for United, and for Sir Matt Busby in particular. The Munich Air Disaster in 1958 affected everybody in the country, and United had been the first English club to play in Europe. It was a very emotional night at Wembley and I know it moved quite a few of the England players who were there.

George played so wonderfully that night and I saw him briefly after the game. We shared a few words and then I left him to his night. I didn't want to intrude.

I was so pleased for him personally. And I thought it was fantastic to be in Manchester at that time when it was the centre of football. It is a big football city anyway, but this was special. There was a camaraderie between the City and United players then. At midweek lunchtimes we would sometimes be in the same pub on the Oxford Road. We were the day I was picked for England and all the United players came over to congratulate me. Many United players came to my wedding early in the following season, and it's ludicrous that people think players from rival clubs can't be friendly off the field. They were civilised days back then, and there are still close ties between the old players. We have great functions together, and that's how it should be.

Winning the League also meant that Manchester City as well as Manchester United would be in the European Cup the following season. The day after we'd won at Newcastle there was a City press conference and Malcolm Allison began boasting about how good we would be. 'We'll terrify Europe,' said Malcolm. 'We won't play the cowardly way that so many teams do with safety-first football. I think we will be the first team to play on Mars.'

That's how invincible we felt at Manchester City in those wonderful days.

I'm the proud 13-year-old captain holding the winners' shield for the Naunton Park
Secondary Modern school team.

Ernie Hun
and myself,
eager 17-ye
olds, ready
for an away
match with
Swindon.

I'm on the far right of
the Swindon squad
preparing for another
journey to a far-flung
Third Division ground.

Celebrating
with Malco
Allison on
open top b
following
Manchester
City's 1969
FA Cup Fi
triumph.

...action at Maine Road.

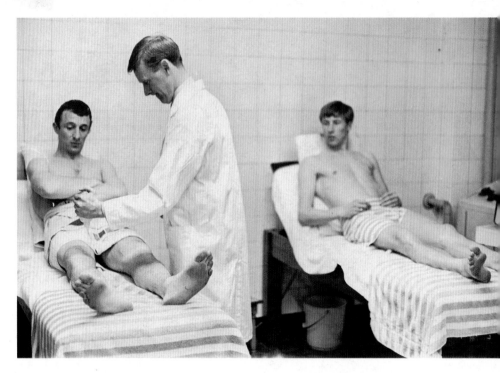

Physio Peter Blakey looks after Colin Bell and myself before we travel late to the League title clincher away to Newcastle.

A typical darts match before the day starts at our Cheadle training ground.

A rare Summerbee goal, scored against Coventry City. My good pal Maurice Setters is the opponent tangled in the net.

THE POPS... THAT'S MANCHESTER CITY

CHAMPIONS!

MAINE ROAD SPECIAL

Drinks in the dressing room with champagne for the champs to celebrate a glorious chapter in the history of Manchester City.

Mike Summerbee opens the scoring with a neat flick that outwits Newca

Mike Summerbee pleads with a policeman to let an over-exuberant fan go free . . . even if he did run on the pitch.

It's No. 4! . . . by courtesy of Lee who dodges round goalkeeper to score

A cutting from my scrapbook when City became champions.

Celebrating our wonderful victory at Newcastle that brought the title to Manchester City.

I'm second left in the b⟩
row between Alex Step⟩
and Bobby Moore⟩
England's squad gathers⟩
Roehampton training grou⟩

9

LEE, BELL AND SUMMERBEE

The Charity Shield in the 1960s featured some of the great goals. There was the one that Tottenham goalkeeper Pat Jennings scored with a drop kick that bounced over the head of Manchester United keeper Alex Stepney. In the same match there was a thrilling strike by Bobby Charlton, lashing home a ferocious shot after a United move that had started by their own corner flag with sublime skill from Denis Law. Commentator Kenneth Wolstenholme said it was a goal 'good enough to win the FA Cup, the League, the World Cup, and even the Grand National'.

So, when Manchester City played in the 1968 Charity Shield against West Brom, we were up for the challenge of creating our own special moment.

Anything that Law, Best and Charlton could do, Lee, Bell and Summerbee could as well.

Our moment came with a free-kick just outside the Albion penalty area. I went to one side of the defensive wall, jockeying with the opposition defenders, while Colin Bell and Francis Lee were stood over the ball. Both of them had fierce shots, and West Brom's goalkeeper John Osborne was no doubt trying to work out which of them would have a go this time. But we had a trick up our sleeves. Colin sold a dummy by running over the ball and Francis rolled it to me. I knew exactly what to do. I let the ball slip just under my foot and then gently played it behind the back of the Albion wall with just enough pace to reach the other side. Francis, quick as a flash, ran past the other end of the wall and smashed the ball into the net as the West Brom defenders and Osborne were left totally bemused and bewildered.

To me it was the classic goal, conjured up out of nothing by wonderful skill and a telepathy that had grown between the three of us. We seemed to know instinctively where the other was on the pitch and we created so many goals for each other. But that's the one that always sticks in my mind when people talk about Lee, Bell and Summerbee. I thought it epitomised the way we wanted to entertain at the same time as produce football that won trophies for Manchester City. The Charity Shield was a side issue, not a piece of silverware that meant too much to a professional footballer, but we thrashed West Brom 6-1 that day at Maine Road, and nobody would be underestimating us any more.

I've often been asked how the Lee, Bell and Summerbee connection came about. I don't have a ready answer. It kind of grew through the years when City had the best spell of winning trophies in their history. I suppose the fact that United supporters used to crow so much about their magnificent trio of Law, Best and Charlton had something to do with it. City fans wanted to show their Manchester rivals they were just as good, and they had their own threesome of Lee, Bell and Summerbee. To them it was proof that City were just as good as United.

The fact that Colin, Francis and myself were the three most high-profile signings also contributed. We were the fresh legs who had been brought in to complement all the very good footballers already at Maine Road. Suddenly, a club that had endured so many years in the doldrums was now thriving, and the fans associated that success with the arrival of us three. It helped, too, that we were all forwards; they are always the glory boys of a football team even though defenders are just as important. And the fact that we all played for England was also significant. The song the crowd used to sing played a part, the one that went: 'Aye-o, aye-o, we're off to Mexico, with Lee and Bell, and Summerbee, aye-o, aye-o, aye-o.'

Supporters want their icons and, for whatever reason, City fans chose us. There was the sheer excitement of Francis Lee's barrel-chested forward play, his arrogance and certainty on the ball. There was the dynamic midfielder play of Colin Bell, his surging forward runs that could lift the entire crowd in a couple of seconds. And I suppose I was a bit of a character, a player who always had a rapport with the fans on the touchline and who had that aggressive streak that supporters know is vital to any team. We all scored goals and, as with the United trio, we were three very different characters.

The fans were wonderful. They were the ones who created the legend of Lee, Bell and Summerbee; they wanted cult heroes in the new age of pop stars. They wanted it so much and we three happened to be in the right place at the right time.

Personally, I always thought it should have been a quartet. I felt that Neil Young, such an elegant player, and the scorer of the goal that won the 1969 FA Cup Final for us, should have been part of the legend. There was a rock group at the time called Crosby, Stills, Nash and Young – the last one a fella also called Neil Young. Why couldn't the City group have been Lee, Bell, Summerbee and Young?

Our Neil Young made such a massive contribution and he was an exceptional player who tuned into the attacking telepathy we had. He was an unsung hero, and that always seemed unfair to me.

It's strange when you become a part of the folklore of a football club – and part of the folklore of the whole game. The insecurity in my nature makes me think: Why me? Did I really deserve that? But don't think I'm complaining. I'm not. It's always nice to be remembered as a player and as a part of that trio, of course it is. I do enjoy the recognition and it is appreciated very much. It is wonderful to know people remember who you are and what you did. Sometimes the legend thing is a bit embarrassing, like when you sign autographs for little lads wearing City shirts and they say: 'Who are you?' It's their fathers or grandfathers who have told them to come up and talk to Mike Summerbee.

You come down to earth very quickly sometimes. I was with my grandson at a City game against Chelsea and I took him to meet Frank Lampard afterwards because I've known Frank a long time. I consider him one of the very best of the modern footballers. His dad is a pal of mine and an old rival from the days when he was a great left back for West Ham. My grandson then asked for autographs from some of the other Chelsea players like John Terry and Ashley Cole, and they looked straight past me thinking I was just another autograph hunter. They had no idea I was an England international at a time when Manchester City were the best team in the country.

That's what we were, a great team. It angers me that our City side seldom gets mentioned when people talk about that era. It's always Liverpool and Leeds and Manchester United, and people overlook us. We were their equals as a football team, and I do emphasise the word 'team'. The one thing that aggravates me about the Lee, Bell and Summerbee talk is that people think it was just us three when I know it was an overall team effort that made us so good. We couldn't have done our stuff without the rest of the players, without the rest of the team. I find the obsession with us embarrassing sometimes. The contribution we made was 20 per cent of the whole thing. Eighty per cent came from the rest of the side.

Lee, Bell and Summerbee – Law, Best and Charlton. They're only words. They're only names. You need a contribution from everyone. The truth is that, at City, we all played for each other. The camaraderie was second to none. We stuck together socially as well. Other sides may have been more skilful, but we were tough and we had a fantastic team spirit and organisation. It's hard to explain how fantastic it was, especially the way the fans loved the team. Maine Road became a fortress. Opponents knew we were tough, they knew we were a fitter team than them, and they knew we could score goals. We attacked together and defended together as a team. The understanding was through all eleven, not just the three of us. Alan Oakes, for example, could always find me with a cross-field ball. I knew that. Mike Doyle was a really good footballer who won five England caps and Glyn Pardoe was right up there with the best left backs.

When people talk about important signings, I always think of Tony Book. He didn't come with a big reputation, but he was quick and a good reader of the game. He led at the back as a captain, and to my mind he was a crucial signing. Off the field he was quiet and unassuming, but he was one of those players whose character changed totally in a game. On the pitch he was a leader, and he led by example. I know I was a better winger for playing in front of Tony.

Colin, Francis and myself knew at the time that the public focus on us wasn't fair to the rest. We didn't play up to the trio thing. We'd be introduced together at opposition grounds before a match, and the photographers always wanted pictures of us three. But you don't see too many, because we actively made sure of that. We allowed the snaps sometimes, but it was never blatant; we wouldn't have that because we had too much respect for all the other players at City.

What was also true, however – and this was something our team-mates appreciated – was that all the Lee, Bell and Summerbee publicity did have a psychological effect on our opponents in some matches. If you had a reputation in the game like that, it did help against certain clubs. There were those who were scared before a match started, and we didn't mind that at all. Every bit of positive talk was a bonus. Jimmy Greaves always said, 'When Summerbee played, City played.' That comment made me proud. Colin Bell also won rave reviews from the moment he signed from Bury in our Second Division season. His influence was tremendous. He could be defending one minute and going through the middle and scoring a goal the next. He created goals. He was an outstanding player, and he was compared to Peter Doherty, the great Manchester City and Northern Ireland inside forward, which is a huge compliment. Every player gained confidence from seeing Colin drive forward in the way he did.

In terms of psychology, though, the biggest impact was

definitely made by Francis Lee when he joined us a few matches into the title-winning season. As I have said, he was the final piece in the jigsaw. He was playing for Bolton Wanderers and everybody in the game could see what a superb forward he was. There had been a lot of newspaper talk about him going to different clubs. But there was also talk that he might even pack in professional football because he was also a very successful businessman in the pulp paper industry. His company made toilet rolls and there was a lot more money in that than in playing football in the autumn of 1967. The speculation was that Francis might buy out his contract and turn his back on the game.

That would have been such a waste, and eventually the silver tongues of Joe Mercer and Malcolm Allison persuaded him to join us at City for a transfer fee of £60,000. We knew Francis was somebody quite different the moment he walked into the dressing room for the first time. He was wearing a smart suit and carrying a briefcase, and I looked at him and thought, 'What the bloody hell have we signed here?' He was different; he had an air, an arrogance about him. Here was a footballer who knew exactly how much he was worth and what he could do – and his arrogance swiftly rubbed off on us for the better.

In the first practice session he came in with a swagger, too. We did a routine with Joe Corrigan in goal where I'd lay up the ball for Francis on the half-volley and he would try to score.

'I'll get ten out of ten,' he said to me, and I laughed. Corrigan was a wonderful goalkeeper and no striker was as good as that. But that's what Francis did. He put all ten in the back of the net past Joe.

I remember as well playing against Sheffield United on a dung heap of a pitch at Bramall Lane. We had a free-kick twenty-five yards out and I stood next to him and he said: 'Just run over the ball, I can see a gap there.'

'Where? I can't see anything.'

'Yes, there's a gap in that corner,' said Francis. So I ran over the ball and he scored right in that corner. That was the arrogance of him. It wasn't big-headed; it was the good kind of arrogance and certainty that the very best players possess.

Francis was a proven and experienced player who could perform at both outside right and centre forward. They were my two positions, and I've been asked if I was worried about my own position when City signed him. The answer is straight – a definite NO. When Francis Lee arrived it came at a time when I really did believe in myself fully.

So, I wasn't worried about him, bloody hell I wasn't. Somebody else might have been scared, but not me. It was a challenge, wasn't it? I had the shirt and my feeling about anyone else, not just Francis, was, 'Get it off me if you can.' That was the same with anybody coming in. They would have had to work bloody hard, too, because I was a very hard worker at my football. I had to look after myself and sometimes look after other people on the pitch as well. The thing about Francis, too, was that we weren't the same kind of outside right or centre forward. We brought different things to each role.

At centre forward I was more of a creative player than a goalscorer, making chances for others. Francis was a classic 'selfish' striker who wanted to score all the time. Yes, I did score some goals, but, as I've said, they were mostly tap-ins, they weren't self-made goals like the type Francis scored. When he played centre forward he created his own goals. He wasn't afraid to have a shot – and he was the king of penalties. I remember one time I'd been injured and came back for a match at Molineux against Wolves. It was a windy day and we were kicking towards the open end, and I'd scored two goals, which was a surprise to me. Then we got a penalty, and Francis said: 'Go on, make it a hat-trick.'

'No,' I said. 'Corners and tap-ins are my thing. It's all yours.'

I really wasn't bothered about the supposed kudos of getting a hat-trick, and Francis went up and smacked it in the corner. That was better for the team, because he was certain to score.

One of the great things was that we could change positions between outside right and centre forward to try to confuse the opposition. It was difficult for people to mark us. That flexibility wasn't something we practised; it was just something we knew we could do.

As well as my own burgeoning self-confidence there was another reason not to worry. It was the knowledge that Joe Mercer and Malcolm Allison always gave you an opportunity. If you had a couple of bad games – and every player does – it wasn't the end of the world. They'd help you in training and talk to you. There were plenty of times I was on the wing and instead of trapping the ball I let it go under my feet. You'd think, 'Bloody hell, eighty-nine minutes of this to go.' But Joe and Malcolm would always give you confidence and tell you to forget about things like that.

With me, everybody knew they would get 110 per cent. I was never going to let anyone down. I might have a poor game, but if I was off form for a couple of matches I always came back, working as hard as I could to get it right. The management understood that. Our team was a proper team. If someone was having a bad time everyone else would help out and get him through. Colin Bell was like me in that he needed to get more confidence when he came to City. I hadn't been sure I could make the step up and I think he was a little the same. But we found that confidence in the Second Division – so that by the time we won promotion we felt we belonged at City.

If Francis was the big, bold footballer who walked around with a swagger, Colin was the ultimate quiet man. He was a very shy fella off the field and I think that if he could have overcome that shyness he would have found other outlets outside the game of football.

I always called him Howard Hughes because he was so quiet, although I didn't say it to him directly. I compare him to Bobby Charlton, who is also a very shy character. But Bobby worked very hard to overcome that shyness and he has become an ambassador for Manchester United. I know he doesn't find it easy – and I don't find it easy myself speaking at dinners. But you have to work at it, and I always wonder if Colin could have found more to do.

For Colin it was enough to play football. And it was wonderful when you saw him burst through an opposition defence and score with a shot that left the back of the net bulging. There haven't been many better sights in the history of English football.

Another thing I loved to see was the way Francis could turn on a sixpence and whip the ball into the net. There was a cleverness about him that way. He always knew what he wanted to do when he had the ball at his feet. He kept his head up; he never ran head down. He drew people to him like a magnet and then he would lay it out wide for me or play a forward pass for Colin to sprint beyond him.

Francis wasn't greedy like that. He was only selfish when it came to grabbing the praise. I remember we played Derby one day at the Baseball Ground on a sticky surface, and we'd been told that afterwards we'd be going to Blackpool for the weekend for special training. Dave Mackay was playing for Derby and he used to tap the ball forward with his foot before playing a pass. That day I nipped in and took it off him about twenty yards inside our half, and started running with the ball. They were chasing me and it was a long way on a muddy pitch. I had to change my stride pattern and as I went towards the side of their six-yard box I could see the Derby players catching me up. But also, out of the corner of my eye, I could see Francis running. He was never the fastest in the world and on a heavy pitch he looked like Freddie Flintoff in full flight, but he was getting there. So I pulled the ball back and Francis tapped it in and then he raced round the back of the goal and was celebrating in front of all the fans as if it was all his own work while I was standing knackered in the box.

He came over and I said: 'You've done bugger all here. I've made it for you.'

'Don't forget we're going to Blackpool for the weekend,' was all he said in reply and jogged back for the restart. That was Francis Lee. He milked the glory for all it was worth.

Francis would always exaggerate his contribution. In our FA Cup Final triumph in 1969 the goal came when he took a throw-in to me. I took the ball, jinked past Leicester defender Alan Woollett, and crossed for Neil Young to score. But if you ask Francis he always claims he made that goal with his perfect throw-in.

Another example was the Charity Shield match at Villa Park in 1972. We wore a new strip of a white shirt with a sash across the front of it, white shorts and red socks. It was a really hot day and about twenty minutes from the end someone played a ball through and I latched on to it. Aston Villa's gangling goalkeeper Jim Cumbes came towards me but I took it past him and he pulled me down from behind. It was a clear penalty and Francis strode up and smashed the ball into the net. Then he walked past and just about acknowledged me. 'Thanks mate', I thought. Jim remembers that game well and I see him quite often now because he's the chief executive of Lancashire County Cricket Club. I always say: 'You must be pretty pleased today; that's the nearest you ever got to me.' He laughs, and reminds me of who took glory for that penalty goal.

Colin Bell was just the opposite, more like me in that respect. He didn't mind who scored a goal, and he always knew who had done the hard work in creating the chance. There was a match against Leeds, on a smoky, hazy day, a game for the connoisseur. A minute from the final whistle I received the ball on the edge of the area with the score 0-0. I got past Terry Cooper, slipped past Jack Charlton and got to the dead-ball line. Then I clipped it back and Colin scored at the far post. It was one of the favourite moments of my career – not so much for the skill but the sheer brute force I needed to get where I wanted to be. Colin came from nowhere and put the cross in with his head. It was an important goal – it was the first time my mother had come to watch me play, and, as I came off the field, Les Cocker, the Leeds and England trainer, walked up to me and said: 'You played brilliantly today.'

That was a massive compliment from an important man, because a vital part of football is about winning respect from opponents, no matter how aggressive you are and however much you get stuck in. It was one of my most pleasing days in football, and what also sticks in my mind is that Colin Bell then came over to me as well and thanked me for making the goal. That summed it up for me. My asset to the side was in creating goals; that was my contribution. There was nothing better in my football life than making a goal. I found more satisfaction in that than scoring – and how often do you see players celebrating with the goal-maker, because they know just how important that part of the game is.

While Colin, Francis and I were all different as characters, there was one sad thing we had in common – that none of our fathers saw us play for England. It is an amazing coincidence because playing for your country is such an important part of your life, and makes everyone around you so proud as well as yourself. Part of the Lee, Bell and Summerbee legend is that we were City's England players, yet none of our fathers saw us in the white shirt.

Another strange fact is that we never played together as a trio for England in the same match. Colin made his debut not long after myself against West Germany in Hanover in June 1968, a match I also played in. By the time Francis was called up for England in 1969 I was out of the side. He won twenty-seven international caps, but the only one where we were in the team together was against Switzerland at Wembley in November 1971. And Colin missed that match through injury.

It was a shame it never happened. For a while it looked as if we would all be in the 1970 World Cup squad and go to Mexico to help England defend the trophy. But I was one of the four players left out in the final cut by Sir Alf Ramsey, while Francis and Colin did travel.

Colin played the most internationals of us, forty-eight times, but Francis was the automatic choice of the three of us as an England player. I was the first of the three to be picked by Sir

Alf, but I didn't find it so easy. I wasn't certain I belonged at that level, but I always tell Francis that I paved the way for him and Colin to take the road from Manchester City to England.

It's many years now since Lee, Bell and Summerbee played together, yet I'm still in touch with both Francis and Colin. While we were team-mates Francis and I became great pals and he is still one of my closest friends today. We go on holiday together to Portugal with our families and we speak all the time. There is a bond between us. Francis became a millionaire through his business acumen, which is rare for a footballer. When I was out nightclubbing, or having coffee with George Best on a midweek afternoon watching the girls go by, Francis had gone out to work on his companies. He created his empire, and not many players could do that. His mind was working all the time.

Our friendship meant I had to say yes to helping out when Francis came back to Maine Road and became the chairman of the club in 1994, when it had gone into a steep decline. He was in a position to help with his wealth, his contacts and his hero status at City. I joined the commercial department and Colin Bell was also on the staff in the youth development section. The trio were all back at City in various ways, but the result this time was not so glorious.

Although results on the pitch were not as good as anyone had hoped for in the bright mood of optimism when Francis took over the club, I believe his contribution was highly significant. It was his passion and persuasion that meant the club moved to the new City of Manchester Stadium built for the 2002 Commonwealth Games. He organised it, he sorted it out; he got the new ground for the club. Whatever people say, he did it. Even when Francis left I remained on the corporate side of the club and try my hardest to help it develop in any way I can.

It was difficult for Francis to switch from business to running a football club that you used to play for. There was a lot of politics involved at so many levels. One small aspect of that was that the relationship between Colin and Francis broke down. Colin was working as a youth team coach alongside Tony Book and a problem developed with another of the coaches at the club. Colin asked Francis, as club chairman, to help sort it out – and Francis said that Colin would have to deal with it himself.

The trouble was it didn't work out, and the situation ended with Colin leaving the club and blaming Francis for his departure. Colin had presumed that Francis was the one who wanted to get him out, but I know that isn't the case. Francis felt the issue was nothing to do with him, and didn't need a chairman's intervention.

While I don't see Colin as much as I do Francis these days we are still friendly when we meet on match days at Eastlands. Colin is quiet and keeps himself to himself, and that's his nature. But we keep in touch, and it is my great hope that Francis and Colin can get together again. All they've got to do, in my view, is sit down and talk to each other, and they'll realise that the situation a few years back was a misunderstanding. I'm certain it's something that could be sorted out with a conversation between them.

I've always said that I hope I'm alive in Manchester when City get a really successful side again – when Lee, Bell and Summerbee are pushed into a back drawer and new champions emerge. I hope the day comes when there are new heroes the fans can revere as club legends.

But my dearest wish right now is that Lee, Bell and Summerbee can be together as friends once more. We shared so many good days together. And I hope we can again in the future.

10

PLAYING TO THE GALLERY

Football grounds were my stage. I felt like an actor playing Shakespeare at Stratford-upon-Avon. Sometimes it was comedy. Sometimes it was tragedy. More often than not it was against a backdrop of blood and guts battles. I loved that – I loved the fun and the fury of football conflict, the eternal duel between a winger and a full-back. Wasn't that exactly what the spectators paid to see?

Some of my best matches were against Chelsea. They had two full-backs, Ron 'Chopper' Harris and Eddie McCreadie, who were everyone's nightmare. They were both good players and tough characters. I had quite a few pull-ins with both of them; I used to get wired into them. Mostly it was a duel with McCreadie, because he was Chelsea's regular left back, and whenever I played against him it was going to be one of those games.

Ray Hatton, the dad of world champion boxer Ricky Hatton, often reminds me about one match when he was sat beside the touchline at Maine Road. In the first few minutes McCreadie came in and gave me plenty. He used to scissor people: he'd tackle with one leg and bring the other one round. He gave me a good 'un, which was the normal procedure. It was a 'welcome to the game' moment. I went down and he thought he'd actually done me, and that I'd be finished for the rest of the game.

So he backed off and ran to his position, but then he suddenly realised I'd got up and he came back to shake hands. I shook his hand, and said: 'Don't make any arrangements tonight, dancing or anything, because you won't be dancing when I've finished with you.' Ray Hatton says you should have seen McCreadie's face when I got up. He knew I was going to get my pound of flesh back. And that was it. We were at each other all through the game. But it happened in a good way. I liked playing in those physical contests. I enjoyed that. You got plenty of stick, but you rode it because you expected it. I never had a problem with opponents who tackled hard but up front like McCreadie and Chopper Harris. I had great respect for them.

You had to be able to handle yourself physically and verbally; give as good as you got. Quite often the verbals in my case would be with Malcolm Allison, who spent the whole match shouting at you from the dugout. I remember I was playing in a Cup match against Stoke City at Maine Road and Malcolm was ranting at me from the touchline, as he always did, calling me a stupid so-and-so and that type of thing. I responded with a few choice phrases as I went past him, and my language was always a little bit strong. The next thing I knew someone was tapping me on the shoulder. It was a policeman with a clipboard in his hand, saying: 'I want your name.'

I couldn't believe it. But he said: 'I'm having you for foul and abusive language.'

And all the while the game was going on. I was looking for the football, for a pass from my team-mates, and PC Plod was insisting on taking my name. It was getting ridiculous until two other policemen came along and took him away, saying they thought he'd had a breakdown recently. The referee, bless him, didn't see a thing.

The crowd had a good laugh at that incident. And laughter was something I couldn't get enough of. I always wanted to make the fans chuckle. When I played against Everton at Goodison Park the home supporters shouted comments about the size of my nose. So I thought I'd show them. Before one match I went and bought a big plastic nose at a joke shop. When I ran down the tunnel before kick-off I waited for the usual comments and whipped out the big nose and put it on for the warm-up. The Everton fans thought it was hysterical, and I've always had a good rapport with them to this day.

Anfield was also a fantastic place to play, and the Liverpool fans were just the same in responding to a bit of fun. We were winning 2-1 there on a Tuesday night, kicking towards the Kop, and we won a corner. The crowd were up for the game and having a go, so I dropped my shorts in front of them to get my own back. Trouble was, Liverpool cleared the corner and immediately went down the other end and scored the equaliser. Then they scored again to beat us 3-2 and the entire Kop was singing: 'Show us your arse now, Summerbee.'

I'd just done it on the spur of the moment, which was how I was. Everything I did in games was spontaneous. I had great pals from the world of comedy and theatre like Kenny Lynch, Jimmy Tarbuck and Michael Crawford, but I didn't need a scriptwriter.

I threw myself into football matches and responded to the drama of the moment.

Another vivid memory is of a derby match against Manchester United at Old Trafford. I was never the most popular person among the Stretford End crowd; they used to give me lots of stick and sing songs about the size of my nose. I didn't mind. It was part and parcel of the game, and if people take notice of you then you must be able to play a bit. In one particular game they were singing, 'He walked a million miles to the end of his nose', so when I took a corner at the Stretford End I put the ball outside the half-moon. The linesman waved his flag like a dervish to make me put it on the line. The crowd, of course, were also having a go, howling all sorts of names at me, so I said: 'Hang on a minute, I need to blow my nose.' And I used the corner flag to do it. They hated that. You couldn't do that kind of thing now – you'd be accused of bringing the game into disrepute. But it was just a bit of fun to get the crowd going.

I did things that you could get away with. I would talk to the crowd and I'd stand there talking to the linesman, I'd take the flag off him sometimes and start waving it. You could do that then. You could have a bit of fun. It was part of my attitude towards the game. If someone was injured in a game I'd go and sit on the wall and talk to the fans while the player was being treated. I wasn't taking the mickey; it was just that I had very close contact with the crowd. I signed autographs sometimes while the game was going on if the ball was on the other side of the pitch – but I never lost my concentration on the match.

The fans knew what to expect with me. They knew I liked a bit of fun and they knew I was a hard player and did things that weren't particularly nice sometimes. But I took everything the opponents gave me and I never complained.

Referees understood the give and take back then. I feel very sorry for officials these days because it's so difficult for them to interpret what's going on when players throw themselves to the ground as if they've been shot by a sniper. If you cheated in our day you knew you couldn't go into the players' bar afterwards. There was a code among pros in those days. It was an unwritten code but it was there nonetheless. Very few players were cheats and so it wasn't so hard to referee the games.

The game today seems all upside down. The cheats are tolerated and the players who want to have a bit of fun, show off a few tricks and entertain the crowd are accused of being disrespectful to opponents and to the game. Something's gone badly wrong with the game in my view. If Cristiano Ronaldo has the ability to do them he should do his tricks. Football is about entertainment as well as winning matches. The fella is an entertainer. Whether people like him or hate him, I think it's a delight to watch him do his tricks. There may be a bit of jealousy from the fans, and maybe from the pressmen because he didn't speak to them after a game. But if you get a player with supreme confidence, I think it's wonderful to see.

When I played you were there to entertain people who'd been working in the factories and on the shop floor and wanted to see something they enjoyed on their day off. George Best could do that type of thing on mud heaps in our day. I dread to think how foreign players would have survived on those pitches and with the toughness of the tackling. I have to laugh sometimes when people today say conditions will be difficult just because it's raining. Raining? Unbelievable. I would have liked to play on the pitches they have today. Our City team of Bell, Lee and Young would have been frightening to play against on them.

I'm sad that so much of the entertainment has gone. We had men like Frank Worthington, Rodney Marsh and Alan Hudson who the crowds loved to watch. They weren't always necessarily good for their side, but they were idolised by the supporters. It's not the same now; players don't play to the gallery like we used to. It's the influence of money, I suppose. Football is so serious, and players who want to entertain are considered to be frivolous. People think they lose their concentration on playing – but I know that I never did, whatever antics I used to get up to.

I think the fun we had was also partly an antidote to the violence in the game. It was tough, and if you didn't have a laugh the game could have become a bit grim. It was also true that the fans were entertained by the physical battles between players. You could hear the crowd respond to a big collision.

People always tend to think that men who are aggressive and hard on the field are born that way. They're not: well, I certainly wasn't. I had to learn, and the only way I could learn was by accepting tackles and going into tackles. If you came out of it and you were okay, then you could take another step forward. But if you didn't take a step forward, you weren't going to get anything. You had to learn to be brave.

I played against some of the greatest full-backs that ever played football, from Paul Breitner of West Germany to England's 1966 World Cup-winner Ray Wilson. But if there was one player who really educated me in the hard realities of professional football it was a man called Mike Thresher. You won't find him in the history books, but Thresher was as tough as any of the celebrated hard men of the game. He played left back for Bristol City, he was only about five foot five, and off the field he was a complete gentleman; softly spoken, just a quiet, unassuming type of person. He wasn't the best player in the world, but he did the job that full-backs did in those days: he stopped the winger from playing.

The first time I faced Mike Thresher was in the local derby for Swindon against Bristol City at Ashton Gate. It was at the time that Tottenham manager Bill Nicholson was showing interest in me, and he might well have been at this match. While everybody else was knocking a ball around in the warm-up as usual, I noticed that Thresher didn't get involved at all. He just stood there waiting and when they tossed the coin he just walked to his position. He never said a word to anybody. I already knew from the other players that this man had a reputation – and he was very different from most footballers. He didn't go over the top of the ball or anything like that. He was just a tough, tough man and if you were in the way of the ball, then he'd take the ball and the man. I'll never forget his first tackle on me. I remember him sliding into me, and he went straight up my legs, ripped my shirt, and finished up giving me a gash over my eye. He didn't say a word, but that was his welcome message. My immediate reaction was to check if everything was still there under my shorts. I was determined, not angry. I had been expecting it to happen, just not as early as it did. The only thought on my mind was, 'Well, he's not hurt me.' I had to get on with it.

I got up, and I continued and I competed against him in that game, and waited until half-time to have a couple of stitches. I ended up having a reasonably good game against him – but if I'd got up after that tackle and thought, 'Ooh, I've had enough of this', then that would have been it. That would have been me finished.

Instead, that was the game that really made me into the

aggressive type of winger that I ended up being known as. Thresher was very far from the most skilful player in the world, but he did a job, as full-backs did in those days. His sole job, with all the press talk beforehand about the Swindon kid going to Spurs, was to put Summerbee out of the game. He didn't hurt me deliberately; it was just the way he was. It was the way Mike Thresher played, and you had to respect him for that. He was a crucial part of what made me into the successful player, because I learned that I had to look after myself. I realised straight away what I was up against. You had to look into your own mind and know that this man could put you out of the game. You had to show you had the toughness and the aggression to cope.

Thresher was what you might call the silent assassin. During the game he didn't say anything to you. He never asked you how you were. But as soon as the final whistle went, he came up, shook hands and said: 'Well done.' That was the longest conversation I ever had with him.

'Thank you very much,' I said. And I hoped I had earned a bit of respect. I certainly respected him. He wasn't the sort who stood above you jeering. He just got on with his job. I played against him two or three times before I got transferred away from Swindon and by the end I really knew how to handle any situation.

That was just as well. I came across some ferocious characters during my career. There was Peter Storey, for one, the Arsenal midfielder who was a team-mate a couple of times for England. He wasn't friendly when you were on the opposing side. There was never any hiding place at Highbury because the pitch was so tight, and there was no hiding from Storey. I always knew what it was going to be like. In one match there against Arsenal I looked up just before the kick-off and there was Storey looking straight at me. He just pointed at my right leg and then made a gesture with his hands like snapping a twig. The message was clear enough – he was threatening to break my leg. Then he went and pointed at the other leg and made the same snapping motion.

'Oh, both legs today, is it?' I said.

'Yeah,' was his gravel-voiced reply.

So that was it. I knew he was going to give me one that day. But he always tried to get me in the game. They knew that I could handle myself in certain ways, so I was a target for them. But that wasn't a problem to me because, as I've said, I enjoyed the aggression and physical contest. I wasn't frightened to take anyone on.

Every footballer of that time had particular players who rubbed them up the wrong way. One of those for me was Johnny Morrissey of Everton, a tough man who played outside left. We had a few skirmishes because we were on the same flank, but after a couple of years an unwritten rule developed between us. The rule was quite simple – he stayed in his half of the pitch and I stayed in mine. We were wary of each other, and the chances were we might both get sent off if we got too close to each other. The rule probably suited our team-mates and managers as much as ourselves.

The Stoke centre half Bill Bentley was another player I had trouble with. There was one Christmas Day when we'd only been playing for five minutes and he went straight through me and split my ankle open. I was taken off and stitched up in the medical room and I lost my temper completely. I was effing and blinding and telling our trainer, Johnny Hart, exactly what I was going to do to Bentley when I got back out. He tried to calm me down but my volatile nature had taken over. 'Don't be stupid,' said Johnny, but I rushed out and went straight through Bentley as soon as I was back on the pitch. Luckily, the referee could see it was rough justice retribution, and he only booked me.

I never broke anyone's leg with a tackle, but my leg was fractured a few times in challenges, although never a really serious break. One of the times it happened was in the 1970 League Cup Final at Wembley against West Brom. Their left back was a fella called Ray Wilson – not the Ray Wilson who won the World Cup with England – but another defender of the same name. He was a decent enough full-back and a tough guy who had sorted me out a couple of times in First Division games. The Cup Final incident happened because the pitch at Wembley was so bad at the time because they also used it for the Horse of the Year Show. It started off being my ball, but then it slowed down and became his ball. You don't pull out of the tackle, of course, and I was caught awkwardly in a head-on collision. There was nothing malicious about Wilson; it was just one of those unlucky things that can happen. Not too long ago I went to a dinner in Sutton Coldfield for a function for a local boys' club. As soon as I walked in the door of the pub where it was being held a gentleman came up to me. It was that Ray Wilson. He lived in the area, had heard I was speaking and said he had to come and see me. I was delighted. That was the mutual respect that existed between 99 per cent of footballers then – even the ones who threatened to break both your legs.

Ninety-nine per cent is about right. There will always be the one per cent who hate you with a passion that nothing will ever change. Top of the one per cent in my case was a player I mentioned earlier, Denis Hollywood of Southampton. He was the crème de la crème lunatic when I was on a football pitch.

He really was a lunatic. The ball would be on the other side of the field and he'd just come up and kick me.

'Why'd you do that?' I asked him.

'I don't like you,' he said.

'The ball's over there,' I said.

'I don't care where the ball is. I just don't like you.'

It was beyond reason, and he must have been sent off five or six times playing against me. I got sent off a couple of times against him as well, as a consequence. I would always retaliate. To this day I don't know why he behaved like that. Most players were trying to get an advantage for their side. He just wanted a fight – and I came to know what was coming. It wasn't difficult; it was just mad.

The difficult games were against the really good left backs, the great players like Ray Wilson of Everton and Terry Cooper of Leeds Utd. Ray Wilson was the best in the business, and I had the greatest respect for him. I'd sat in the stands at Wembley and watched him win the World Cup, and when I played against him in the First Division I found out why he was so good. Even though he was ten years older than me he was still superbly quick and he could read the game so well. He was a great tackler, but the way he assessed the play he didn't have to tackle all the time. His positional sense was just incredible.

When I knew I was playing against him I'd spend the whole week beforehand thinking about what would happen on the Saturday. How would I perform? How would I cope with Wilson? What should I try? You played all the possibilities over and over in your head. I knew that people were coming to watch the duel between Wilson and Summerbee and I had to give myself every chance of doing well. But I very rarely got the better of him. I remember we played Everton once just before

Christmas and I did reasonably well. By that I mean I'd kept Ray on his toes and kept him looking for me; I'd got past him a couple of times and got the crosses over. That was a very good game against Ray Wilson. He was simply the best. Against him it wasn't so much a physical battle as a mental and tactical battle. And he was the master of that.

I saw Ray Wilson of Everton not so long ago as well. I was at a function with him and Danny McGrain, the very fine Scotland and Celtic full-back. Danny came up and said to Ray: 'It's such a pleasure to meet you. You were my hero.' I sat there listening in awe. That tells you how good Ray Wilson was. Yet when you meet him you wouldn't realise who he is. He's such a quiet and humble man; there is no shining light on his head saying, 'Look at me, look at me.'

Terry Cooper was another brilliant full-back, a lovely man and a really clever and exciting player. The first time I played against him was when Leeds started this new thing called overlapping full-backs. I thought it was a terrible idea. To me the so-called 'wing backs' are neither one thing nor the other. They can't do either; they can't defend and they can't cross balls. But Terry was so good that he could do both, and we knew that. So Malcolm Allison's response was a psychological ploy – and I followed it to the letter.

We kicked off and I said to Terry: 'If you're going to go running up front I'll see you later because I'm staying on the halfway line. And remember this: when you cross a ball it's an art, and if you can't cross a ball the keeper will catch it and he'll throw it straight to me where I'm waiting on the halfway line and I'll have fifty yards' start on you. It's up to you whether you go down the wing or not.'

Well, he didn't go, did he? He knew he'd be in trouble. That was the type of banter you had. And it was fun. But keeping Terry back in defence only worked up to a point. He was such a good left back that I rarely got past him,

Another left back who was never easy was Frank Lampard senior of West Ham. I was always geared up for a tough challenge with him, and he was unusual because most of the time the West Ham players weren't physical. I didn't like that, and very often I didn't play well against them because I preferred a battle. It got me going. Frank was tough, though, and one time I caught him and he had to have stitches in his leg. I remember also that we had a laugh about it afterwards in the players' bar.

I'd like to mention two more outstanding left backs. One I never played against in a competitive match, but he was responsible as much as anyone for making me the player I was. Glyn Pardoe of City was my opponent only in practice routines in training. He was a really high–class full-back who'd been converted from centre forward. He was so difficult to beat in the week, and he made many Saturdays so easy for me because then the left back was second rate by comparison. I think people forget how good he was.

The other is a player whose name I guess that most football fans have never heard of. He is Bobby Noble, who was an outstanding young talent at Manchester United in the late 1960s. I played against him a couple of times and he really sorted me out in a way that almost nobody else ever did. I thought he was going to be the very best left back, an absolute certainty to play for England for years. He was tough and hard and clever and quick; he had all the attributes you needed. I had such respect for him. Sadly, his career was ended by a car crash when a vehicle he was in skidded into a lamp-post. He never played again. Many years later his son was stabbed to death outside a pub in Sale. I don't see him very often now; the tragedy has affected him. I thought Bobby Noble ranked alongside the best I ever played against. He was only young and had such potential. Life can be devastating at times and when his son was killed I wondered just how unlucky can someone be?

I often think about the players I encountered from that time in the 1960s and 1970s. What strikes me is that most of them were very humble people. Many were shy and quiet until they crossed the white line and ran on to the football field. That's where they became sure of themselves. But take them out of that environment and they are humble. I saw that recently when most of the 1970 Brazilian World Cup-winning team came to Manchester City for a function. They were fantastic players but humble men. When Rivelino's luggage was lost at the new Heathrow Terminal Five he didn't make a fuss; he just went to the shop and bought an England football shirt and wore that everywhere. Most of the great English players were the same – Bobby Charlton, Ray Wilson, Colin Bell and many more.

I know that's how I am. The fiery entertainer on the field is an ordinary fella out and about in real life. I find it very embarrassing when people come up to me and say: 'Oh, you were a great player, you were a legend.' That doesn't strike home with me at all; it never has done.

If I'd thought more of myself as a footballer I might have been more successful as an international player. But I think I was a little in awe of the people I played alongside with England. In my own mind I didn't really think I was good enough to do it.

Doing the rounds at Manchester City before matches I sometimes go into the Sky TV box and Andy Gray says: 'Oh, the legend's coming in.' You talk to them, and I say the same thing every time. When people say I was a legend or a great player, I reply: 'No, I was just a good player. The great players are men like Tom Finney, Stanley Matthews, Dave Mackay and Duncan Edwards.' Greatness is very rare.

I was fortunate that I had the sort of personality that meant I could mingle easily with people in all walks of life, from football to show business. But there was also an essential shyness in my nature, a lack of belief in my ability as a footballer, and you had to overcome that doubt. My personality helped me to overcome it, but sometimes that personality was a bit of a charade. It was a way of hiding things. That's why I have the greatest respect for Bobby Charlton – because he is a shy man. It's the same with Nicolas Anelka. People look at him and think he's aloof. But when he was at Manchester City he told me that it is just shyness. And I can believe that.

Perhaps the nature of the players of my generation was also down to the very different climate we played in. With so little live football on television there were no TV interviews, and no chance of boasting about this or that in front of a camera with all the world watching. Nor were there a thousand and one reruns of every minor incident; skirmishes weren't blown up to be more important than they really were.

You were on TV so rarely as a player that when your game was on *Match of the Day* you had to find somewhere to see it on a Saturday night. I can remember watching with George Best in his digs at Mrs Fullaway's, and trying to find a bar that had a TV on. That's why you see the same old clips of George in action played over and over again. Most of his genius was never captured on film. I am for ever grateful the 'Ballet on Ice' was lucky enough to be covered that day.

The publicity of football then was nearly all in the newspapers. They were an integral part of the football show. We'd talk to the pressmen after the game in the tunnel, and then I'd say: 'I'll see you later.' Modern players would throw their hands up in horror at the idea of having a drink on a Saturday evening with the football reporters, but that was our routine after a game. We'd go to the Grand Hotel in Manchester and have a pint with the pressmen who were covering the match. It was there that we had the proper conversation; it was there they'd tell you the real truth about the match that afternoon. They'd praise you for a good game and tell you if it had been poor.

'What happened to you today? Did you have a late night?' they'd say, that type of thing. And you'd listen to them. Supporters would always come and say that you'd played well even when you knew as a professional that you hadn't. You could walk away from a ground deceived by the fans. But reality was always there in the bar at the Grand Hotel. And I wouldn't have changed that for the world. It was an essential part of my football education.

Another change that hasn't been for the better in football is the intense scrutiny that referees are now put under all the time. TV coverage has changed it all. Everything is seen and analysed endlessly. In our day the 'over the top of the ball' tackle was a common thing. Today it is brought into focus and causes a huge commotion. I feel sorry for the refs today. When I was playing I'd say to the refs: 'Look after me today.' They used to laugh, but they did it. So many big games are ruined today because someone mistimes a tackle early in the game and gets sent off with a straight red card. It changes the whole concept of the game. In our day, if you were sent off you deserved to get sent off. The refs didn't make a fool of you when they booked you. They just stood next to you and did the job quietly. I remember being booked once at Anfield for a tackle on Ron Yeats. He was enormous, a giant of a centre half. Bill Shankly called him the colossus.

'Look at the size of him up there,' I said. 'What's it all about, ref?'

'Name?' was all he said. And Ron stood there grinning.

The refs were a different quality then. They understood the game and the players. I was never sent off when I didn't deserve to be, and probably would have gone a few more times but for a little leniency by the officials. I was sent off for tackles, never for bad language or verbals. Once I got sent off for sticking my head into someone at Southampton, the wing half David Walker, who had come from Burnley. Francis Lee had raced forward and Walker sliced him. I made a comment and Walker turned round and came to me so I just stuck my head in his face. The ref was over immediately, of course.

'Don't say anything,' I told the ref. 'I'm already going.' And off I went.

My temper made me do stupid things like that occasionally. It's all right being aggressive, but you let your side down if you got sent off and the player you were involved with stayed on the pitch. You had put your team-mates under pressure. The unwritten rule was that if you got sent off the other fella either got carried off or he was also sent off. Some of the time I let the side down. The red mist descended sometimes. Perhaps it's in the family. My brother is the same, and remember the only time I saw my father play he was also sent off.

It was quite hard to get sent off in those days, but I even managed it once in a testimonial. Nobody could believe it. The game was just before Christmas against QPR at Loftus Road, a supposed friendly in aid of someone's good cause. Rodney Marsh went off because it was too cold and Francis Lee wouldn't come out for the second half. It wasn't the weather that bothered me – it was the way QPR's full-back Tony Hazell kept kicking me all through the first forty-five minutes. I hadn't gone all that way to be kicked in a testimonial match, and I was boiling with anger. We started the second half and immediately Hazell kicked me again so I went straight through him and was sent off. As I was walking back down the tunnel Joe Mercer was only just coming out to watch the second half. He couldn't believe I'd got myself sent off in a testimonial – and it didn't go down well with the boss.

As it was, Terry Venables used his considerable powers of persuasion as the PFA union man to get me off an FA charge. And the next day we went to the children's hospital at Great Ormond Street in London to visit the kids there. That soon stopped me feeling sorry for myself. I remember that we saw a little boy who looked just like Gary Lee, Francis's son, who had a bad heart problem. There were tears in our eyes and Francis was very upset. I looked at Joe and said to him: 'I only got sent off, you know.' It was a reality check for all of us.

The truth is that I wasn't a dirty player; I was an aggressive player. Some of the defenders I played against gave it out to me. I knew what I was going to get – and they knew what they were going to get in return. All wingers were meant to have peas for a heart, but that wasn't the case with me. I would respond to any aggression – that's the way my life was. I didn't break anyone's leg, and I never went out with the intention of doing anything like that. I left my foot there a couple of times, but that's just the way I was. It was about being able to look after yourself. I can't remember any arguments or punch-ups in the players' lounge after a game. Sometimes they limped in, and sometimes I limped in. But we all had a drink together. I never showed it if I was hurt or had any damage done. That was about pride as much as anything. And the crowd expected to see that, too. They wouldn't tolerate weakness and making the most of injuries back then. It was all part of being on the football stage.

And there were so many wonderful stages. One of my favourite grounds was always Stamford Bridge, even though it had a dog track round it in those days. That made it big and open, and we always seemed to play well there. I enjoyed it. I knew it would be tough; no messing around with Harris and McCreadie. But it was a great atmosphere.

Goodison Park was another particular favourite. I had a wonderful rapport with the fans there, and I liked the way you had to step up on to the pitch. I really did feel like an actor treading up on to the boards. Old Trafford was brilliant, too. We won quite a few matches there and it was easy to rile the United fans. The atmosphere was magic.

Villa Park was a special place for me as well, more than anything because it was the ground I went to so often as a boy to watch big matches. Every time I played there I felt so privileged to have a career in the professional game. I also remember after one match against Aston Villa that three City fans had missed the train home, so they came on the team bus and we gave them a lift home. When we played in London we'd go on the train and talk to the fans on the journey home. The football club was like a big family, and there was no separation between players and supporters, no 'them and us'. I always thought it was so important that we were accessible to the fans. We'd go and have lunch sometimes in the supporters' club that was just outside Maine Road, and it wasn't unusual for me to give a couple of fans a lift to the ground on a Saturday afternoon.

My favourite ground, of course, was Maine Road. That was

my home arena, and it was a fantastic stadium. The pitch was beautiful, certainly compared to some of the dung heaps we played on elsewhere, and it was the widest pitch in the First Division, which was perfect for a winger in a team that played with width. It was great for a home winger, too, because the main standing area, the Kippax, was on the side of the pitch rather than behind the goal, as it was at almost every other ground. When you were on that side you had 30,000 City fans helping you out.

I remember we played Leicester City in the FA Cup when we were in the Second Division. We were 3-1 down and eventually drew 3-3. The full-back kicked me up hill and down dale; he cut me to pieces. It was a particularly tough match, but the crowd were really with me that day.

When I went on a run they were with me – and then I got applauded all the way back. It happened all game, and made the difference between losing and getting a draw. Sometimes we used to run up the Kippax in training and it made you realise how many people it could hold.

I don't think there was a better crowd anywhere in football. And, for me, there was no better stage to be a football entertainer.

11

THE THREE LIONS

The first hint that I was getting close to playing for England was when Sir Alf Ramsey sent me a Christmas card in December 1967. It came through the letterbox just two months before my proud debut against Scotland – and it's a curious memento to look at now. There's an extremely dull picture on the front of the 'Centenary Room at the Football Association Headquarters'; just a photo of some tables and chairs, with nobody in the room, and not a hint of festivity.

Why did he send it to me? I must have been in his thoughts then, I suppose, although I'd only won a single Under-23 cap against Turkey and I didn't think the match had gone very well.

Apart from that, the only other time I'd come across Sir Alf was when I'd been selected for an FA touring party that played a few matches at Expo '67 in Montreal. That trip was a riot, one long and often drunken party that didn't involve anything like serious football. Some of the 1966 World Cup-winners were there – Bobby Moore, Gordon Banks, Alan Ball and George

Cohen among them. There were also up and coming players like me, and some old-timers near the end of their careers like the great John 'Budgie' Byrne. They all said it was the best trip ever.

Sir Alf had expected us to be staying in the same kind of top-class hotel that the England team was used to, but they put all the teams in the Loyola Jesuit College dormitories, and the facilities were basic to say the least. We couldn't have cared less because it was a holiday really. Sir Alf lined us all up and personally handed out spending money to us as if we were schoolboys. It was about twenty Canadian dollars a day. Then he said: 'I don't want to see you for seven days.' And he didn't. We got up to all sorts while the Russian team, who were one of the other sides in the tournament, had to train in the blistering heat every morning.

One time we trotted to a café round the corner while the Russians sweated, and I remember walking back past their practice with Budgie Byrne, who was a bit overweight at the time. We were wearing shorts, sandals and sunglasses, looking like the tourists we were. Suddenly a loose ball dropped out of the sky from the Russian training game and Budgie trapped it on his chest, rolled it round his neck and down his back, before flicking it up and volleying the thing back to the Russian players. They were gobsmacked.

After a week we had to start playing matches. Sir Alf had seen us boozing too much and he wasn't particularly happy. He nearly cancelled our participation as well because the pitch was so bad; it had been used for a fairground and a circus and was covered in manure and sand. Diplomacy for the FA meant we had to play, and diplomacy towards Sir Alf meant we had to win the tournament.

The Russians were strong, but we beat them and two club sides, Standard Liège of Belgium and León of Mexico. That put us into the final and we beat Borussia Dortmund 3-0. Only then did Sir Alf smile.

Looking back, it may seem obvious that being selected for that FA touring party was a precursor to playing for England. But that wasn't how I felt at the time. I didn't think I was of a high enough standard to play for the world champions, and, even when there was press speculation that I might be called up, I took it with a pinch of salt. I'd seen so many headlines in my career that came to nothing that I had learned not to take any notice.

When it did happen in February 1968 it was a big surprise. They were different days, as that Christmas card proves, and at that time when an England call-up came it was by letter sent to Manchester City. The club were informed first and then our manager, Joe Mercer, came and told me the news and everyone was chuffed because I was the first City player to be picked by England for a long time. It was a dream come true to a player like myself who'd come through from the lower divisions. It was a tribute to the City team more than anything. There were no big stars at Maine Road; we were all about teamwork. Francis Lee and Colin Bell were both better players than me and they would go on to play more times for England.

Although I played most of my career as a winger, the selection came at the time when City had switched me from outside right to centre forward. I'm sure what helped me get into the England team was that I was an unknown quantity to First Division centre halves, and because of that I got away with it for a year. I did very well at the time and I scored eighteen goals in the season City won the League title. I was also making things happen around me, and maybe Sir Alf picked me for that. Nevertheless, I wasn't a real goalpoacher and to be chosen ahead of Roger Hunt and Jimmy Greaves astounded me.

I've already told the story of that day and my debut against Scotland – all except for the aftermath. While the rest of the England team left straight after the game for a flight back to London, I had to stay overnight in Glasgow with Bobby Charlton because we were flying back to Manchester the next morning. I remember walking out of Hampden Park with Bobby, a black plastic bag under my arm containing that white No. 9 England shirt and my football boots and shin pads. I couldn't have been happier.

Bobby already had social arrangements that evening, but, back at the hotel, Billy Bremner, the fiercely competitive Leeds and Scotland midfielder, saw that I was alone and said: 'See you in the bar.' It was more a command than an invitation, and I was on cloud nine as I dumped my boots and pads and England shirt in the room and went down for a drink with Billy. He bought me a gin and tonic, and, as he was paying, more than a few Scotsmen asked him what he was doing socialising with 'that Sassenach bastard'.

Billy and I had a few run-ins through the years on the pitch when City played Leeds. There was one time when I caught him with an elbow and cut him over the eye. Another time I left my leg in and caught him on the knee. He went off to be stitched up and then came back and spent the entire match chasing me round the pitch trying to kick me. There was still a bit of blood dripping out of his plaster in the players' lounge afterwards, but now he was smiling and I bought him a drink. We had respect for each other.

So, while he'd been a sworn enemy on the Hampden pitch

the afternoon I made my England debut, he was my best pal that evening in Glasgow. He got very shirty with the loudmouths giving me stick and threatened to fight every last one of them to defend the Englishman drinking his gin and tonic. He took me out in Glasgow that evening and the same scenario occurred a few more times. The city was quite a dangerous place in those days and you had to be careful what you were doing. Each time Billy had his fists up ready to fight for the Sassenach and each time they backed down.

It was a perfect illustration of the camaraderie of professional sport. Billy was a wonderful man who died far too young, and his friendship and protection that night summed up football for me. It's tough out on the pitch, and there were times when you had to look after yourself the best way you could. You did everything in your power to help your team and your team-mates, and you tried to enjoy the game on and off the field. Football is meant to be fun, and it was that night with Billy Bremner.

Bobby Charlton and I flew back to Manchester in the morning and that lunchtime I met Cecil Green, the director of Swindon who had given me my biggest break in football. He had gone to Hampden to watch me play, although I didn't know it that day. But I knew I had everything to thank him for, and when we met at the Midland Hotel in central Manchester I gave Mr Green my No. 9 white shirt from my England debut. More than anyone's it was his faith that had enabled me to fulfil my dream of playing for my country. He kept the shirt until he died and then his family presented it back to me. I'm not one for souvenirs, though, so I handed it on to Manchester City, and now it hangs up on the wall in one of the rooms at the Eastlands.

The 1-1 draw with Scotland had meant that England qualified

for the quarter-finals of the 1968 European Nations Cup. That was going to be a two-legged tie home and away to Spain, the reigning holders of the trophy. And Sir Alf picked me for the team again. That was so pleasing. After all the doubts I'd had about the Scotland game, and whether I was good enough for international football, here was the best possible proof that the manager had seen something in me. I was excited because it was also my first match at Wembley.

We stayed at Hendon Hall and trained at the Bank of England sports ground at Roehampton, where afterwards you'd have a shower and a lovely roast beef meal. Then there was a little team meeting in a room that was so hot that Bobby Moore fell asleep as Sir Alf was speaking: 'Bobby, just remember to tuck in, mate,' said Sir Alf as he looked over to his famous captain. 'Oh, I won't wake you up,' continued the manager. 'No need for that. Bobby knows what to do anyway.'

Sir Alf had a very dry sense of humour and he thought that situation was incredibly funny. He was such a nice man, a proper Englishman. He loved the Three Lions and knew that the players he picked would never let him down even if they didn't play as well as expected. Sir Alf must have believed in me to select me for such a vital and difficult match, and I went into this clash with much more self-confidence. We won 1-0, Bobby Charlton scoring the goal, and I know I did quite well. I had a few opportunities and felt more at home.

I also remember the thrill of playing against some of the great Spanish players from Real Madrid, like José Santamaría, Pachin, the full-back, and the flying winger, Gento. There was one moment when Gento received the ball when he was stood next to me. He just back-heeled it and was gone like lightning. He was a tiny man but with so much speed.

After the game I went to a club in London for a few drinks with Jackie Charlton and Bobby Moore. The captain was always a critic, and if I didn't play well he would tell me. It's no good saying you played well when you didn't. That night he told me I'd had a good game and when you got that acknowledgement from Bobby you knew you weren't doing too badly. What they don't want in an England side in a crucial game is someone who isn't going to be able to do the business for them. You have to be able to play at that level. I didn't have the touch of a Bobby Charlton or an Alfredo di Stéfano, but I worked very hard indeed for the team.

The return leg against Spain was scheduled for three weeks later in Madrid. I had done well enough to be selected for the squad again, and was looking forward to travelling to a city I had never been to – and to playing at the great Bernabéu Stadium. It was going to be the biggest week of my football life. The match against the Spanish was in midweek, sandwiched between the two final matches of the First Division season that Manchester City had to win to become League champions. Unfortunately, I sustained a bad ankle knock in that penultimate match at Tottenham. I knew as I hobbled out of White Hart Lane that it was bad news.

When I'd been picked for the squad I had to give all my contact numbers to Sir Alf, and on the Sunday morning I was at Tina's family house for lunch. The phone rang and Tina's brother David answered with his usual line: 'Yes, Puffin Island Embassy.'

'Oh, I do apologise, it's Sir Alf Ramsey here.'

David was mortified and handed the phone over. But Sir Alf understood the humour perfectly well.

'I'm sorry, I'm not fit enough to play,' I told Sir Alf with the heaviest of hearts. It was the first time I'd had to pull out of anything due to injury but I knew I had to be 100 per cent fit to make a contribution for England.

'It's disappointing,' said Sir Alf, 'but thank you, Michael, for being so honest. I do understand.'

He couldn't have been as disappointed as I was. I had spoken to Joe Mercer and Malcolm Allison after the game at Tottenham but nothing had been said about saving myself for City's title-deciding game the following Saturday at Newcastle. That just wasn't the case then that you might miss an international match for the selfish sake of your club. It was my own decision to pull out of the England game, and there was nothing else I could do. As it was, I just about recovered for the Newcastle match, but it was touch and go, just as it was for Colin Bell, who had also had to tell Sir Alf he couldn't go to Madrid.

When I put the phone down so many thoughts passed through my mind: does he believe you? Does Sir Alf think you're messing him around and you don't fancy going to Spain? Will he ever pick you again? Will he put you to one side now you've let him down for this important game by not playing? Such thoughts probably never even crossed his mind. But they did mine. The self-doubt was always lurking somewhere in the background.

England went to Madrid and won that match 2-1 and so qualified for the mini-tournament final of the European Nations Cup to be held in Italy. Our opponents in the semi-final would be Yugoslavia, while hosts Italy played the Soviet Union in the other semi. And I was in the squad.

The ankle was still troubling me enough that I was left out of the first warm-up match for the tournament, a home fixture with Sweden that we won 3-1. But I got to play in the next game, which was away to West Germany in Hanover, the first time the countries had met since the World Cup Final in 1966. It was five days before the semi against Yugoslavia, a red-hot day when the Germans played their full World Cup team.

Prior to the game there was a major kerfuffle. I always wore Adidas boots, as did most of the players. Their great rivals were Puma, a breakaway company formed by Rudi Dassler, the brother of Adi Dassler, founder of Adidas. Derek Ibbotson, who was working on our fitness at Manchester City, was also a rep for Puma and he approached the England players with a financial deal to wear Puma boots in this game. The money was good and nearly all the England players agreed, apart from Bobby Moore, Geoff Hurst and myself. I always wore Adidas and I wasn't going to switch. I was also very friendly with Horst Dassler, Adi's son, and I wouldn't let him down.

It was a hot day and hardly conducive to wearing brand-new boots, but the players had gone for it and they warmed up in their Pumas. Horst Dassler arrived in the dressing room and was deeply upset, and so was Sir Alf Ramsey who said sternly: 'No, you're not wearing new boots in this match. Nobody is wearing Puma boots.'

The trouble was that some of the players had thrown away their old boots and had no option. But instead of their boots sporting the bold Puma stripe along the side, the Puma marking was blacked out and three white stripes painted on to make it appear as if they were Adidas boots. The German players knew all about this, and must have been laughing at us.

It was a tough enough match anyway without all this distraction. It was also Colin Bell's debut for England. The Germans had Helmut Haller playing, but it was Franz Beckenbauer who was decisive. He hit a shot from twenty yards that deflected in past Gordon Banks for an own goal. We lost 1-0. I did okay, and I remember having a tussle right through the game with Wolfgang Overath, who was a magnificent midfielder but an irritating type of player. He was always trying to get hold of me, and it's fair to say we didn't hit it off. I was also directly up against Beckenbauer, and he was an amazing player, in a different world from me. He always had time on the ball and was never caught in possession however hard you chased him. The ball seemed glued to his foot when he moved forward. Sir Alf always said that if you gave the ball away against the top teams you didn't get it back. And that day I found out how true his words were.

From Hanover we flew to Florence for the Nations Cup semi-final. I thought I had a chance to play, but Sir Alf picked the same side that had won in Madrid in the quarter-final second leg. I felt as if the ankle injury had come back to haunt me – and I had to watch from the bench, wondering what might have been. The showdown with the Yugoslavs turned out to be a ferocious match. I played in some tough games, but nothing as brutal as this one.

Sir Alf had asked in the dressing room for someone to keep their playmaker Ivica Osim quiet in the game, to keep him out of the action. Fury took over when a tackle from Norman Hunter put Osim out of the game completely. The match had begun normally but suddenly the Yugoslavs turned. They were so incensed and they were tackling waist-high. They became animals, and I mean animals. If that incident hadn't occurred I believe they would have carried on playing their normal football and we might have won. Instead, the other key moment came when Alan Mullery was sent off amid all the mayhem. Eventually, we lost when Dragan Dzajic scored the only goal with five minutes to go. Dzajic was a wonderfully skilful player, not a kicker at all, but he couldn't change the ugly mood by himself.

We had to fly on to Rome for the third-place play-off, which we won 2-0 against the Soviet Union, while Italy beat the Yugoslavs in the final after a replay. I had to sit on the bench again in Rome, but I wasn't angry. I felt fortunate to be with the squad at all, and to be very close to the team. My feeling was that it proved I was one of the best twenty players in the country and if Sir Alf didn't pick me in the first eleven then I'd do all I could to support from the sidelines. First and foremost, you wanted the right result for England, and I played eight times for my country, which is more than I ever thought I would.

I missed out again on the Mexico World Cup squad. I was in the original forty, but was one of the final few players to be axed. I wasn't surprised. I hadn't played for England for two years, and I was now playing back at outside right for Manchester City at a time when Sir Alf didn't really use wingers. Perhaps that was a factor. I also had a bad run of injuries in the months leading up to the summer of 1970, and that can't have helped my case. I broke my leg — a hairline fracture, but bad enough — in the League Cup Final, and it went again in the final League match of the season against Sheffield Wednesday, which meant that I missed the final of the European Cup Winners' Cup with City. It would have been a gamble for Sir Alf to take me to Mexico. I thought I could have done a job out there if I'd been in the squad, but I respected the decision when he rang himself to say that I was staying at home. I'm not sure Sir Alf thought I had the real cutting edge for international football that he required. I was always someone to call on if he was in a bit of trouble and short of players.

As it turned out, three full years went by before I was needed again. I was in consistent form for City in the 1971–2 season where we went close to winning the League again, and in November 1971 I had another call from Sir Alf to put me in the squad to face Switzerland home and away in European Nations Cup qualifiers. The away match was first, in Basle, and I was only on the bench as we won 3-2. But for the game at Wembley he switched Francis Lee to centre forward and I came in with No. 7 on my back for England for the first time. It was the only time Francis and I played for England together and we both did well. It wasn't a good game, but I remember it with great affection, because I scored our goal in a 1-1 draw. Not only had I played for my country, but now I'd scored for my country, too.

If Francis had scored that goal, he would no doubt tell you about the terrific skill involved, but the truth is it was just about the softest headed goal you'll ever see. The ball came over and I got a head to it and it went looping up high and dropped into the far corner of the net. I didn't intend it to go there, but it was a wonderful feeling to score for England at Wembley. Francis was laughing, and so were some of the others. No, it wasn't spectacular, but they can't take it away from me. It's in the record books: goalscorer – Summerbee. And the fact is that it helped the team, it helped England to qualify for a quarter-final against West Germany. That's always the test for me: did you make a contribution? I did that night, and I felt I deserved the celebration drink afterwards at a club in Berkeley Square.

The two quarter-final matches with West Germany are famous in the history of English football. I wasn't involved in the first leg at home, a 3-1 defeat at Wembley when the team were thoroughly outplayed by a brilliant display from the Germans,

Happy days as Tina and I become engaged.

Celebrating m[...]
first England [...]
up in proper s[...]
with George [...]

The official
engagement
photograph.

e wedding of Manchester City's
ke Summerbee saw best man
orge sporting a short-lived
ustache

The only wedding photo where all eyes are on the best man.

Preston's 1938 FA
Cup Final squad.
My father George
third from left in
back row standing
next to Bill Shank

Football on the beach at San Rafael
in Portugal with my son Nicholas
(far right of the front row).

On holiday in Dubai with
(far left), former West Ham pl
Ken Brown and his wife, and D
Pleat, a man always on the ph

...oying an Oasis concert at the Old ...ford cricket ground in a group ...ed by Paul and Rachel Beck.

My son Nicholas at Wembley before playing for Sunderland against Charlton in a play-off final.

My elder brother John
with his daughter Leah
and son Luke.

I've never seen anyone
so happy to become a
fiftysomething as Tina.

Nicholas and my daughter
Rachel on holiday in Portug

...a seems even happier to celebrate ...60th birthday with myself, Nicholas, ...hel, and her husband Stephen.

Samuel Summerbee loves watching football at the City of Manchester Stadium just as much as his grandfather.

I'm holding the play-off trophy won by Manchester City the company of my friend John, a recovering alcoholic.

The players of 1968 at a reunion dinner with Mrs Joe Me in the pink and Mrs Roy Clarke.

What is there to say?
Lee, Bell and Summerbee
join forces with Best, Law
and Charlton at the launch
of videos of us all in action.

with Günter Netzer the orchestrator in midfield. Sir Alf decided we had to be more aggressive in the return match in Berlin a few weeks later, and maybe that was one reason I got the call to join the squad that included Peter Storey and Norman Hunter, among others. I came on for the second half with the score still 0-0 in the big Olympic Stadium and I did quite well in the game. We couldn't get the goals to worry the Germans but we did restore some dignity by not losing. Some of the newspaper critics, though, attacked us for being too rough and brutal. One of them, Brian Glanville, picked me out for treading on some-one's hand. But that hadn't been deliberate; it was just an accident. And we hadn't tried to 'kick the Germans off the park'.

It was an aggressive game, that's all. We got stuck into them, and we had to because Netzer was playing and the link-up between him and Beckenbauer was fantastic. They could so easily make you look stupid. Glanville said that Sir Alf had brought on animals like Hunter and Summerbee, that we were cloggers. Glanville thinks he has great knowledge of the game, but he got that wrong. It's easy to criticise like that, but I don't think you call someone an animal because he goes on to the field with an aggressive attitude. If you assess any international side you will always find players with an aggressive streak. Sometimes you have to try to shake up the opponent who can knock the ball around and take the piss out of you. We weren't kicking lumps out of people; we just got into the Germans.

Sir Alf never told us to kick lumps out of players. I came on in the second half and did the best I could. I was up against Paul Breitner and I fared pretty well against him. I got wired into him, and the Germans did the same to you. Despite all our efforts they controlled the game because they were such a good side. Netzer was a magnificent player, and they were the best team I ever played against. Every one of them could play and they could grind out results even if they weren't on top form. They had ability right through the team.

Off the field, I was fascinated by the city of Berlin. I was a war baby and an avid reader of history books, particularly about the Second World War. I went through Checkpoint Charlie and walked round the Brandenburg Gate. We also passed by Spandau, the jail in which Hitler's deputy Rudolf Hess was imprisoned. As I walked around I wondered what it must have been like living in Berlin during the war. There were still areas of rubble then which hadn't been cleared. I didn't go with the attitude of a victor, just with a fascination for history. The stadium in which we played was where Hitler had held some of his rallies, and the platform from which he used to speak was still there. Bobby Moore and Alan Ball would also come out with me looking at these historic places; we thought it was a better use of time than just sitting round the hotel getting bored and fed up.

This period was my best in an England shirt. Not long afterwards I was in the squad for the Home Internationals. The opener was against Wales, and we won 3-0 at Ninian Park in Cardiff. There were three Manchester City players – myself, Colin Bell and Rodney Marsh, who had joined us a couple of months earlier from QPR. They both scored and I made their goals, and I came off the pitch feeling chuffed. It was the first time I'd felt really good in an England shirt. Then I showered and changed more quickly than in any other match I ever played.

Sir Alf had given us the weekend off after the match and a pal of mine, Mike Cornall, was having a party back in Manchester. He said he would come to watch the match and then drive me back north himself. I told him to be outside the ground at five o'clock and I'd be there. So, ten minutes after the final whistle I'm outside Ninian Park and Mike drives up in his Porsche and we are away. By quarter to seven Mike was pulling up in the car park of the Swan at Bucklow Hill, just outside Manchester, to have a drink.

I was standing at the bar and this fella walked in and said: 'Blinkin' hell. I've just seen you on the television playing in Cardiff. How did you get here as quick as that?'

'Don't bloomin' ask me,' I said. 'Just check me trousers.'

Mike had driven at 130 mph in his Porsche, and it was the drive of death. I think the party was just about worth it.

In midweek we were playing Northern Ireland at Wembley. There was no party there. We lost 1-0 to a goal from Terry Neill and I pulled a hamstring near the end of the match. None of us played well and it was a big deal because it was the first time England had lost to Northern Ireland at Wembley. Terry Neill has never let me forget it. George Best played very well that night, and he was pleased. But he didn't make anything of it; he wasn't a gloater. Sir Alf was very unhappy, and so was I. The injury meant I was forced to miss the last match of the Home Internationals, away to Scotland at Hampden Park. I was bitterly disappointed because I wanted to go back and put on the kind of show I was now convinced I was capable of in a Three Lions shirt. Instead, the season was over – and the boots were in the skip.

Another whole season went by before my eighth and final match for England in June 1973. Having been overlooked for all the games during the season I was picked for the summer tour to Czechoslovakia, Poland, the Soviet Union and Italy. I had been playing well all season, but I was probably only chosen as a stopgap. I didn't mind that. I was back with Bobby and the lads, and whenever Sir Alf picked me I treated it as a bonus – whether I played or not.

I wasn't needed for the friendly against the Czechs, but I was on the bench for the next game, a vitally important World Cup qualifier away to a really good Poland side. I was so frustrated that day because I was sitting on the bench as we went 2-0 down, thinking there was a real opportunity for me. I had noticed the left back wasn't up to standard and I was willing Sir Alf to put me on because I knew I could have done a job on the left back and maybe pulled something out of the fire. It was the only time I felt so certain with England, and it turned out to be such a significant result. It was the match in which Bobby Moore made a mistake and the defeat cost us dearly, preventing us qualifying for the 1974 World Cup Finals and not long afterwards ending the managerial reign of Sir Alf.

I always remember going back to the hotel afterwards. Alf had been quiet and he told us to have an early night because we were going on to Moscow in the morning. Bobby Moore was in a big room at the end of the corridor with all the kit and this time was rooming with Alan Ball. I was rooming on my own because Colin Bell had gone home because his wife had problems with her pregnancy. The phone went, and it was Bobby, inviting me down for a few drinks with him and Bally. We were having a chat, and drinking some gin and tonics, when who knocks on the door but Alf.

He came in and said: 'I thought I told you boys not to have a drink and to have an early night.' He paused for maximum effect, and then said: 'But I'll have a large gin and tonic, thank you, Bobby.' I don't think it was an accident. He knew where he'd find a G and T. Alf knew everything.

Moscow wasn't the nicest place in the world, but it was fascinating. We went to Red Square and looked at Lenin's tomb in the Kremlin. I watched in amazement at the precision of the guards. As the clock sounded the guard would slam his rifle butt on the ground at the same moment with absolutely perfect timing. I was so impressed I told the others and we went to see it five times. We were transfixed by the precision of it.

The weather was boiling hot in a Russian summer and we were staying at a huge hotel near Red Square that boasted a thousand rooms. Shame none of them was any good. The heat was unbearable because the air conditioning didn't work, the beds were rock hard and the noise never stopped because people were constantly walking past the hotel right through the night. At least there was a nice view out of the window to a garden full of lavender bushes.

I couldn't get any sleep for a couple of nights, and when it was just the same the night before the match I thought I'd had enough of that. So, I got my pillow, put my tracksuit on and wandered over the road into this garden looking for somewhere to have a kip on a bench. Looking around, the first thing I saw was Bobby Moore, already asleep on one seat with his head on a hotel pillow. We both ended up kipping there. We were like vagrants in England tracksuits. When it was light we walked over to the hotel, had a shower and got on with the rest of the day.

That day I played my final international, coming on as a substitute for Micky Channon in a 2-1 victory against the Soviets. There were 100,000 in the crowd and Leonid Brezhnev was the Communist leader then. When he came on to the pitch before the match you could hear a pin drop in this massive stadium. He shook hands with everybody and sat down and then the place erupted. The Soviets had a good side, but I enjoyed that game. I thought I'd done quite well again.

Last stop on the tour was Italy. It was a helluva long season when you were still travelling with England in June across Europe, and it was my final journey with Sir Alf. We flew to Turin, and I was sat with Allan Clarke at the front of the plane near Martin Chivers, Peter Storey and, inevitably, Bobby Moore and Alan Ball. Sir Alf stood up and in his clipped voice gave the orders: 'Right, you're having bacon and eggs, and one glass of champagne each,' he said.

The girls on the plane ignored him, and so did we. We drank a lot more than one glass and got off the plane speaking Japanese. We were all ready for our holidays.

In training it was pretty clear that I wasn't going to be involved in the match, not even as a substitute. Sir Alf may even have told me that straight, or perhaps Bobby let me know. Anyway, my season was over so I ritually threw my football boots out of the hotel window, which was about three floors up, and into the alleyway behind the building. A little while later I was out for a walk after a coffee and Alf passed by and said matter-of-factly: 'You're on the bench tomorrow.'

Suddenly, it was panic. I had no boots, and I might well be playing for England the next day. I raced back to the hotel and, fortunately, nobody had been in the back alley and I found the boots. Just as well. Nobody else had the same size feet as me, and I didn't carry a spare pair. I only ever used one pair a season, even if they finished with a few holes in the side or whatever.

As it turned out, I never left the bench as we lost the game 2-0.

The Italians did leave us with one present, though. They presented Bobby Moore with some beautiful Capo di Monte porcelain in recognition of his outstanding contribution to world football and his century of international caps. We had so much of it that when we arrived at Heathrow we pushed Mooro along in the trolley with his cargo. My wife Tina had flown down to meet me at the airport because we were going straight off on holiday the next day, and some of the other wives were there, too. We all ended up in a hotel opposite the airport, sitting in the pool bar in the water with our suits on – Mooro, Bally, me and the girls. And that was it; that was my final moment as an England footballer. I had no regrets. How can you have regrets about playing for your country? How can you regret being lucky enough to play for Sir Alf Ramsey?

12

THE ROCK OF MY LIFE

You know how it is. You're out on a Saturday night and you see a beautiful girl go dancing by. You think she could be your girl, and you'll make a complete fool of yourself having a go.

I'm so glad I did. Tina has been the rock of my life.

It was at the Phonograph disco and she went dancing by with her boyfriend. I was sitting with George Best and Selwyn Demmy and I said: 'Cor, look at that girl there.' Selwyn knew everybody in Manchester and he told me her name was Christine Schofield and that she worked at the Midland Hotel as a beautician. He said she lived in Stalybridge and her father was in the travel goods business. Selwyn asked her over, and joining the company of George Best was always an attraction. As it happened, she sat next to me and I thought she was gorgeous.

I spoke like a farmer then, and I tried to chat her up out of the corner of my mouth with my West Country accent. It didn't go down too well. I asked her if she'd like to go out and she looked at me as if I was a piece of dirt. Then she disappeared with her boyfriend.

She was on my mind all the time after that, and a couple of days later I rang the Midland Hotel. They put me through to her. She said hello in a posh public school accent and I reminded her of our meeting in the Phonograph and asked if there was any chance of taking her out. She said: 'I beg your pardon. Where did you meet me? I don't remember you.' And she put the phone down.

She had no idea who I was, she wasn't interested in football and it was hardly as if I was Robert Redford. I rang again and she said sorry, she wouldn't go out. But I kept thinking about her as I played my football and went gallivanting around with George. One day I went to the Midland to see a man called Maurice Rubin, a lawyer. We were having smoked salmon in a special tea room at the hotel and I saw Tina again as she walked by. I thought I'd sneak up and say hello, but I couldn't find her. So, when I was home, I rang again and said I'd continue to ring to see if I could take her out.

I said: 'Let me take you out and if you don't like me, well, okay. And I promise you I'm not a lunatic.'

So, finally, she gave in and agreed to a date. I was to pick her up at the family house in Stalybridge. I don't know what I expected but it wasn't the lovely long driveway and the Ferrari in front of the house that belonged to her brother. This was another world from the one I'd grown up in. The only thing I had on my side was that I was driving a P1800 Volvo, like The Saint had in the TV show. It was a stylish motor, but that was my only plus. I wasn't wearing a suit and Tina came out all dressed up. I thought, 'Phew!' and she said: 'Which restaurant are we going to?'

'Isn't there a good pub round here?' I said, but it wasn't what she wanted to hear.

I drove up into the Derbyshire hills, and I had a record player in my car that played 45s. It was specially built for a car so that when you went over a bump it didn't move and continued playing. I was playing stupid songs and we went into a pub near New Mills. I was excited because she was a darling. She had a whisky and dry ginger, and I ordered my normal pint of Mackeson, a bag of crisps and a jar of cockles.

We talked and talked. It was one of those things. Tina has a great personality and we just got on. I thought we had anyway, and I gave her a kiss outside. She'll always tell you she wondered if I could kiss. A kiss means a lot. When I asked to see her again and she said yes, my heart leapt.

I don't think her family were too pleased that she was going out with a footballer. They were all rugby people. But we were together for about six months and then she went to Majorca for a holiday with her girlfriends. She had a great time – and she wasn't married or engaged at the time. But I didn't think it was right. It was an egotistical thing on my part and I packed it in between us and didn't see her after that for a long time.

Tina decided she'd leave the Manchester area after that. She worked as a beautician on a cruise liner and then went to live in London and became an air hostess for British Caledonian. I kept in touch a bit, and that was cheeky on my part. When Manchester City were staying in London for a match, which was usually at the Waldorf Hotel, I would ring and ask her to come and see me. There was still that spark between us, but we only met for coffee for an hour. Then I met her in Manchester just before she was due to fly off to Canada and she looked so lovely. She was wearing a black miniskirt and was tanned from a trip to the Caribbean. She seemed so pleased to see me as well, so I just said: 'Pack your job in and I'll marry you.' And that's what she did.

There was no rush to get married, but we had decided we wanted to be married and live together, and so the fact that the season had just started and that it wasn't the best time of year for a footballer to arrange a wedding didn't seem to matter. We just picked the best date we could find – and it was on a Monday lunchtime, the day before Manchester City were flying out to Turkey to face Fenerbahçe in the European Cup.

My choice of best man seemed obvious to me – my best pal. That was George Best, and he was brilliant. We decided to stay at the Piccadilly Hotel in Manchester the night before the wedding, but first of all we drove up to Tina's house in Stalybridge because she had insisted on seeing George to read the riot act and make sure he turned up. George was banned from driving at the time because of a speeding offence so he had a chauffeur ferrying him around, and the driver dropped us off back in the city at nine o'clock. We weren't going to watch *Z Cars* on the telly so I went with George for a drink at the Brown Bull in Salford, which was a favourite place of ours. It wasn't the brightest move because most of the wedding guests happened to be drinking there that night – Malcolm Allison, Tony Book, Pat Crerand and a few others. The Brown Bull would stay open late and we got to bed at a quarter to five in the morning.

George's driver picked us up a few hours later and I was still more than a little the worse for wear, so we sneaked in round the back of the church in the village of Mottram-in-Longendale on the edge of the Peak District. It was a rainy, windy day and the vicar came up and put his Primus stove on to make us a cup of tea. As we were waiting to go in for the service, George beckoned me out to the door.

'See that wall over there?' he said. 'You've only got to run down there, jump over it and you'll be away. You won't have to get married, and you'll be as free as a bird. They'll never catch you.'

I looked at George, with his hair cut short and big moustache, and thought he looked like a Mexican bandit. That's how he wanted to live – with that freedom of action. But I was a different kind of man. I knew that getting married was serious but I had found the right girl, and settling down with a family of my own had always been my goal. It wasn't hard to ignore his advice, and then we walked into the church from round the back and you could hear the sighs of relief. A lot of people had thought George might not show up.

The wedding went brilliantly, and we had a reception up on the borders of the Derbyshire hills. Lots of people turned up there including Joe and Norah Mercer, my City team-mates and the drinkers from the Brown Bull. George was lovely, and spoke about our friendship and how lucky I was to meet Tina. I often wonder what went through his mind that day, whether he wanted to have the same opportunity. I wonder what would have happened if he could have met someone and been able to be more settled. Knowing the person he was it might have helped him – but maybe there was no way round it and that was the only path his life could take. Maybe it was impossible for him to meet the right person given who he was – with his aura and his looks.

Tina and I couldn't have a honeymoon because I was off to play football the next day. It's something a couple look forward to and it was quite strange not having one. Instead, we went home to a house we'd bought in Timperley, just south of Manchester. We'd had weekends away. But this was the first moment we had lived together. We didn't live together before we were married, as people do today. Tina had been at home and I was in digs.

I always remember the next morning we were sat facing each other having breakfast and thinking that this was the reality of life. It was an unusual feeling for me. I'd never had regular meals living in digs. I'd always been in cafés in the morning before training. It was totally different. We had bought the house and made everything perfect but we hadn't lived in it until we got married. After breakfast I went off to the airport to fly to Turkey. That was hard for Tina, but that's how it is in professional football. The job comes first. It has to be the predominant thing. I think Tina found it difficult to accept that. She went to Liverpool and stayed with a friend while I went off to play.

It took me some while, I admit, to get used to the changed routine of life. I came back from Turkey in a bad mood because we'd lost the game 2-1 and been knocked out of the European Cup, and a couple of days afterwards Malcolm Allison said he was going to watch a game at Burnley and did I want to come along. I said yes without thinking because that was how it had always been. I went, and it didn't go down well at home. I hadn't thought about it. I hadn't had a family life since I'd left home at fifteen, and my memory of my father was that he was rarely in the house when he was working in football.

Before the wedding we'd had a couple of narrow escapes when we thought Tina might have become pregnant. And as soon as we were married we thought, 'Let's have a little go', not really thinking through the consequences. The first time we really tried, it happened. The next minute Tina was expecting our Rachel. It didn't go down well with her father. He was a businessman and he hadn't been too keen on his clever daughter marrying a footballer; in those days people thought that footballers ended up running pubs when they retired. I came home from training the next day and found Tina crying. She had told her father the good news and he'd said: 'How silly can you be – you hardly know each other.'

Tina was so upset and I rang him up and said: 'Mr Schofield, no disrespect to you, but Tina is my wife now. I look after her. We do what we do. And don't you worry about Tina. We want a baby, we're having a baby, and that's it. You're going to be a grandfather. You don't have to worry about looking after her financially. I will look after her. She's my responsibility.'

He took it – and it broke the ice with him. It was fine after that. He accepted the situation. He had just been a bit shocked. And we were, too. We hadn't expected it to happen so quickly. I was in and out playing football and it wasn't a normal married life for a girl who had come from a different background. Tina had seen the world and had had her freedom. Suddenly, it wasn't there any more, and instead there was so much responsibility.

Once Rachel was born there was the further clash of interests between family and football. Tina was getting fed up with the end of her pregnancy and I'd heard the rumour about a spoonful of castor oil and a cup of coffee helping to encourage the baby to arrive. It's not recommended today. Tina had two weeks to go, but I gave her the remedy and within a couple of hours she was in labour and off to Southfields maternity hospital in Bowden. Me? Well, I was due to play for Manchester City against Ajax the next day in a pre-season friendly over in Amsterdam.

I took Tina into the hospital and the labour ward and she said to the matron: 'Can you get him out of here. I don't want him in here.' I was a nuisance rather than a help and I didn't particularly want to see my wife in agony in that situation. Each to his own, but I don't believe in men being there.

I went out of the room and down to reception and there was a young lad there whose wife had just had a baby. He was waiting for a taxi, so I said I'd give him a lift home. I had a drink with him and came back to the hospital to find it all locked up. I knocked on the door and Tina had already given birth to Rachel. She was too tired to see me, so I went in and saw the baby then I was gone. I caught the early flight to Amsterdam and I told the lads and everyone was chuffed.

We drew 3–3 against the great Ajax team of Johan Cruyff, Arie Haan, Rudi Krol, Johan Neeskens and others. Afterwards, we went out to wet the baby's head and the Ajax players came with us to a club. So there was Johan Cruyff celebrating the birth of our Rachel, and I hadn't even spoken to Tina yet. I flew home and we got into the routine of life with a baby in the house. Rachel wasn't the easiest to start with, crying all the time, but I was so happy to be a father. I knew this was how it was meant to be and there is a picture at home now of Tina when she was pregnant with Rachel. It means the world to me; it is my favourite photo.

That routine was pretty set until one particular morning when we'd been in the house in Timperley for about twelve months. Tina read the *Daily Mail*, and in those days before you reached the sports pages there was a little supplement on houses. That day she was reading the paper before I went training and she saw this house that she knew in Romiley in Cheshire. It was for sale for £10,000, a lot of money in 1969. It was for a footballer earning £75 a week anyway. She said she would go and have a look at it and I went off to City. I didn't think anything of it but when I'd just come out of the shower after training there was a message that Tina was on the phone and would I take the call in the office.

She said: 'Well, I've got it.'

'You what?'

'I've got it.'

'What do you mean, you've got it?'

She said: 'I've bought the house that was in the paper this morning. I went to see it. It's fantastic. I've fallen in love with it.'

The thing about Tina, which has helped me throughout my life, is that she's a good decision-maker. There's no messing around, no shilly-shallying. She sorts it out and we deal with the consequences later. She has been a good, steadying influence on me.

'How did you do that?' I asked her.

'Well, I phoned Daddy up and he sent over a cheque for the deposit for the house.'

So, I'd gone from being a normal young married man living in a house that was affordable to something that was like a mansion. It had six bedrooms, a tennis court, orchards and a big garden. We drove to have a look and the good thing I noticed was that it was opposite a pub called the Spread Eagle. The house was called Hatherlow House and Tina knew the family who lived there. The furniture in the whole house in Timperley would have gone in a corner of the lounge, but I went along with it. And it became the most wonderful home a family could have. We lived there for more than twenty years. The children had space to play and it was fantastic for having guests. It was hard work financially at the start because we were living beyond our means for a while. But fortunately I continued being successful at football and the rewards could go back to the family. Football had to come first.

A couple of years later we had another baby and that was our Nicholas. It wasn't easy to run that house but Tina threw herself into it and we had so many wonderful people coming to stay with us. There were sports stars like Bobby Moore, Gareth Edwards and Colin Milburn, and showbiz pals like Kenny Lynch, Jimmy Tarbuck and Michael Crawford. Looking back on it, I can see that I led a selfish life. I had the all-consuming pull of football and I kept the freedom of going out on the town and coming home late at night. My life didn't change that much even though I was married. But it did for Tina.

I met Michael Crawford when I was invited to take part in a pilot show for a television quiz programme. He was also on the panel and we became friends even though the programme was never taken up.

Michael had just done the show *No Sex Please, We're British* in London, but unfortunately his marriage to his wife Gabrielle had collapsed. He was a bit down at the time and he came to stay a couple of times at the house. Then I rang him just before Christmas and he said he had chickenpox. He was living alone in a small apartment in Earl's Court in London and I invited him to stay with us. He arrived on Christmas Eve. I tried to get a doctor for him, but the only chap I could get was the local vet who came and gave him an injection. Michael recuperated with us and not long afterwards he started appearing in the TV sitcom *Some Mothers Do 'Ave 'Em*.

He became very close to us, and one day he said to me it might be a good idea to get Tina some help in the house to give her a little freedom of her own. It must have been like being locked in a cell for Tina, for a young woman who'd been round the world and enjoyed life. I hadn't thought about that; that was me being selfish again. Michael had sensed the situation, so we made some inquiries. There was a French lady in the village, married to an Englishman, and she said that her seventeen-year-old sister would like to come and do an au pair job like that. She was called Christine, too, and she immediately lifted the pressure off Tina. She stayed with us right through the children growing up and became part of the family.

Michael Crawford became a superstar after that. But he was a star for me in helping my marriage to stay on course.

There was another time when Michael came to play *Billy Liar* on the stage in Manchester. I helped find him a flat for the duration because he said he wouldn't stay with us all the time. The reason was that I was too tidy for him. I wanted everything to be just so, and I do go round the house making sure all the cushions are just right. Once when Michael had stayed I came home to find a note saying he'd gone back to London. Then I saw the lounge – where he had got all the furniture and stacked it up in the middle of the room. There was another message on the top, saying: 'Sort that lot out then!' He used to say I was puffing up cushions as he was trying to sit down on them. That's the way I was.

I suppose that sense of tidiness and smartness is what attracted me to the shirt-making business. Although I'd pulled out of the Edwardia boutique I set up with George Best, I knew it was a good idea to have a business away from professional football that might make some money and provide a future once my playing days were over. The start of it was over a drink in a pub, which was the usual procedure in my case. I met a chap called Fred

Jones, who came up to me and said he was a cutter in a shirt-making business, a bespoke shirt company. He showed me some shirts that he made in his own time with material he'd accumulated and wondered if I wanted any. They looked good, so he measured me up and three weeks later came back with some fantastic shirts.

A seed had been sown and a little while later I met an ambitious lad called Frank Rostron who worked in one of the Manchester boutiques. We were talking and the idea of starting up a shirt-making business became a reality when I put up some money to get it going. I went back to Fred Jones, who agreed to pack in his current job and become our cutter. He brought a couple of machinists, too, and suddenly we were up and running from back-street premises in Manchester.

My name as a footballer helped to bring in customers, Frank did the measuring and the orders and Fred did the cutting. It grew by word of mouth, really, and we developed a good customer base within Manchester and among my showbiz friends like Jimmy Tarbuck and Michael Parkinson, and sportsmen like Bobby Moore.

Bobby was a big pal of mine, and similarly obsessed with looking smart at all times. He became interested and opened a shop of his own in London, and we took on a contract to make some of Bobby's shirts for his business. As our firm grew so we moved into a shop in Chapel Walk, next to the famous Manchester restaurant Sam's Chop House, and it seemed like the perfect move to the perfect location. Then I came back from my last international trip with England, the summer tour of matches in 1973, to discover that Frank Rostron had also been away on holiday in Bermuda, a trip that must have cost the kind of money I didn't know he had. I knew something was up and the partnership split and he took away a lot of customers and business to set up on his own. His firm became very successful.

I, however, was left nearly high and dry, but I was determined to carry on. You learn from your experiences and I set up Summerbee Shirts, which is still going today. I learned how to measure and slowly began to build up trade. It was very small at first, but I had one great break from Michael Parkinson, who had started life as a sportswriter in Manchester before going into television. He liked the shirts and arranged a meeting in London with the writers of a new TV programme, *The Sweeney*, who were looking for good clothes for their characters. I went down to see John Thaw, Dennis Waterman and the producers at Euston Films and they decided to use my shirts for the main characters. When you see John and Dennis in big floral shirts with penny round collars, those are the ones I made.

It was a business I thoroughly enjoyed, away from football altogether. And the day after I finished my football career at Stockport County in 1979 I threw myself into it. I sold thirty shirts the first day and it was like a breath of fresh air. I was never a massive businessman like Francis Lee, but it was fun, and Tina supported me brilliantly. I came through it all because of her, the beautiful girl who just happened to go dancing by on a Saturday night.

13

THE CUP OF DREAMS

Marriage distracted me from my football, but not for long – just as long as it took Malcolm Allison to work the greatest psychological trick of my time at Manchester City. My one really poor spell at Maine Road came at the start of the 1968–9 season when we began the campaign as League champions. There were a number of reasons for that poor spell, and one of them was probably that I'd become a bit cocky and complacent, having tasted success and won a couple of England caps. The other was adjusting to married life. I became a bit lethargic because, instead of being a party animal and going out at night, I was staying at home quietly. It sounds all about face but I think it was the change of lifestyle that really did affect me, and perhaps being burdened by a sense of responsibility because now I had a wife to look after.

At the time I couldn't understand what was happening. I'd done the same pre-season as normal but I was struggling in the games, even when they put me back to outside right, a position

I knew and understood so well. Allison didn't care why it was happening. His imperative was that it had to stop – and so he pulled off a classic con trick. He found some of my mates and told them casually in conversation that he thought I was finished as a footballer. He knew word would get back to me, which it quickly did.

I was so angry. I went round to his house, knocked on his door, and told him straight I'd show him who was finished. By coincidence my mother Dulcie was up in Manchester for a visit at the time, and unbeknown to me she also marched round to Malcolm's house and demanded to see him. I don't know how their conversation went behind closed doors, but I bet Malcolm was very happy to see her. His trick had worked a treat, and it probably ended up saving my career. In the next match all I had in my head was that I was playing not against the opposition but against Malcolm Allison. I would show the bastard I could play and that I was far from finished as a footballer. Needless to say, I had a great match and never looked back that season as we went on to win the FA Cup. The episode made me realise you could never afford to be complacent even for a couple of matches in professional football.

The use of psychology was one of Malcolm's great attributes. He would often tear me off a strip in the dressing room, almost to the point of humiliation. But he knew I could take it, and that it worked. He seemed to be able to read people's minds. He would say nothing at all to Alan Oakes or Mike Doyle, because they were the Mr Reliables of the team.

In a sense we lived Malcolm's life for him – and we won the trophies for Malcolm's life. Once his own playing career had been cut short by TB, he threw himself into us. He transferred his own ability and confidence into us. This may sound strange, but for City players at that time, if you were in love with anyone, you'd have said you were in love with Malcolm Allison. That's not meant in a gay way – it was about the shared obsession for the game and for winning for Manchester City.

The wives weren't particularly happy. Tina wasn't the only one who used to say: 'You think more of him than you do of me.'

I said: 'You're right, I do.' I had to think that way because it was the only way to be a professional footballer. In my day we always had to put 100 per cent into the game.

In my day, as well, the greatest single prize was playing in the FA Cup Final. Every small boy dreamed of going to Wembley, and I grew up with that feeling. So, even though winning the League title is obviously the more significant achievement in pure football terms, for me winning the Cup in 1969 was the ultimate moment as a club player.

I'd been involved in a few good Cup runs before with both City and Swindon, but this year we seemed destined to go all the way. I don't know why; it was just a feeling we had. Our defence of the League title was already beyond repair by the time the Cup started in January and we had been knocked out of the European Cup in the first round by Fenerbahçe. So it was the FA Cup or nothing for a team that had so much skill and a passion to do well.

I can't pretend the third round was memorable. We beat Luton Town 1-0 with a goal from Francis Lee, and I only know that because I looked it up in the record books. The truth is that not every game sticks in your mind. But the fourth round that year does. We drew 0-0 against Newcastle in a dour match at St James' Park, but the replay was all fireworks. I exploded in the wrong way. I was having a personal battle with big John

McGrath, the Newcastle centre half, who was a fierce competitor. He was trying to wind me up all through the first half, and doing a pretty good job of it. He knew I had a short fuse and that I might go. He was right that day. My anger was brewing and eventually I went into a silly challenge in the centre circle and was sent off for leaving McGrath in a heap on the ground.

I was really stupid and I got a deserved bollocking from the boss at half-time. I could see that Joe Mercer and Malcolm Allison were very unhappy with me. I had put the team in danger, but luckily the rest of the players responded to win the game 2-0.

The fifth round draw wasn't kind – away to Blackburn Rovers at Ewood Park. The match was postponed four or five times because of shocking weather; there were blizzards and all sorts. By the time we played the game the pitch was in an atrocious condition, really heavy and muddy. But we didn't care about that. We were good enough to play on any surface and we took them apart, winning 4-1 with two goals each from Francis Lee and Tony Coleman. I remember the goalscorers (I didn't have to look them up this time) because this is a match that has stayed firmly in my mind. I remember it because I was well below par that day; I hardly made a contribution at all. I recall a sense of relief that we got through despite me playing poorly and I remember thinking that we were now in the sixth round and that going to Wembley was a distinct possibility because the draw had already been made. We would be at home to Tottenham.

Mostly, though, I remember that game because I got the silent treatment for three or four days afterwards from Malcolm. He and Joe Mercer had two usual ways of getting more out of me when my contribution hadn't been up to scratch. Sometimes I got a bollocking, and sometimes I got the silent treatment – which was even worse. A straight bollocking for me was good. The silent treatment, where you said 'Hello' to them and they just turned their heads, was horrible. I hated it, and Malcolm was very good at that. I got the message all right.

We played the quarter-final against Spurs only a few days later. Tina's brother was getting married that day, but she had to go alone. I had a battle with Mike England to look after. He was an exceptional player, a Welsh international centre half and also a nice person. But Mike had a temper on the pitch and he did not stand on ceremony in a game. This was a tough match, and a closely fought one. The prize was high and Mike England and I had a couple of run-ins during the play. I was at outside right and not long before the end it was still 0-0 and I saw Mike rushing out from the penalty area to the wing with a look in his eye that said he was going to do me on the touchline.

I saw it coming, so I left it in there for him and I caught him on his ankle. He went down, of course, and it was a stretcher case. The leg wasn't broken; it was ligaments or something like that. I just said to him as he went off: 'Bad luck, Mike. I might see you in a few months' time playing again.'

That didn't go down very well. He looked daggers at me. He had come over to really sort me out and I just managed to get the ball away and I left it in. It wasn't a standing foot; it was a foot in the air. After the game you don't feel proud that someone has been injured but Mike's intention was to sort me out, so I had to look after myself. I had grown up knowing how to look after myself and Mike would have been aware of that. It was a matter of self-preservation, really. Just before the final whistle Francis Lee curled in the winning goal out of the blue;

he moved in from the right flank and hit the ball on the volley past Pat Jennings. I was in the FA Cup semi-final for the first time in my life.

Our form was now as good as it had been patchy before Christmas. Before the semi-final we had a derby match away to Manchester United at Old Trafford. We won 1-0 and I scored the only goal with a shot that I flicked over the head of Alex Stepney. We were on a roll and couldn't wait for the semi against Everton that was to take place at Villa Park. We had that wonderful, invaluable feeling of self-confidence, and we knew the opposition would be afraid of us. Sure, we'd be thinking about their midfield trio of Colin Harvey, Howard Kendall and Alan Ball, but they'd be more worried about Lee, Bell, Summerbee and the rest. I knew we had a great chance, and maybe the one and only chance of my career.

Everton were staying out in the country, but we stayed right in the middle of Birmingham, at the Albany Hotel near the Bull Ring. There was a bit of a party going on on the Friday night so we got out and had a bit of a mingle to take our minds off the game. Nothing could, though. I couldn't stop thinking about the Twin Towers and going up Wembley Way, yet we were only in the semi-final. I thought about when I was a boy and watched the Stanley Matthews final and the Tom Finney final the following year when his Preston team lost to West Brom. I thought about the chance of following in their footsteps and eventually had to take a sleeping pill to calm myself down and knock myself out.

I remember it was a greasy day for the semi-final. There was a bit of mist from cigarette smoke at the stadium and a haze in the air. Then there was Sandy Brown, the Everton left back. He didn't particularly like me, which was nothing unusual. And he was his usual self in the game – he kicked me all through the ninety minutes. Brown kicked me for the sake of kicking me. If he got the ball as well it was a miracle – and while the rest of the match was played we had a private battle.

The first half was end to end and both sides had chances. Then Mike Doyle went down after a tackle and looked as if he was in deep trouble. Our trainer Ken Barnes came on and tied Mike's legs together and took him off. It may have looked dreadful to the supporters but Ken knew about Mike and the lads knew Mike. Sometimes things weren't as bad as they seemed to be. We didn't bring on a substitute, and played on with ten men for the fifteen minutes up till half-time. A couple of minutes before the break we suddenly saw Mike Doyle come sprinting out of the tunnel and back into the match. Malcolm Allison had guessed there was nothing too much wrong with Mike. It's one of these things; it happens to people. It's a weakness. Malcolm had been strong and taken the gamble of playing for fifteen minutes with a man down, and was proved right.

In the second half we put a lot of pressure on Everton and started to attack them and create chances. Two minutes from the end we forced a corner. Neil Young took it and the ball came through a ruck of players to me. The goal was behind me, but I could see our centre half, Tommy Booth. So I knocked it back to him and he rammed it past me into the top of the net. The final whistle went almost straight away and there was pandemonium. We were in the FA Cup Final. Champagne corks were going everywhere in the changing room and then the chairman Albert Alexander came in. Joe Mercer was so happy, especially doing it at Villa Park where he'd once been manager. Suddenly, Joe saw the chairman, who was only five foot tall. He had grey hair, a bowler hat, a detached collar, a pinstripe suit, and shoes so shiny you could see your face in them. He was an immaculate man, but the size of a jockey. It went dead quiet as Joe encouraged Mr Alexander to say a few words.

'Well done, lads,' said the chairman. 'I am very, very proud of you. And the great thing about it is we can now earn some extra money and go out and buy some decent players.'

The silence was tangible. The lads were gobsmacked as he went round shaking the players' hands, not realising for a moment what he'd said. It is a speech that has gone down in football legend for its incredible insensitivity, and I still hear it quoted to this day. Harry Redknapp made mention of it after Portsmouth won the FA Cup in 2008. But we didn't hold it against Albert Alexander. We knew he was just a very excited old man and we actually thought it was very funny.

Back home the phone didn't stop ringing. That was the impact of reaching the FA Cup Final in 1969. George Best rang. Bobby Moore was on the phone. So was Jimmy Tarbuck. It meant everything to a footballer to be going to Wembley.

Our opponents in the final were Leicester City, who were struggling in the First Division and battling to avoid relegation. We had to play them in the League a month before the final and I remember that game vividly. It was one of the best I played for the club – and I did so running on pure adrenalin.

For many months of that season I had been visiting Pendlebury Hospital to talk to a young Manchester City fan called Michael who was gravely ill with cancer. We had gone initially as a team group at the instigation of Joe Mercer, who had been contacted by the hospital. The boy was said to have only a few weeks to live, yet he was so glad to see us. He was in a soundproof room and obviously very unwell; the doctors said he had cancer throughout his body. All the walls were decorated with City scarves and pictures, and the next time we went along we brought more souvenirs and presents. He was so delighted and I kept going to see him each week. He looked really well for a time and we talked about so many different things, and you couldn't but be inspired by his courage. I also met his family, and one day I asked Tina if she would come and meet him, too. She agreed but as we were walking into the hospital I saw a nurse coming towards us.

'Mike, he has just died,' said the nurse, and I'm not ashamed to say I wept a few tears that day.

The boy Michael was from a Catholic family and I was invited to his funeral, and I knew I had to attend. But it was to be held on a Saturday lunchtime, at 12.30 on the day of that League match against Leicester. The funeral was about five miles from Maine Road, and I told Joe Mercer I wanted to go and he said okay. I said it would be a rush to get back for the match because I knew the team sheet had to be handed in at two o'clock, an hour before kick-off, and that you have to be at the ground then. Joe told me to go to the service.

It was a big funeral and quite traumatic. It had been a very upsetting situation, and at a quarter to two the service was still not finished. I left quietly at the back, found my car, and saw a policeman on a motorbike.

'Do me a favour,' I said. 'Can you give me a police escort to the ground. I have to be there in ten minutes.'

'Come on, let's go,' said the cop. He must have been a City fan.

I jumped in and he took me all through the traffic lights on red. There were no hazard lights on cars in those days so I put my headlights on and I chased him all the way to Maine Road.

It was that late I had to park right outside the main door to get in on time. I walked into the dressing room a minute before two o' clock and my name went down on the team sheet. You can imagine that my blood was pumping and the adrenalin flowing. I didn't have to warm up. I just got changed, went out for the kick-off, and scored both goals in a 2-0 win that all the newspapers said gave us the psychological edge ahead of the Cup Final. That was the furthest thought from my mind. I had played for Michael. I had scored the goals for the boy. That was that game. How could I ever forget?

The surgeon at the hospital wrote to Joe Mercer not long afterwards thanking everyone at City for what they had done, and saying that our visits had played a part in helping Michael to live months longer than had been expected. It brought home to us the privileged position we were in, not just as sportsmen doing something we loved, but also as people with the ability to help others. I vowed that I would always try to help in any little way I could. And that's what I've done throughout my life since.

Tina was heavily pregnant with our first-born Rachel at the time, but she wanted to go to the Cup Final. I was obviously with the team, so Bobby Moore invited Tina to stay with him and his wife on the Friday night and then took her to Wembley. We stayed out in Esher, in a Temperance Hotel where no drinking was allowed. It sounded like a good idea for a football team, and it was a beautiful, big place. But Malcolm Allison had other ideas. He thought it helped us relax to have a glass or two of wine with a meal the night before a big match so he took us all out to a Polynesian restaurant in Weybridge. His psychology was right again, at least as far as I was concerned. I slept like a log. Then, in the morning, after an impromptu five-a-side game on the hotel lawn for a bit of fun, we put on our suits and made the bus trip to Wembley.

That was like no other football journey. Miles from the ground people were waving to us, and, while we all knew it was a massive occasion, that just drove it home that on this day you were becoming a part of football history. The closer we got to the stadium the bigger the crowds and it was a drive through the masses up Wembley Way. I remember that was just a fantastic feeling. I had played at Wembley before for England, but this was different again. The nerves were jangling as we walked into the changing rooms, and it felt as if I needed to go for a wee six times a minute. We did the traditional walk on to the pitch and talked to the TV reporters from both BBC and ITV – Malcolm had done an 'exclusive' deal with both of them apparently. We were so high we'd have talked to anyone. The pitch was a disappointment; it was almost dead in places because once again it had been used for the Horse of the Year Show. But we were used to playing on crap pitches, and we could cope with that. The occasion made Wembley seem huge, but it didn't seem like a big pitch to me when you were playing on it. I always felt claustrophobic playing there.

Back in the changing room there was a bit of fuss because someone had heard that Jackie Blanchflower was outside and couldn't get in because he didn't have a ticket. Jackie was one of the Manchester United players who survived the Munich Air Disaster but never played again as a result of the injuries he suffered. I hadn't changed by then, so Malcolm Allison told me to go outside and spirit him into the dressing room. I did that, and Jackie sat on the back of our bench watching the Cup Final.

On the day of the final many people were saying it would be an easy match for us because Leicester weren't a good side. Yes, they were eventually relegated that year, but they had signed Allan Clarke for a big fee and he was a very good forward. They had Peter Shilton in goal and David Nish, and some other top-class players. When you think that they were relegated that season, it shows how strong the First Division was in those days. Although we were rightly considered the favourites, our attitude was spot-on. We were expecting a tough match, and there wasn't an ounce of complacency in our team.

As we walked out on to the pitch the noise of the crowd was simply amazing. In the changing rooms you could hear the supporters singing 'Abide With Me', and the moment you were out of the tunnel behind the goal there was an incredible roar. It was the ultimate noise for a footballer then. You knew that everyone in the world was watching the FA Cup Final – and for me it's the worst thing about modern football the way people and teams have pulled down its reputation in the last few years. The Cup Final is history; it has a special place in English culture. As we walked out I looked up to try to see Tina and Bobby Moore, but you couldn't spot anyone. I knew that well enough; three years earlier I'd been in the crowd at the World Cup Final watching Bobby play.

We were introduced to Princess Anne before the game, and as she went along the line my one thought was that I didn't want to walk off with a loser's medal. Officially it's called a runner's-up medal, but I couldn't think of it like that. The match was all or nothing. We felt confident and we attacked and created chances in the first half. Leicester also had chances for Andy Lochhead and Peter Rodrigues as well. Clarke was magnificent for them, and I had a good duel with Nish. That was always a battle, but I had the legs on him and that allowed me to make the goal in the twenty-third minute. Francis Lee took a quick throw-in to me and I was free of Nish. Then Alan Woollett came over to me and I forced my way past him to the dead ball line. You have a split second then to decide what to do with the cross – and that's where the telepathy and teamwork of playing together for years comes in. I spotted Neil Young in a familiar position just to the left of the penalty spot and I clipped the back across to him and he hit a beautiful left-footer past Shilton. We were 1-0 up.

After that it became difficult. Maybe we were a little over-confident, maybe it was the strength-sapping nature of the pitch; I played with my socks rolled down to the ankles in the second half. Leicester came into it more and both teams had more chances. By the end my legs had gone a bit and it was a relief more than anything to hear the final whistle. I was desperately tired. I was that drained I was the last City player up the steps to receive my winner's medal. Even so, the thoughts of history were on my mind as I dragged my feet up. I thought particularly of the great Tom Finney, who never had that feeling of winning the Cup. I thought about my father, another Preston man, and I only found out later that his brother, my Uncle Bunt, and my cousin Raymond were about twenty yards away in the crowd when I collected my medal.

I know I had a good day at Wembley. I made the contribution I wanted to make. But it was a team effort, and every man in the team was English, which has been very rare throughout the history of the Cup.

I was delighted, too, for Malcolm Allison, who had been banned from the dugout by the Football Association for some minor bust-up. I thought that was a stupid decision on their part. Malcolm was a real character, like José Mourinho now, and the game needs people who say interesting and sometimes controversial things. When the TV cameras pan to the touch-lines you need real characters there, not the sight of someone writing notes or a letter to their auntie. Malcolm wasn't allowed on the bench at Wembley that day, but he found a seat low enough in the crowd so that we could hear his shouting as usual.

The razzmatazz of winning the FA Cup continued all through the evening. I went back to the hotel to collect Tina and there was a reception at the Café Royal. We ended up taking the Cup to the Sportsman's Club on Tottenham Court Road in central London where they put it on display. Tina was very pregnant, and we decided to leave much earlier than I might have done normally. I walked out first and three lads at the door started being funny and causing a scene. Tina went back inside and found Francis Lee who rushed up and started pounding all three of them until some policemen came in and broke it up. Francis certainly sorted them out, but his Cup Final suit was ripped in the process and we were invited to finish the incident down at the police station while someone made sure Tina got safely back to the hotel.

It could have been a very nasty incident for me if Francis hadn't come to the rescue, and he was far from happy with his ruined suit. The lads were all the worse for drink and the police let us off after a bit of finger-wagging. Thankfully, no charges were brought. That would have caused a real problem. Nevertheless, it wasn't the best way to finish FA Cup Final day, heading back to see the wife at half past two in the morning after being taken to the police station. I got the usual rollocking.

I had been full of myself for winning the Cup and sometimes you neglect the person you love. Football takes over, which is understandable, but when you look back at it you can see you were a bit of a bastard, to be honest. Anyway, I learned another lesson that day, and it swiftly brought me down to earth. The only way to appease Tina was take her to look at the Queen's special coach, which you could see at Regent's Park. I got up early and recovered some brownie points.

It had to be early because we were taking the train back north in time for a celebration open-top bus ride. We stopped at Wilmslow station and my worry was that there would be nobody there. Who would want to watch us having a party? Well, how wrong I was. We got on the bus and there were thousands of people there at the start of the bus ride. It was unbelievable. All the houses were painted blue and white and flags were waving everywhere. Literally, thousands and thousands of people lined the streets all the way to Manchester through Didsbury village and so on. As we came into Oxford Road, even more people were there and we moved at a snail's pace the last half mile of the journey to Albert Square. It was phenomenal; I thought so because I remembered my first match at Maine Road barely four years earlier when there was an attendance of 8,000. They reckon three-quarters of a million people were on the streets of Manchester that Sunday to celebrate us winning the FA Cup.

What came to me at the very end of it, when we won the Cup, was remembering how it was when I was a boy out on the parks the day after the Cup Final, pretending to be a player I'd seen in the match the day before – pretending to be Stanley Matthews or Tom Finney or Stan Mortensen. When we won the 1969 Cup Final I wondered if there was someone down on the Rec in Preston or Cheltenham wanting to be Francis Lee or Allan Clarke or even Mike Summerbee. When I was young the greatest dream was to play in the FA Cup Final. You must have your dreams, but most people can't fulfil them. I was lucky enough to live my dream.

14

FALL AND RISE IN EUROPE

Malcolm Allison's pride set us up for a great fall. The moment we won the League title in May 1968 he was boasting about the way Manchester City would thrash all-comers in the European Cup. 'We'll terrify Europe,' he said. 'We won't play defensively as I have seen teams such as Gornik and Real Madrid play. Too many of these foreign coaches are cowards. We won't let Manchester City play in away legs like so many of these European sides. They play with fear implanted in them by their coaches. I believe pride is a better driving force than fear. We like to take on opposing teams and that is what we will do in Europe.'

Joe Mercer was more sensible. At the same time he told City fans: 'We may have to develop a mean streak in Europe and play tight in defence.'

Few people remember the wisdom of Joe. When we were knocked out of the European Cup in the very first round by the unheralded Turkish club Fenerbahçe, it was the booming confidence of Malcolm that was thrown back in our faces. He had said we would be the first team to play on Mars. As it turned out, we didn't even leave the ground.

The truth was that, despite Malcolm's overblown predictions, we were novices in European football. And it showed immediately. We thought winning the title stood us in good stead, but there was a different approach and mentality in Europe. It wasn't like playing in the First Division. It was a vast step up, particularly playing against unknown quantities and teams and players with an entirely different footballing mentality. We had been drawn at home against Fenerbahçe in the first leg and we dominated the match at Maine Road in terms of possession and chances. But we struggled to cope with their totally alien way of defending. Fenerbahçe's defence was more organised than we were used to, and they were very cynical in their tackles, blatantly body checking, something that was unheard of in the English League then. There were also players spitting at you and putting fingers in your eyes, that kind of thing, to try to niggle you. And it did. We thought we knew all about the game, but here was something completely unknown to us. We shouldn't have been so easily put off our game, but that's how it was. Even so we should have won the home match. I happened to miss a sitter – and it really was a sitter. It was my usual tap-in opportunity, but when the cross came over I just missed the ball completely. It was a bad mistake and it did cause me a few problems. Quite a few of the crowd turned against me because of that miss and it took a long time to win them back.

The game finished 0-0 and we were very disappointed by the result. Malcolm had put pressure on us by saying we would destroy everyone and the backlash was inevitable when it didn't happen. It was a normal thing for Malcolm to say – and we had become conditioned to believe what he said was correct. But this time he wasn't right, and it was a profound shock to all of us.

Nowadays, a 0-0 home score line in a European knockout tie is considered quite a good result, but then it was a hammer blow to our confidence. We had expected so much better. Even so, Fenerbahçe were not one of the best teams at that time, and if we'd been more experienced there would still have been a chance to progress in the away leg.

It was a manic time for me before that return fixture. I got married on the Monday before we flew to Istanbul. All the players came to the wedding, and many of the United side, and then I left Tina and went off to play football. My honeymoon was spent with the team in a place where it felt as if you'd gone back in time fifty years. Istanbul was full of souks and back-alley warrens, and they had communal taxis where everyone could jump in. Things weren't at all smooth in preparation for the game; the training ground was poor and when I woke up on the morning of the match there was a tremendous noise in the distance, a huge roar like a plane or a train coming in. It was about nine o'clock in the morning and the noise kept coming in waves in a crescendo. I couldn't understand what it was until I asked in the hotel lobby and they said it was the football stadium a couple of miles away. It was already full with Fenerbahçe fans and the game wasn't kicking off for another eleven hours. We heard the noise all day, even as we went out shopping in the city. I remember going with Tony Book looking for some designer-label shoes to take back for my bride. I had the size and everything and I found the perfect pair of Dior shoes and put them safely in my travelling bag.

The tension grew as the day wore on. We all felt it rising

through us and we knew it was going to be the most difficult game of our lives so far. Nothing had prepared us for this occasion. We had the obligatory police escort to the ground, and for all the fervour and noise it wasn't a smart stadium at all. It was more like a bull ring, and we were cast as the hapless English bulls. The changing rooms were a mess; all the windows were broken, the place was filthy and there were only stand-up toilets, a nightmare for someone like me with my pre-match routine. I had never known such an intimidating atmosphere. We could hear the incessant roar of the fans outside as we got changed, and the boss spoke to us about the game. He told us to be careful on the field, and not to retaliate whatever the provocation, because that could cause problems. When the bell went for time to leave the changing room I was pretty much shitting myself – and I wasn't alone.

As the door opened we were met by a group of soldiers – one for each player. They all had guns. I said to mine: 'What are you doing?'

'I will look after you, don't worry too much,' said the unsmiling Turkish guardsman.

This was like no other football match I'd been involved in. We marched out across the moat that surrounded the pitch to keep the fans away from the players and discovered the pitch was in a terrible condition. It was an incredibly intimidating occasion, and once the protection of the soldiers had disappeared the Fenerbahçe players did everything to us they could think of, knowing that it would be folly for us to retaliate. We actually did okay in the game. Tony Coleman gave us the lead, but once the Turks equalised they took control. The match flew by in a whirl of heavy tackling and ferocious body-checking, and Fenerbahçe scored another goal towards the end to win 2-1 on aggregate and leave us crushed at the first hurdle in Europe.

It had been a swift and brutal education in the ways of European football, and I was so disappointed. Malcolm had threatened the world and we hadn't survived one round. Although the education would prove immensely valuable for future years, that was no consolation as we flew back home. There was further backlash from the crowd in the next League matches, and I could hear from the comments that they weren't too happy with me. Some of them turned quite badly, but it didn't affect me. I knew you couldn't please all the people all of the time. It was hurtful, but I knew the truth of the matter – that no footballer will be for ever judged on one bad game and one big missed opportunity.

More aggravation lay in store at home. I gave the Dior shoes to Tina, thinking I'd at least got one thing right in Istanbul, and discovered they were a size too small. It seemed like another piece of education – about the dangers of being ripped off abroad. I'd heard the stereotypical stories about Ali Baba and the Forty Thieves and thought I was another victim. The shoes were no use, so I thought I'd send them back to the shop in Istanbul with a little note. And, blow me down, within ten days another identical pair of shoes, but the right size this time, arrived at the door. So there was another lesson – that it was all bullshit about Ali Baba and the Turkish people.

The education on and off the field stuck with me. You had to understand that you were dealing with different cultures, and you certainly couldn't travel to play in foreign countries with stupid assumptions that your way of football and your way of life were better than theirs. If we'd understood that before the Fenerbahçe match maybe we would have had a real go at winning the 1969 European Cup. As it was, it was a year too soon and the glory would come the following season in the European Cup Winners' Cup, for which we'd qualified by winning the FA Cup in 1969.

We heeded the harsh lesson of Istanbul immediately. This time we had a really tough first-round draw against Athletic Bilbao, one of the top sides in Spain. As soon as I heard the pairing I wondered if it would be like Fenerbahçe again. That feeling only intensified when we played the first leg away in their San Mamés Stadium and were 2-0 down inside the first twenty minutes. We seemed underprepared again – Bilbao's manager was Ronnie Allen, the former West Brom and England centre forward, and he'd sent us to a training ground that was a shit hole, with a terrible pitch and showers that didn't work. The actual pitch for the match, though, was beautiful and with drizzle in the air it was a slick surface that was ideal to play on. I loved it, and that match is probably the best game I ever played for City.

Two-nil down looked a hopeless situation, but I picked up the ball and went at the full-back to see what he was made of. I raced past him and he just stood there and I knew instantly that I had the beating of him. The same thing happened every time I received the ball and we began to put a lot of pressure on the Bilbao defence. Neil Young scored to make it 2-1 at half-time and Malcolm gave the orders at the break.

'Just get the ball to Mike,' he said.

Bilbao made it 3-1 but I constantly had the ball and was getting to the dead-ball line and creating chances. Tommy Booth scored one from a cross and then another time I clipped the ball in and Luis Echeverría put into his own goal. Final score 3-3, and I knew I had played brilliantly that night. It was the kind of stadium I relished, with the fans so close you could almost shake their hands as you ran along the line. I remember getting to the dead-ball line one time, clipping over the cross, and then my momentum carrying me over the touchline and into the crowd. There was a Basque fella with a beret on with his daughter next to him. I pretended to kiss her, and all hell was let loose. It was only a bit of fun, but this gentleman couldn't see that. Nobody would have minded in England but the Bilbao fans were very upset.

Nevertheless, I took real pleasure from that match. It was a special performance and I think it put me back on a better standing with the City fans who had seemed to have become disillusioned with me. That evening we celebrated in the hotel, having a drink among ourselves and with the air crew from the charter flight that took us there. At two in the morning there was a fella beside me on the edge of a sofa who gently rolled off and fell asleep drunk on the floor of the hotel lounge. He was the pilot who flew us home a few hours later.

On the flight we played a trick on Joe Mercer. We were sat at the back of the aircraft and Francis Lee noticed that Joe was in an aisle seat, next to a man we didn't know. Now this was an aircraft chartered especially for our trip and there couldn't be anyone we didn't know. So Francis called over a stewardess and gave her a message he'd written for Joe. The boss looks at the message and it says, 'The man by the window next to you is a suspected hijacker, please keep him talking. Don't panic!' Joe kept him talking for a couple of hours. He turned out to be part of the relief air crew.

The home leg against Bilbao was a doddle. We won 3-0, but it wasn't the same feeling for me. I had an ordinary match that night at Maine Road, but the job was done. The real triumph had been out in Spain, proving that we could cope in hostile and intimidating foreign venues and proving we had the ability to overcome problems. Everybody knew that Bilbao were a decent team and that it was a good achievement to progress.

Lierse of Belgium were the next opponents, but this was just about the easiest match we had in Europe. We won 3-0 away and 5-0 back at Maine Road, where I scored one of the goals. It was the first match Lierse had played at this level, and they were completely overawed. For us it was a matter of learning what lessons we could. One of the most important was to keep the ball and not give it away easily. Against Lierse it wouldn't have mattered, but it was vital against the good teams to come. Another particular lesson for me was to keep my cool when the tackles were flying in. I had to keep my temper.

There was a long wait through the winter for the quarter-final against Académica de Coimbra of Portugal. At home we had reached the final of the League Cup, and that game against West Brom was being played only three days after the European away leg. The timing wasn't great, and there was a balance between doing well against Académica and saving some energy for Wembley, where we knew the pitch was going to be a quagmire. Coimbra was a lovely place, a university town in the centre of Portugal, and we were lodged in a royal palace that had been turned into a hotel. Underneath there were huge cellars full of port, and the hotel manager promised us a bottle each after the game if we didn't lose. We hardly needed the incentive, but a 0-0 draw in 80 degrees' heat took us back to the cellars where I chose a forty-two-year-old bottle of port. That was pot luck rather than a connoisseur's choice.

I missed the second leg which we won 1-0 to reach the semi-finals of the Cup Winners' Cup. I suffered a hairline fracture of my right leg in the League Cup Final and was out of action for a few weeks until I returned in the first leg of the semi away to German club Schalke '04, based in the town of Gelsenkirchen. I came through the match okay and we were a little unlucky to lose 1-0. The German international Reinhard Libuda played very well for Schalke, but overall we weren't worried because we had this great confidence that we could beat them at home.

That confidence wasn't misplaced. To be honest, I don't remember too much about the second leg. We won it 5-1 and there was a great atmosphere at Maine Road to celebrate reaching a European club final. Our superior fitness really told in that match, and even though Libuda was outstanding again we had far too much firepower for the Germans. We penned them in for most of the match and played our normal aggressive attacking game. I do remember Mike Doyle scoring the fifth goal near the end and thinking that we had now arrived as a real force in Europe. A big victory in a big match against one of the best teams from Germany couldn't really be argued with.

My own contribution was average. My leg was still not right from the fracture sustained at Wembley, but I wanted to play in these significant matches, and Joe and Malcolm wanted me to play, too, because we had several other injuries. There were two League matches between the semi and the Cup Winners' Cup Final against Polish club Górnik Zabrze in Vienna. I sat out the first of them against Leeds but was brought back for the second against Sheffield Wednesday even though I knew I wasn't 100 per cent. If Joe Mercer told me to play, I played. But in my heart of hearts I knew it wasn't wise to take part in that match and within twenty minutes I was involved in a tackle with Don Megson and the leg was knackered again. After the game I was back in a plaster cast, and my chances of playing in the European final were gone.

I went to Vienna for the final; of course I did. The club were still hoping I could play, but I knew I would be no more than a passenger. The injury was too severe. City gave me a fitness test anyway, but perhaps that was just for show, to keep the Poles guessing. The club doctor, Sydney Rose, was sticking needles in my leg to try to freeze the pain, but it didn't work. If I had tried to play I would only have let the side down. I did get a medal from the match, and someone has told me that I was down on the official records of the final as a substitute. Well, I might have sat on the bench and people misinterpreted that as me being a sub, but I couldn't have played in that game. I was hugely disappointed and upset, but I wasn't fool enough to think it was a good idea to take part.

As a professional, I knew the only important thing was City winning the match, not my personal feelings. You always feel out of it when you can't play, initially anyway, but I remember watching the game with great intensity, living every moment on the touchline. It was a super match and we were always going to win after two first-half goals from Neil Young and a Francis Lee penalty. They didn't seem to miss me at all, and my replacement, Ian Bowyer, did ever so well. It was a filthy night of teeming rain and there were only about 10,000 people in the giant Prater Stadium. There were also no live TV cameras, so the only footage you can see is five minutes of news coverage of our goals. Górnik had a great team then, with Jerzy Gorgoń and the scintillating talent of Włodek Lubański. They pulled a goal back with twenty minutes to go but it was one of those nights you knew your side was destined to win. I just wished I could have been out there on the pitch.

The plane journey back was a little sombre. Some City fans had been killed in a car accident on the way to the airport, and that put a dampener on our mood. Back in Manchester, however, there was a party going on. The open-top bus was there again waiting for us, having just been serviced because we had been using it so much. The crowds were magnificent, and it was wonderful for the supporters. City fans are a different breed. They can take defeat – and they've had to take a fair amount of that down the years while seeing Manchester United win trophies regularly. But at that time City fans could walk around town knowing their team was the one always winning prizes. I was glad to give them that pleasure. It was a special time back then, and it tasted good.

One trophy we didn't win was the Anglo-Italian Cup, a tournament that often featured brutal matches. We played against Bologna early in the season after we'd won the Cup Winners' Cup. Malcolm Allison made the travel arrangements and we knew he wasn't taking this contest too seriously when he booked us into a hotel in Rimini, on the Adriatic coast, about one hundred miles from Bologna. We just relaxed and enjoyed ourselves, and I was looking forward to playing against the great Luis Suárez. He was approaching the end of his career, but the fabulous touch on the ball was still there. I couldn't be as complimentary about the Bologna left-back, though.

I pushed the ball past him and as I went to run forward he blatantly body-checked me with huge force. He did a complete job. When you play rugby you prepare yourself for being hit like that. When you're playing football you're not expecting it. And when it happens out of the blue, as it did that day, you think you're going to die. Every bit of wind is knocked out of you; you can't breathe and you're down on the floor. This one really shook me up and it took a little time to recover. Once I had, I thought I'd better sort him out, which I did about ten minutes later. The fella had to go off on a stretcher; there was nothing broken, but he was even more shaken up than I had been. It sparked all sorts in the crowd, they were throwing cushions and everything out of the stands at me. Luckily for me, the referee was a Mr Smith from Stonehouse in Gloucestershire, who I had first encountered when I was playing in schoolboy matches. He knew me well from those Cheltenham days and he always used to look after me a little when I got into trouble on the pitch.

He walked over this time and said: 'I really should send you off, Mike.'

'Don't do that,' I said. 'Just give me a booking. Pretend you're really serious with me, but keep me on the field.'

That's what he did – and then the cushions started flying again. I should have been sent off but the other fella should have gone for what he did as well. I was through on goal and he was so cynical. As it was, we lost the match 1-0. In the return leg at Maine Road I was only a substitute. I guess that may have been a bit of diplomacy from Joe and Malcolm. Anyway, the full-back was there and he laughed as he walked past me when he saw I wasn't in the team that day. We drew 2-2 and were knocked out, but nobody gave a damn really.

What mattered was trying to defend the Cup Winners' Cup. The first match was against Honved, and that fascinated me because I'd grown up on the tales of the great Hungarians who beat England in the 1950s. Honved was the club of Puskás, Hideguti and Groscis, and I watched the famous game on television when Wolves beat them at Molineux. Hungary had beaten England 6-3 at Wembley and then 7-1 in Budapest.

They had educated us about a new way of playing the game, and now here I was going to play in that same stadium in Budapest.

I remember that we played ever so well, and that there was a nasty incident just before the end of the game when Colin Bell went down. The Honved fella kicked him, and then kicked Colin's head when he fell down, leaving a big, bloody gash. That riled us and we got really aggressive with the Hungarians and won the match 1-0. The trouble hadn't finished, though. On the way back, unbeknown to us on the aircraft, our plane developed engine problems. We were having a bit of fun in the back, downing a few drinks as usual. As it landed someone noticed that fire engines and police cars were racing along by the side of the plane. As we got off the aircraft there was a big commotion, with lots of pressmen asking us how scared we had felt on the flight. We hadn't a clue; we were happily drinking our champagne.

A 2-0 victory at home put us in the quarter-finals where our opponents were the same Górnik team we'd beaten in the previous year's final. The away leg was first, and it was freezing cold as we flew into Krakow and then had an hour's drive to Katowice. It was snowing hard and to me it looked just like a scene out of *Dr Zhivago*. It was minus ten by the time we got there, and we went straight to the ground for a training session. It was a big, open stadium also used for speedway and the ground was just ice. We couldn't imagine the game could be played, but of course it was. And we were totally underequipped for the weather. I always remember standing there in the tunnel wearing a normal football shirt and Lubanski standing next to me in their line-up.

'Mike Summerbee – are you stupid?' asked Lubanski.

'What?'

'Look at you,' he said. 'And look at me.'

So I did. He was wearing thick gloves and body stockings and I was jogging on the spot vainly trying to get my blood going. When we walked out of the tunnel it was like going into a deep freezer. The pitch was even more icy and we were lucky to lose only 2-0. I have never been as cold again in my life. Near the final whistle Francis Lee said: 'As soon as the ref blows we all run to each other and start jumping up and down as if we've done really well.'

That's what we did, patting each other on the back. Górnik stood there watching this charade, but I don't think it fooled them. They knew they'd beaten us easily enough and we'd never looked like scoring. After the game we had to stand with our boots on in the showers because the floor was just a block of ice, and I don't think I was the only one who caught a cold in the kidneys.

The journey home was a nightmare, too. The snow was now so heavy you couldn't see anything out of the window as we drove back to the airfield in Krakow.

'Right, lads,' said the pilot. 'Strap yourselves in because we are going to take off straight away, we're going straight up, not gradually. I'm going to have to give it everything otherwise there's no way we'll get off the tarmac.'

One or two of the players like Mike Doyle and Stan Bowles were not good flyers and they looked very worried. The engines started up and the pilot came on again, saying: 'Sorry about the bumps, lads. I'm just trying to find the runway.'

Even I felt it then. I never had a problem being on a plane, but that day things started to flash through my mind about Munich. That tragedy had been a problem with ice on the wings and snowy weather, and this was a frightening moment for us all. True to his word, the pilot took off and was heading up straight away. Once we were above the clouds the relief was heavenly.

We won the home leg 2-0, but I watched on crutches. In the next League match after the first Górnik game we were playing Derby at the Baseball Ground. Dave Mackay was in their side, and I've already mentioned his habit of touching the ball forward a little before playing his pass. I spotted this and nicked in front of him to get the ball. As I did he caught me and I had another broken leg. I was back in plaster and it drove me daft. It didn't help my mood any having to catch the train everywhere. One day some school kids recognised me and as I limped on to the platform they shouted: 'Whoever did that should have broken the other leg as well, you bastard Summerbee.' Charming.

I was still out of action when we had a quarter-final play-off against Górnik on neutral territory in Copenhagen. I still travelled to the match and my main memory is of going out in the evening and wanting to join in the celebrations after the lads had won 3-1. I was rocking and rolling with them somewhere and what happens but I break my plaster cast falling over. The boss was far from happy.

This stress fracture was one of my worst injuries, and it still hadn't cleared up by the first leg of the semi-final. This was against Chelsea, who had won the FA Cup in 1970, and I think it was the first time there was an all-English clash in a big match in European competition. I remember there was a lot of hype and pre-match talk about who was the better team. We were, of course, but Chelsea won the first leg 1-0 at Stamford Bridge, and we had a couple more injuries to contend with for the second leg at home. I was out of plaster by then, and with an injury crisis they pushed me back into the team for that match. I was still limping, but the physio Freddie Griffiths injected painkillers into my leg and they built a very light plaster to go on the side of my leg.

Of course, I was up against Ron Harris, who was never the easiest. He didn't spare me anything, and I tried my best to unsettle him. In one tackle my studs went down his dark blue sock and then I tapped Ron on his shoulder as he was getting up. He swung round ready to defend himself and I just said: 'Excuse me, but do you know your nylons are laddered?'

He wasn't a happy man, but we were too depleted to have a real chance that night and lost the game 1-0, and so lost the Cup Winners' Cup. We lost because of missing and half-fit players and I was sick that Chelsea, not us, were going to the final to play Real Madrid. Our squad just wasn't big enough to cope, and although I was always willing to play with pain that was a match I really shouldn't have been involved in. City did bring me back too early a few times because I was needed, but if Joe Mercer had told me to jump off Mount Everest I would have done it.

My final match in Europe with City was special because one of the greatest players in the history of football, Alfredo di Stéfano, was the manager of our opponents, Valencia. It was the first round of the UEFA Cup in the 1972–3 season and we drew 2-2 at home. Then we flew off to play in their atmospheric Mestalla Stadium, a tight ground with no room at all to breathe, similar to Highbury or The Dell, Southampton's ground. There was no hiding place and they had an animal of a left back who spent the whole match trying to rip my shorts off. He tried every trick and you couldn't believe his tackling. I remember coming out for the start of the second half and seeing Di Stéfano standing there.

'Would you mind getting him off,' I said to this legend of a man. 'He wants my shirt and shorts and everything.'

'There is nothing I can do,' said Di Stéfano slowly, with a big smile on his face. And that was it. We lost 2-1 and were out immediately, just as we had been against Fenerbahçe in our first European venture.

Somehow it didn't hurt as much when Di Stéfano was involved. Everybody idolised him, and I was glad to meet him again a few years ago when he brought the Champions League trophy to Manchester on behalf of Real Madrid when Old Trafford staged the 2003 final between Milan and Juventus. I was in awe of Di Stéfano, a player who had inspired me when I watched his great Real Madrid team win the 1960 European Cup Final 7-3 against Eintracht Frankfurt in perhaps the greatest club match ever played.

I thought then how privileged I had been to be on the same continental stage for a while myself, and to have won a European trophy with Manchester City.

15

TURBULENT TIMES

Within the Manchester City dressing room I never had a nickname. It was always plain Mike. But it was a different matter with the fans. Some tried to christen me Pinocchio because of my long nose – and what some of the opposition supporters called me is unprintable. The name that stuck among the City crowd, though, was Buzzer. It came from my name ending with bee, and because I used to buzz around the pitch when I played. I didn't mind at all. It was a contact word and I would acknowledge it. But it was never used in the dressing room.

The name that came to mind when we played Southport at the start of a run that took us to triumph in the League Cup Final was my boyhood name, Tich. Playing against Southport was a trip down memory lane for me because my father, George, had played for them and my mother, Dulcie, used to work in the town. It was a sentimental journey and I remember the big pitch and the fact that it was a difficult match even though we eventually won 3-0. So many of those kinds of matches are lost in the fog of time, but I felt an emotional pull that day – and I like to think there was a little fate involved in the match being the start of another journey to Wembley.

In the next round we played Liverpool, and I remember that match for one of Malcolm Allison's tactical ploys that worked a treat. In the team talk Malcolm told everyone that I had the beating of their left back, Alec Lindsay, and told the other players to get the ball to me all the time. He told me to take on Lindsay at every opportunity, and that I would beat him so often that it would force Liverpool's central defender, Emlyn Hughes, to come across and cover. That in turn, said Malcolm, would open up space for Colin Bell to surge forward into. It was a beautiful autumn night at Maine Road and the strategy worked a treat as we won 3-2 against a very tough Liverpool side. I also remember that Lindsay cottoned on to the tactic and refused to come towards me.

'Come on, come on,' I taunted him, both of us knowing that if Lindsay committed himself the chances were that I would whip the ball past him. I'll admit there was a bit of theatricals involved but I wasn't trying to embarrass him. It was just the psychology of the moment. 'Come on, come and get it if you want the ball,' I shouted at Lindsay so all the crowd could hear.

And I remember Liverpool's wonderful manager Bill Shankly, my father's great friend, shouting in response to his player: 'Alec, smack him one,' roared Shankly. 'Give him one. Just come and get him.'

I turned round to Shankly and said: 'Dulcie wouldn't like to hear you saying that. Talking about me like that.' He laughed, but he didn't stop.

Our progress in the competition continued with home

wins against Everton and QPR, which put us in a two-legged semi-final against Manchester United. They were massive matches and we won the first leg 2-1 at home in a really good contest. So it was a slight advantage to us when we went for the showdown at Old Trafford. We scored first but United came back to lead 2-1 and put the scores level on aggregate. All that set up one of the most dramatic goals of my career, one that took us to Wembley again.

It came near the end of the semi-final when we had a free-kick awarded at the Stretford End. The ref signalled it was indirect, and I saw that; I saw his arm raised, but few others did. Francis Lee certainly didn't, because he took one of his trademark run-ups and smacked the ball straight towards goal. If United's goalkeeper, Alex Stepney, had let the ball fly past him into the net, the goal would have been disallowed. But Alex got his palms to the ball, which dropped down into the six-yard box and I buzzed in to tap it into the net. Alex had made a mistake and I just acted on instinct. I nearly missed it, though – and it was only two yards out. The ball just crept under the crossbar. I remember there was a stunned silence when the ball went into the net, and the crowd probably thought the ref would say the free-kick would have to be retaken. He didn't though.

That game gave me particular joy, I had been abused for many years by the Stretford End; they were always going on about the size of my nose. So I just stayed there when I scored, and everyone came over and celebrated right in front of the Stretford End. It was a fantastic feeling. We were in the League Cup Final, we'd overcome United again and I had scored the winner. It was an unforgettable moment of one-upmanship. That wasn't the case when I spoke to Alex Stepney after the final whistle. He was a pal of mine and I was respectful towards him. I wasn't laughing or crowing or gloating at Alex about the incident. I asked him about it and he said he'd thought the free-kick was direct and he'd had to save it. It was just a mistake by Alex. Maybe the wall had obstructed his view and he couldn't see the referee's arm raised. It wasn't the most difficult goal I scored, but it seemed so at the time. I didn't score too many goals but they were often significant ones. This was massive – 10,000 people had been locked out of Old Trafford that night.

A month later we lost 3-0 to Manchester United in the FA Cup fourth round. That was a rare victory for them in that era. We tended to win most of the derby clashes, and they were often significant results because they led to trophies. I remember that FA Cup game because I went off after twenty minutes following a collision with Brian Kidd. It wasn't a bad tackle; Brian just fell awkwardly on my knee. I'd played every game of the season until then, but it was the start of a bad run of injuries that disrupted my pleasure in a year in which we won two trophies, the League Cup and the Cup Winners' Cup.

Looking back, our preparation for the League Cup Final must have been the worst any team has ever had for a prestigious match. We had played away to Académica de Coimbra in a European quarter-final on the Wednesday night and flew back to Britain the next afternoon. That was the plan at least. But Heathrow airport was snowbound and our plane was late departing and had to be diverted to Birmingham. We didn't land there till one o'clock on the Friday morning and then we had a bus journey down to our hotel near London in the middle of the night. We were totally knackered and the weather was still so bad on Friday afternoon, the day before the game, that we didn't even get to train on the Wembley pitch. Instead, we stayed at the hotel and adjusted from the 80-degree heat of Portugal to the freezing temperatures in London.

I don't suppose it made any difference not going to Wembley the day before. We couldn't believe how bad the pitch was, churned up as it was by a combination of the weather and use of it, yet again, for the Horse of the Year Show. The dignitaries being presented to us before the start had to walk on duckboards across the mud to be introduced to us. It was unbelievable that they could allow Wembley to become such a quagmire. It took us time to get into the game, which wasn't surprising, and Jeff Astle gave West Brom the lead by half-time. We were up against it and we'd been playing twenty minutes of the second half when a ball was played between myself and the Albion left back Ray Wilson. I've described earlier how it turned from being my ball into his because of the conditions and how he caught me and left me with a hairline fracture of the leg. I didn't know the extent of the injury at the time; all I thought was that I was struggling a bit. I went to the touchline, covered in mud from head to foot, and the trainers sprayed some water on my leg and sent me back on to the pitch.

Soon afterwards, someone took a throw-in and the ball came to me out on the touchline. I instinctively flicked it back over the top into the middle and Mike Doyle ran through and scored. We had equalised and I had set up the goal with a broken leg. Of course, I couldn't play on, and had to come off the paddy field. The match went to extra time and the hero that day for us was Francis Lee. He played so many great games for Manchester City, but that was his very best. He was a Trojan, and played on the quagmire as if it was the bone-hard ground in Coimbra. The psychological impact he made on West Brom was immense and it had to be him who knocked the ball through for Glyn Pardoe to score the winner. I know that from people telling me and watching the highlights later on television. I didn't see it at the time – I was in hospital, where they said they couldn't see anything wrong and sent me back to Wembley.

In fact, I could hardly walk and the pain was terrible. Another winners' medal was wonderful but I knew something was seriously wrong with my leg. Back in Manchester they took some proper X-rays and they showed up the fracture that left me a passenger really for the rest of the season and missing out on playing in the Cup Winners' Cup Final.

Injuries are always an occupational hazard for a professional footballer, and the science then was nowhere near what it is today. Another infamous broken leg in the history of Manchester City is the one suffered by Glyn Pardoe in a match against United in November 1970. It was in a collision with George Best and there has always been great controversy about that tackle which resulted in Glyn nearly losing a leg. I wasn't close to the incident and people have said it was an intentional act by George. But I have never believed that. I know in my own mind he wasn't a person who could do that kind of thing. It was just something that happens in matches, as it did to me in the League Cup Final. And I know that the serious injury to Glyn affected George very deeply.

When the incident happened we were 1–0 down in the game, and our immediate reaction at the nasty sight of Glyn being carried off wasn't squeamishness but an intense desire to win the game. It was an inspiration to us and we took United apart and won 4–1. I can't remember ever being so motivated on a football field.

We were capable of some great football at that time, but we couldn't find the consistency in the League that won us the title in 1968. In the next three seasons we finished thirteenth, tenth and eleventh. All the time Malcolm Allison was hoping to become the team manager, a role allegedly promised to him by Joe Mercer when they first came together in the summer of 1965. While we were winning various cup competitions, the pressure to give Malcolm full control of the team was resisted. Why change a winning formula that worked so well, with Joe and Malcolm working together to their strengths? That's what I thought, and probably what most City fans thought, too.

I knew Malcolm's huge ego was driving him to want to be the manager, and I could see that he wasn't always happy. It was obvious when he wasn't – and I also knew that he and Joe couldn't go on for ever. But while it was working I didn't see the need for change and I told Malcolm that myself once when I was feeling particularly bold. It didn't make any difference, of course, and eventually Malcolm got his wish from the City board of directors, not long after the start of the 1971–2 season. It's easy to say with hindsight that the split came too soon, but I knew it at the time.

In my view they didn't treat Joe very well. The boss was pushed upstairs as general manager when he could have gone on to the board and been a club figurehead for the rest of his life. He deserved that because he is the greatest manager Manchester City have ever had. Instead, he ended up leaving for Coventry at the end of that season and I was upset about that. City should have looked after a hero like Joe, not have discarded him completely. While I had immense respect for Malcolm as a coach (I repeat that he was the best this country has ever produced) he was not a good manager of a football club. He lived his own life too freely to be able to impose the essential rules and regulations and discipline that every football team needs. I respected him so much, but City lost the momentum of those great years when his partnership with Joe Mercer ended. While Liverpool found the secret of keeping the system going and passing control from Bill Shankly to Bob Paisley, the fact is that Manchester City didn't. And the club has suffered for it ever since.

For a few months, however, that didn't seem to be the case. One great signing for us was the Welsh striker Wyn Davies. When he came to play it was fantastic. You knew very well that if you played the right kind of cross he would be there to head it with all the power he had. He frightened goalkeepers to death. He caused so many problems. That was wonderful for me.

I could always cross a ball just as Jimmy Greaves could always score a goal. It was a natural thing. To me, there's nothing better in the world than seeing a centre forward going for a ball in the air that's been crossed on the perfect spot for him. I know it sounds stupid, but that's how I feel. I remember one goal in particular I made for Wyn, and it was against Tottenham. I picked up the ball fifteen yards inside our half, made a short run forward and then sent a cross from deep towards him at the near post. Wyn headed it in and the ball hit the back stanchion before Pat Jennings had even moved. He just caught it perfectly. The goal was on the opening credits of *Match of the Day* for ages and ages as the theme tune played, and it had to be good for that.

With Wyn leading the line we were once again strong challengers for the League title, and with nine games of the season left were top of the table. Then Malcolm Allison tried to be clever and signed Rodney Marsh from QPR for £250,000, to add even more flair to our team. He thought it would be the move that clinched the title. What happened instead was that it denied us the glory we should have had.

At the time of the deal I was pleased that we had signed Rodney. We could all see his ability with a football and I thought he would be a plus for us. I helped to make him feel welcome. He spent his first night in Manchester at my house and Francis Lee and I took him out on the town a couple of times. There was no animosity at all towards him personally, but the fact was that he didn't suit the style we had been playing that season with Wyn Davies leading the line. Rodney was also a little overweight when he arrived and his fitness wasn't up to the City standard. He came on as a substitute for Wyn in his debut against Chelsea and we won 1-0. But it didn't work. We lost vital matches at home to Stoke and away to Southampton over Easter and our momentum had stalled.

If Malcolm had left Rodney out until the next season to get fully fit it would have been much better. That was the advice he received from Joe Mercer in his reluctant role as general manager, but Malcolm ignored it. Our football that season was a quick, attacking game and when Rodney came into the side it was a problem because he wasn't passing the ball to players where they were used to receiving it. By the time we beat Derby in the final match of the season it was too late. Brian Clough's side were already out of reach for us and they claimed the title.

Rodney is a good friend of mine to this day and he knows the way I feel. We have spoken about it. Losing the title that season was not solely down to him, but his arrival definitely disrupted the performances of what had been a settled team. We should have been champions again that year. It was a great shame that we failed, but it happens in football. I remember there was a lot of upset among the supporters, and it was only to be expected. They had come to enjoy success because we'd won so many trophies and when we threw it away they were bound to be disappointed.

The next season Rodney became a firm favourite with everybody. He won lots of games for us when the team was struggling. Rodney loved the ball and he was a great entertainer. He also had a deaf ear – and I could never work out which one it was. It always seemed to be the ear on your side when you were calling for a pass. Rodney is a lovely man, but buying him was one of Malcolm Allison's big mistakes.

That summer of 1972 Joe Mercer left Maine Road for Coventry and before the end of the next season Malcolm was gone, too. And my time at Manchester City wasn't the same without the two men who made me the player I was. Perhaps inevitably, there was a period of instability that affected everyone. Johnny Hart became manager for a few months but resigned through ill health. Tony Book was made caretaker for a little while, but the board wouldn't put their trust in an untried boss so they opted for an experienced manager with a hard-man reputation in Ron Saunders. He arrived in November 1973 but he too was gone before the end of that season.

When Saunders came he found it very difficult to handle the players we had. By that time Denis Law had also been signed from Manchester United and the forward line consisted of Denis, Francis Lee, myself and Rodney Marsh. We were all experienced professionals with big characters and he seemed overawed by the challenge. He just couldn't manage us. Mike Doyle was a City blue through and through and he couldn't get on with Ron either. All Saunders had to do was treat us normally, but he didn't. He got us in for training before the rest of the team and had us doing different things. I suppose it was classic sergeant-major tactics, but that wasn't going to work. It was ludicrous.

I remember going to training one day and he had the Futcher twins there for shooting practice. Behind the goal was a quartet of ballboys – Law, Marsh, Summerbee and Lee. That was the mentality of Ron Saunders. I didn't think I was getting the respect I deserved and I am sure I wasn't the only one who felt this way and was upset as a result. Having said that it can't have been an easy situation for Saunders with so many international players and the club struggling after all the success with Joe and Malcolm, but I can't help but feel that he tried to change something that didn't need changing. It wasn't a case of player power against him; it was just a case that when senior professionals are not treated with respect it is bound to cause aggravation. But we weren't stupid. We kept on training hard and playing hard because we were never going to go out on the field and make fools of ourselves.

Despite the antagonism in the dressing room we reached the final of the League Cup in 1974, where we faced Wolves. It was my last game at Wembley but I don't recall it with any fondness. We lost 2-1. We had some chances and didn't take them and what I remember above all is sitting on the coach next to Denis Law as we left the stadium and seeing how much losing had hurt him. Denis was one of the great players of my era, of any era in football in fact. I remember saying to him on the coach that at least I could tell my grandchildren I had played alongside Denis Law in a cup final. It was a corny line and it didn't cheer him up, but I meant it all the same.

I felt I had reached a stage at City where I was getting a little stale. I was thirty-one and I felt a change would do me good. It almost happened, too, when Don Revie made a bid to sign me for his superb Leeds United team. The match after the League Cup Final was away to Leeds at Elland Road and we lost 1-0. Afterwards, Billy Bremner came up to me and said: 'You'll be here next week.' He knew that Revie was making a bid, and it was obvious he was keen on me joining up with their outstanding group of players. The following match was the derby at home to Manchester United, and it was a 0-0 draw, which was very rare at that time. My mind was racing ahead with the prospect of joining Leeds. I knew the deal was on, and the day after the United match I left for London on the six o'clock early morning train on business with my shirt-making company. I told City where I was going and left contact numbers. It was just before the transfer deadline, so the move was now or never.

I remember going into an Italian restaurant in Mayfair for lunch, and it was there that the call came from Ron Saunders telling me to get back to Maine Road because I was going to be transferred to Leeds for £30,000. My heart was jumping. I knew it was going to happen and I got a taxi back to Euston and was on the first train north. I was excited because it would have been a huge challenge to play for Leeds, who went on to win the title that season and reach the European Cup Final the following year. I felt I had given everything to Manchester City, and that it was time for a change; a fresh ground, a fresh dressing room, a fresh situation. Playing with new team-mates can give you an extra lease of life, and I was young enough for that to be so.

When I reached Maine Road the place was almost deserted. Eventually I found the secretary, Bernard Halford, and he told me the deal was off, that Don Revie had pulled out. Bernard couldn't or wouldn't tell me why so I phoned up Revie myself. He told me he had agreed a £30,000 transfer fee with City, but that Ron Saunders was trying to buy Stuart Pearson from Hull, and when the fee for Pearson went up City tried to load the extra money on to my transfer price.

'City reneged on our deal for you, Mike, so I pulled out,' said Revie. 'I did want you, Mike, but a deal is a deal with me.'

I was very disappointed with City's attitude. It was clear enough that the team built by Joe Mercer and Malcolm Allison was beginning to break up and I had given the club good service. Leeds were the top club in England right then and it was a boost to know they wanted me to play for them. I didn't feel nearly as wanted at Maine Road in the spring of 1974. Another reason I was keen to join Leeds was that they were such a professional side in every department. When you played against them it was a proper match for the connoisseurs of the game, who liked to see different players working against each other. It was footballing brains pitted against each other, and the contests were enthralling.

Ron Saunders didn't last much longer as manager. He couldn't the way he treated so many of the City players. From the League Cup Final onwards we won only one of twelve matches, and that poor run of form must have persuaded the new chairman, Peter Swales, to ditch Saunders and make Tony Book the full-time boss. That was what should have happened when Johnny Hart stepped down.

All that was left that season was pride – and a match on the final day against Manchester United at Old Trafford. It was the game Manchester City won 1-0 and famously condemned United to relegation, when Denis Law scored the goal he never wanted to. Let me say that City were not the reason United went down. They had been poor all season and we just applied the finishing touch. Denis had joined us after being kicked out of Old Trafford by the latest United manager, Tommy Docherty. My pal George Best was still at the club but having even more trouble with the Doc than I had with Saunders.

The pitch wasn't good that day and the moment all football remembers from that game started when I pushed the ball wide to Francis Lee on the right wing. He crossed it, a nothing cross really, and Denis back-heeled it casually into the net. It was a tribute to his magical ability that he could do it, but my feeling was that he didn't really want to score. His first love was always United. When the goal went in Denis showed no emotion; there was no trademark arm in the air. He kept his hands by his side and trotted back to the halfway line a shattered man. He didn't want United to go down.

Privately, I don't think many other City players did either. I always loved the derby matches; I looked forward to them more than any others. I felt it was better for United to be in the same division as us so that we could play them and beat them – which, as I've said, we usually did in those days. I didn't feel elation at the goal. It was a nothing feeling. I liked the players. George Best was my great friend and I admired Sir Matt Busby.

The ugly part of that day was that the game didn't finish. Denis walked off and then the Stretford End fans came streaming on to the pitch. I already had stitches over my right eye from an aerial collision with Jim Holton. We had clashed heads and I came off worst. As the supporters invaded the pitch someone hit me on the back of the head with a big stick; maybe it was the corner flag. I know that I didn't see it coming. It split the back of my head open. They were frightening scenes as the game was abandoned and I took off my blue shirt to try to hide the fact that I was a City player. It didn't make any difference; they must have been looking at my nose.

That was the first hooligan violence I encountered personally, and today they would close the stadium if it happened. Afterwards, the press questioned me about the stitches all over my head. How had it happened? I said it was all part of the clash with Holton. I didn't want to make an issue of it. If I had done it would have caused a lot of trouble for Manchester United. It was my decision to keep quiet about what had happened. I was concerned about the way Denis Law was hurting so much. I wasn't concerned about myself. I could take a bit of pain – I had more stitches in my head during my career than I'd eaten hot dinners. It was a nasty way to finish, though. That night I went with Denis and our wives to watch Rod Stewart playing a concert at Belle Vue. We went backstage to see him afterwards, and the atmosphere was so much more civilised.

We had one final match that year, a friendly away to Panathinaikos in Athens after the League season had ended. It was meant to be a relaxing trip, but Tony Book had not long taken over and wanted to show who was in charge. After the match we were invited into a taverna in central Athens to have drinks with Ferenc Puskás, then the manager of Panathinaikos. He was one of my heroes, and when Tony said that we all had to go back to the hotel after dinner and miss out on seeing Puskás, I rebelled. I wasn't going to snub one of the legends of world football and Francis Lee said he was staying with me, too. So while the others stuck to Tony Book's orders we got merrily drunk with the great Hungarian and rolled back in the middle of the night.

I guess that was the end of the road for Francis and myself at City, even though we still had something to offer. Francis was luckier than me – he got a £100,000 move to Derby just before the start of the 1974–5 season and ended up winning another League title with them. He was as unhappy as I was at the way we were being treated, and he found the exit door quickly. I was stuck for another season, and played as many games in the reserves as the first team.

The writing had been on the wall from the moment Peter Swales became chairman. The first thing he did was take down the pictures in the boardroom from the previous era when we'd won every trophy going. He didn't want any association with the past regime, but I couldn't understand that. You can't change the history of a football club, and this was a history to be proud of. But Swales wanted it all out of the way, and he wanted to get rid of influential people who were aligned to that era.

I don't blame Tony Book for the problems. I roomed with him as a player for many years and he is still a friend. It was difficult for him when he became manager because the chairman was such a dominant personality with an ego to match. It wasn't easy for Tony to make the transition, and it made my final year at Manchester City less than enjoyable.

My last game for the first team was at home to Coventry City in March 1975. I have no memory of it at all. It was a 1-0 win, probably routine. But I had no idea it would be the last time I'd wear a City shirt in the First Division. I was in and out, sometimes playing in the reserves, and I wasn't finding that easy as a thirty-two-year-old who'd been an England international.

In my mind I always knew it would come to an end because I had been brought up in a family where my father spent most of his career in the reserves. I knew the realities of professional football well enough, but it doesn't stop it being a shock when it happens to you. It was a very strange feeling to be pushed to one side when I had been such an important player in the team for so long. But it comes to everyone. In the end, you are just a commodity as a footballer. When you have lost your usefulness you are out of the door.

16

PARTING SHOTS

In the summer of 1975, a year too late, it was obvious I would be leaving Manchester City. The only question was where I'd be going – and to which division. I felt I could still contribute in the top flight and the fact that I'd been granted a free transfer by City would help. A message came through fairly swiftly that Burnley were interested, and that delighted me. They were a big, solid First Division club and close enough to home that I wouldn't have to upset the family by moving house.

Burnley manager Jimmy Adamson and his assistant, Brian 'Dusty' Miller, came over to talk and to sell me the idea of going to Turf Moor. I was thirty-two but I had never been in that position before. I was the one who had initiated contact with Joe Mercer when I left Swindon for City, and none of the possible transfers in the next decade ever got as far as personal talks with the other club. I had no agents or advisers, and all I knew was that being on a free transfer might allow me to be given a lucrative signing-on fee.

That prospect flew out of the window when, with Burnley's interest becoming very strong, the City chairman Peter Swales suddenly reneged on the free transfer deal we had and demanded a £25,000 fee from Burnley. I was very angry. My wages had been £40 a week when I started at Maine Road. I had never been an expensive commodity for the club, set against all the effort I'd put in and the trophies won while I was there. I had given blood, sweat and tears to City and I'd often played with bad injuries for the sake of the club when I knew it wasn't good for my body. I was more than disappointed in Swales, and I told him so to his face. But it is impossible to argue or reason with ego, and it's particularly difficult when someone is in love with himself. He wasn't on the same wavelength. Swales probably loved the game of football, but he had no cause to do what he did to me. He could have given me a reward to say thank you for my service to Manchester City. But he didn't.

I met Jimmy and Dusty two or three times and I agreed to join Burnley. The Northamptonshire cricketer Colin Milburn was staying with me when I got the call to go to Turf Moor to sign terms and he came over with me. I was a little apprehensive, a little afraid of meeting the Burnley chairman, Bob Lord. He had a fearsome reputation within football as a Lancashire man of steel who never stood on ceremony. Everybody knew that if you didn't get on with Bob Lord at Burnley you were out.

All I was interested in was a fresh start and first team football, and Burnley gave them to me. I went into the boardroom and there was Bob Lord stood behind the directors' table. In front of him was the contract with a pen beside it. We were introduced; he was wearing a light-grey suit with an England badge on the breast pocket because he was on one of the FA management committees.

He gave me the contract and I could hardly believe it. Burnley were going to pay me around £200 per week, which was significantly more than I'd been earning at Manchester City. And it was an inflation-proof contract, which was a great thing to have at a time when inflation was running at 13 per cent. It was a wonderful deal, and there was appearance and bonus money as well.

I looked at it, and I said: 'Well, that's fantastic, that.'

'You deserve all that,' he said.

'For what, Mr Lord?'

'Because in all the times you've been with Jimmy Adamson and Dusty you've never mentioned money. So you're coming to Burnley Football Club because you want to. And that's your reward for doing it.'

I thanked him – and I signed up smartish. I was elated by the deal, and I was elated to be at a club like Burnley. Then we went down to the pitch and had a few pictures taken in the claret and blue kit along with Willie Morgan, who had joined on the same day. That was very satisfying. I've always had a love of claret and blue football strips. I don't know why, but I always liked it, always thought it looked good. Maybe it was from watching Aston Villa so much as a young boy. I'd have joined Burnley if they played in pink and yellow, but the colours seemed just right to me.

There were some great lads at the club – Alan Stevenson in goal, Colin Waldron, Leighton James, Brian Flynn, Paul Fletcher and Peter Noble. I came with a reputation and they treated me with respect. I suppose I was an elder statesman of football in their eyes, and I didn't mind that status. It was a lot better than being an old man in the reserves. I felt it was an adventure, and it certainly was in pre-season training when they took us up on to Hartshead Pike on the moors. We all went up in a bus and it was a long climb to the top with gorse everywhere. There was a plateau near the top and gorse as far the eye could see, with no landmarks and no trees. We walked thirty yards into it and it seemed like it was the middle of nowhere.

Dusty got us running and doing different exercises and then he said: 'Right, lads, back to the bus.'

We turned round but we didn't have any idea where we were. 'Where do we go?' I said.

'Back to the bus,' said Dusty, and then he disappeared.

So we split up into groups. I was with Noble, Fletcher and Flynn, and we headed off in one direction, completely the wrong way, and we ended up in Skipton, about fifteen miles from Burnley. We were in our club tracksuits, we had no money and we were supposed to be back at the club for afternoon training. A bus driver took pity on us and let us on without paying the fare but by the time we got back to the training ground everyone else had finished and gone home except Jimmy Adamson. He couldn't believe it, and must have wondered what he had signed.

The pre-season was fun, and one of the friendly matches was away to Plymouth. For some reason, and I still can't figure out why, we were to take a bus down the motorway to Bristol and then catch a train to Plymouth. It seemed a strange arrangement to me. Jimmy said they would pick up Willie Morgan and myself at Knutsford on the M6 at two o'clock. We were waiting as we'd arranged on the roundabout, but by a quarter past two nobody had turned up. We went down to the service station just beyond, and the team bus had been waiting there and had gone five minutes earlier. Again, Jimmy must have been wondering if he'd made a foolish mistake in buying me.

Standing there, wondering what to do, we saw a bus pull up full of the blue rinse brigade going to Cheltenham. So we thumbed a lift with them and told the driver we were trying to catch the Burnley bus. He was young, and the ladies who thought they were going for a sedate drive down suddenly found themselves speeding off at 70 mph. It was a bit of fun. We got to Keele services, but once again the team bus had just left. So we got off the coach and saw a police car.

'Look, we're in deep trouble,' I said to one of the policemen. 'We're trying to catch the Burnley team bus. Can you help?'

'Hop in,' they said, cleared the traffic cones off the back seat and started off down the motorway. The blue light was going some of the way, but we didn't catch the bus until it was just turning up into the entrance into Temple Meads Station in Bristol, well beyond the remit of the police car. But they finished off the job in style, sirens and lights going as they pulled up in front of the team bus. The other players looked on in hysterics.

'Sorry, boss,' I said. 'But we're here now. Can you bung the policemen a few quid?'

'No, it was our pleasure,' said the cops. And Jimmy Adamson didn't say a word. He was gobsmacked.

My start at the club had been haphazard, and that was the mark of the whole season. We began well enough with a 0-0 home draw against Arsenal, and I enjoyed playing for the side. But I had lost a bit of pace, and that was something I had always relied on in my game. Sometimes I played in midfield, but it wasn't my position really. With results not going well, Jimmy Adamson was sacked by Christmas. This was the ruthless streak that Bob Lord was known for, and there was sadness in the dressing room about Jimmy's departure.

I wished I had gone to Turf Moor a season earlier. I always tried my hardest but I don't think I gave real value for money at Burnley. If it had been a big transfer fee I would have felt embarrassed. Nevertheless, the Burnley supporters were brilliant to me; they were as good as any set of fans in the country. I could sense the time was coming when I had to do something else with my life. I didn't want to make a fool of myself – and it's quite easy to do that, you know.

Relegation arrived in a way I didn't appreciate. A defeat at home to Manchester United was the result that sent Burnley down, and they have never returned to the top flight since. What I do remember with some affection is my last ever match in the First Division. It was away to Newcastle and I knew that my loss of pace meant I would never again hack it with the best defenders. It was a midweek match and we won 1-0 at St James' Park, and I remember going out on to the pitch afterwards and just standing and thinking, 'This is where I won the League Championship.' It was just a little moment alone with my thoughts, a private thing. I knew it was the last match and that I would never be playing these games again.

Maybe I should have quit playing football then. But I had a good contract at Burnley and I reckoned I would be able to get by at Second Division level. I also wanted to repay their faith by trying to help the club get promotion back straight away. It was soon clear that that was a foolish dream. Soon after the start of the season I suffered a strange and horrible injury. As the ball came across the box I tried to flick it between my legs and I felt something go in my stomach, like a snap. The pain was excruciating. I'd had a few uncomfortable injuries in my life but nothing like this.

And it was weird. I could run, but I couldn't pass the ball

because the pain was so bad. I didn't come out for the second half and after the game the whole area stiffened up and the pain was awful. But there was no swelling and no visible problem. By Monday morning I knew something was very badly wrong. The only way I could get up in the morning was by rolling out of the bed. I had to roll out of chairs, too. Trying to pass a football was impossible, and obviously I was out of the team.

Rest was thought to be the cure, and it did ease the problem sufficiently to convince me I could carry on playing. And by the time Blackpool came in for me in December 1976 I thought I'd overcome the problem. I hadn't played for a little while, but Blackpool were going well in the Second Division and I hoped it would make a fresh start. What I didn't know was that it was all the Blackpool chairman's idea and that the manager, Allan Brown, didn't fancy me at all. Almost as soon as I arrived at the club I knew I was in trouble. The injury was still there and making it very hard to play, and the manager wasn't keen to pick me anyway. In hindsight, I did a stupid thing by going to Blackpool, and I played only three matches for them in the six months I was there.

They did try to help me with the injury, sending me to a clinic in Roehampton. I was lowered into a special bath where they treated people who had arthritis, trying to improve their mobility. It felt a little better after a weekend of treatment, but not much. The next idea was to see a specialist recommended by Manchester City. He said my pelvic muscles had opened up and that I might as well pack in football right there and then.

'You'll never play again,' he said – those fateful words that no professional sportsman wants to hear. I didn't know if he was right, but my instinctive reaction was not to believe him. There had to be a solution, and I was still enjoying my football enough to want to carry on playing a little longer. Like so many players, I guess, I didn't want to give up.

The last-chance saloon for me was the Manchester City physio, Freddie Griffiths. He had always been a hard taskmaster, and I trusted him more than anyone. The easiest thing for a footballer on a Monday morning after a weekend out on the razzle is to claim to have a slight strain and go into the medical room. But you didn't do that with Freddie. It was harder in his medical room than it was doing normal training.

So I went to see Freddie about the injury. I had to. He diagnosed me with torn pelvic muscles and within a matter of minutes he said: 'Mike, forget what the surgeon said. If you do what I tell you to do, you'll be playing again in a fortnight.'

One day my career was definitely over, the next day I was being told I could be out on the pitch in a couple of weeks. I believed in Freddie, and I got permission from Tony Book to train at City. Blackpool thought I was finished, so it didn't matter to them, and this was my last, desperate hope of playing football again.

I came in to work with Freddie Griffiths once he'd finished with the City players. The first thing I did was some bench work. I sat with my head above my hands and couldn't bend forward an inch without being in terrible agony. Freddie said I had to keep trying, and slowly it improved. After a week I could go a foot down.

Then it was the wallbars in the gym. I had one leg up on the bars, the other on the floor, and I had to bounce back and forward a hundred times, to work the pelvic muscles.

After a fortnight of progress Freddie put me on the wooden horse in the gym. I had to sit on the top while he held my legs and then I had to pull my head down as far as I could. I went so far down that my head was nearly touching the ground. I came back up and I never felt a thing. It seemed to me to be a miracle. Within two weeks of being told by a specialist that my career was finished I was doing things I hadn't been able to do for months.

Next Freddie got a football out and I had to tap it to him. He was a yard away at first and then gradually increased the distance between us. I kept sidefooting it to him. Eventually he told me to hit it with the full instep. I was back thirty yards by now and he said to drive the ball at him with full power. I did so, and never felt a thing. I did it fifty times and I was back to normal. I had another chance of playing.

Blackpool still held my registration but they weren't going to gamble on my fitness. I knew Freddie Pye, the chairman of Stockport County, and he asked me if I'd like to play for them. I joined on loan initially at the start of the 1977–8 season and signed for County on a free transfer in October. It was a final opportunity for me, and I'd always had a soft spot for Stockport since the days George Best and I used to watch them, together, standing on the terraces on a Friday evening on 'Go-Go County' nights. George played three matches for Stockport in 1975. I would play nearly a hundred games as it turned out.

I really enjoyed the days at Edgeley Park. It was a friendly club and I could have a bit of fun again. There was a match against Barnsley where it was snowing. We were winning 1-0 and as I went to take a corner I was bombarded with snowballs by the away fans. I took the cue and demanded the referee organise some police protection.

The manager when I arrived was the youngest in the Football League by far. He was a boy called Alan Thompson who was only twenty-six and had come from Sheffield Wednesday as player-manager. At one stage we were chasing promotion but after a run of defeats Alan was relieved of the manager's job and went back to being just a central defender. Freddie Pye asked me if I'd take over as player-manager, and although I had no coaching experience, and hadn't even really considered the prospect of being a boss, I thought I'd give it a go.

I didn't care that I had no background in doing the job. I didn't need any. I'd been in the game all my life and seen the way things had been done. I'd watched my father do the role when I was a young boy and I'd seen the genius of Joe Mercer and Malcolm Allison. I learned from that. If you didn't learn from them and how they handled footballers and a dressing room, you couldn't learn anything.

The very first thing I did was to introduce the warm-up routines and the hard physical sessions that Malcolm had used at City to such good effect. I brought in a fitness expert, Peter Keeling, a former athlete. I wanted to get all the players really fit and I worked them hard. Then it was trying to find a few extra players. One boost was persuading Arsenal winger George Armstrong to join us for a spell.

I don't think you have to go to managerial school to become a manager. Your education comes as you go along in the game, and I had played in the lower divisions so I knew what football was about at that level.

Another matter I insisted on was help as a player-manager. I needed people alongside me and I had two excellent assistants in Trevor Porteous and Eric Webster. I was still a player and I had to do the training, and I couldn't be making assessments while I was buzzing about in matches. Trevor and Eric were both older than me and I told them they had to be in charge while I was playing. If I wasn't doing well in a game, I had to get a bollocking at half-time if that was required. Right or wrong, that's how I approached it. The only time I was the 'manager' was during the week, when there was work to do or players to sign.

We started quite well in my time as the boss, and I was quite proud of some of the changes I made at Stockport. One of them, strangely, was initiated by the club's hosting of the World Lacrosse Championships. It so happened that the Edgeley Park area was the headquarters of lacrosse in Britain, and some of the tournament matches were going to be played at our ground where the showers were swinging off the walls, the tiles were cracked and everything was so ramshackle. I told Freddie it would be an embarrassment, but the club didn't have the money to sort it out. Then I remembered a contact who might be able to help.

He was a fella called Eddie Quiligotti, a wealthy businessman in the bathroom industry who was a big supporter of Manchester United. I had been in a restaurant a few years before, playing for City at the time, and I was sat having a meal a few days before a derby match. A man at the next table recognised me and said: 'Hey, Summerbee, we'll beat you on Saturday.' That was Eddie. I bet him £10 they wouldn't and he said okay. Eddie's firm did marble tiles and the like and after we beat United in that game, as per usual, he got in contact and asked me where I lived. Then he came to the house and laid a wonderful black and white marble floor in my hall.

So now I phoned up Eddie and told him about the problems at Stockport with the lacrosse tournament, and how I didn't want the town or the club to be humiliated and the world's best lacrosse players thinking they'd come to a dosshouse. Eddie came to the ground, had a look and sorted out a fantastic renovation of the dressing rooms, done by his apprentices. The price to the club was two tickets in the directors' box whenever he wanted to come to a match. He rarely did. I thought it was a brilliant gesture.

Another contact who helped us was my old friend Horst Dassler from Adidas. I told him how terrible our playing kit was and he asked me what colours we wore. 'Blue and white,' I said, and he organised a short-sleeve and long-sleeve version of the Argentina national team strip. They had just won the 1978 World Cup Final. He had another Adidas team in that World Cup playing in yellow and green and he gave us that for our away strip. Then he gave us thirty-five footballs and asked for the shoe sizes of all the players and sent flats, rubbers and boots for each man. He gave us all that, and when we played the first game of the 1978–9 season against Walsall we came out looking just like Argentina. We were the best-dressed side ever in the Fourth Division. It was just a shame we couldn't play like Ossie Ardiles and his pals.

I tried to get the team playing football, although you couldn't really do that in the division. But I do know the fans enjoyed that period at Stockport. And there was no doubt about the highlight of my season as a football manager. It was a League Cup match against Manchester United. We were drawn at home but the chairman decided to concede that advantage and play at Old Trafford for the big payday. I could understand that, and the players were excited at the prospect of a game at Old Trafford. I wanted us to try to approach it as a First Division club and Adidas even sent us a special all-white strip to use for the occasion.

Just before the game Alan Thompson, the former manager, came up and asked what the team would be getting in cash for playing at Old Trafford. I said: 'Playing there is your reward, simple as that. It's an opportunity to go out and prove to people how good as players you are. That's it. Just go and enjoy yourselves.'

I don't know if that made me popular in the dressing room, and I certainly wasn't popular that night among the fans on the Stretford End. But the Stockport players responded brilliantly to the challenge. We played so well and we were the better side. If real Manchester United fans read this book they will know that I'm not lying. For spells we played them off the park. We were getting beat 1-0 at half-time to a goal by Joe Jordan but we'd had chances. The occasion was magnificent and men like Les Bradd lifted themselves from being Fourth Division players to the top level for a night. I also remember that I got under the skin of Lou Macari and he seemed to spend the whole game chasing round after me. Jordan topped me on the halfway line at one point, but that was no problem. I expected stuff like that.

In the second half we kept on playing the same way and we took a 2-1 lead. Thompson converted a penalty and Terry Park got a second goal for us. We were still in the lead with only five minutes left when it all went wrong because of the referee, Peter Willis. He was a policeman, and the man who sent off Kevin Moran in the 1985 FA Cup Final. I'm still convinced to this day he was doing everything in the world to make Manchester United win against us.

Five minutes from the end there was an incident between Derek Lowey and United centre half Gordon McQueen, who had committed the foul. McQueen spat at Lowey and the ref sent him off. But he also decided to give the free-kick to United when it was clearly ours. They chipped the ball up into our box, the keeper caught it and took only three steps, but the ref blew for an indirect free-kick on the edge of the six-yard box. United took it and a shot from Sammy McIlroy ended up in the back of our net. Two each – and that was heartbreaking enough. But with just a minute to go Thompson came out and won a clean header and the ref gave a penalty for climbing on Joe Jordan's back. Jimmy Greenhoff scored and that was that.

'Don't go off,' I shouted to the lads at the final whistle. 'We'll run right round the pitch because you deserve it.'

The United fans stayed behind and applauded us because they'd seen how we'd been cheated, and I appreciated that. It was a classy thing to do. When I see situations today where managers complain about decisions going in favour of the big sides I have to smile. It's nothing new. It's always happened in football. There is one law for one, and one law for others. That was certainly driven home to me that particular night. We were robbed, plain and simple.

In my career I had some great nights at Manchester United, but if we'd won that evening it would have been the most pleasurable of all – for the way we played and the way we went down in defeat. I was so proud of that.

The trouble was that the players had performed well above standard. They could never match the intensity and feeling of that night again, and, as so often happens in football, there was a negative reaction. It was absolutely guaranteed that we would lose the next game in the League at home to Halifax. It began a slow process of decline and we finished the season just below mid-table.

I knew my professional career was coming to a close at the end of the season. The moment that truly decided it for me was when I tried to sprint down the right touchline and saw the linesman speeding past me. It was time to go, and while I'd enjoyed being a player-manager at Stockport I didn't have any ambition to go into full-time management. I was never committed to that because I'd seen what had happened to my father, and I had a shirt-making business that would make me a decent living. As it was, the board at Stockport weren't too keen on me and Freddie Pye was good enough to warn me, and give me the chance of resigning before I was sacked. He got me the money I was due as well.

So I finished my football career where I started – at the bottom. I'd worked my way to the top, played for my country, won all the trophies, and was back at the bottom having fun. I'd enjoyed it, and what I missed when I finished wasn't the playing so much as the camaraderie. It's that sense of fellow feeling, the knowledge that you are doing something together that you love doing. Not many people are lucky enough to have that in their working lives.

The final game of the season, the final game of my League career, was at home to Barnsley. We had beaten them 1-0 at Oakwell earlier in the season in a match played in deep snow. Their centre half, Mick McCarthy, had kicked lumps out of me for the whole game. Mick wasn't my favourite man at the time, although he's a friend now, and became a player at Manchester City for a while. I asked him if he got pleasure out of kicking an old man, and he just laughed. In that last match he was doing exactly the same. Eventually I'd had enough, so I turned round and gave him a whack with a big tackle and got sent off. It was a good tackle all right, and by the time the referee came over I was already on my way. I knew what was coming.

That was my last moment in professional football – being sent off for making sure that a tough defender didn't think he could mess around with a supposedly lily-livered winger. In the dressing room I threw my boots away. I wouldn't need them again.

17

ESCAPE TO VICTORY

The phone call came out of the blue. 'Hey, Miguel, how are you?' It was Bobby Moore on the line, and that was what he called me. 'Fancy being a film star?' he said.

My immediate thought was that he meant a football documentary or something like that.

'No, I'm serious,' said Bobby. 'This is a proper film, with Michael Caine and Sylvester Stallone. If you're in London next week we can meet some of the people connected with the movie.'

I think Bobby rang me because we got on very well; we always had done since the day we'd met in the Upton Park dressing room as teenagers after a reserve match between West Ham and Swindon more than twenty years earlier. We were similar in so many ways. We enjoyed the fun in life, we had a similar outlook on the world and we were both very smart and tidy men, traits I'd inherited from my father. When I'd played for England we'd roomed together and we'd stay at each other's houses if he was coming north or I was going south. Both our wives were called Tina, and they got on, too.

It was the spring of 1980 and I'd been retired as a professional footballer for nearly a year, and trying hard to make a go of my business. It didn't take me five seconds to wonder about being a film star. Of course, I'd meet Bobby in London and see what the deal was. It didn't take long when we met the film company to realise this was a serious venture. They talked about the actors: Caine, Stallone and others like Daniel Massey, Tim Piggott-Smith and Maurice Roeves. Then there were the other footballers: Pelé, Ossie Ardiles, Paul Van Himst and many of the Ipswich Town side like Russell Osman and John Wark. There was also the fact that we'd spend six weeks on location in Budapest. And then there was the money: the basic was good and there was spending money on top, and it was far more than I'd ever earned as a footballer. It was Bobby's request that I play a part in the film that was going to be called *Escape to Victory* about a football match in a Second World War prisoner-of-war camp. And they agreed.

The closest thing I'd ever done to acting was taking part in the Manchester City club pantomime at Christmas for a few years. Francis Lee and I enjoyed that, and we'd go up on the stage for three nights and have a bit of fun. But I had always admired the world of showbiz and I had a few very good friends from the stage. I didn't think I'd feel out of place being thrown into a film set.

Bobby, of course, was a fantastic footballer, one of the greatest England has ever produced. He was the captain who won the World Cup in 1966 and he lived and played with such dignity. When I came into the England set-up he was the one who made me feel welcome. He insisted on rooming with me and helped me overcome my apprehension. Our room was a sight. While so many others had clothes strewn all over the place, we had all our shirts folded immaculately in the cupboards. Bobby was astute, too. I remember that he would always say at a function to put any empty wine bottles under the table and never to loosen your tie. His logic was that it would never look as if we'd had a few drinks even when it was a racing certainty that we had. The way you appear in public is vitally important, he would always say. Even when he played football he always looked just so. West Ham were the smartest team on the field; they looked as if they were going out for a photocall rather than a match.

He didn't get nasty on the field either. I remember playing at Upton Park against Frank Lampard senior in front of the old Chicken Run Terrace where the dockers used to stand. They were giving me terrible stick and in one tackle I caught Lampard and zipped him down the front of his leg. It wasn't intentional but there was blood everywhere. The crowd were going mad and Bobby ran over and stood there, and just said: 'Mike?'

It was the look on his face that went straight through me, the look that said, 'What did you do that for?'

'Sorry, Bob,' I said, and sorry wasn't a word I ever used on a football field. 'It wasn't intentional.' I felt guilty as hell.

When Bobby finished his career he had a go at management like myself, but it didn't work out. I don't know that it suited him. As well as linking up in the shirt-making business, we had a firm together with a businessman called Maurice Keston that did leather goods. Bobby also set up coaching schools round the country and he'd come and stay with us if he was in the Manchester area. We'd have a few gin and tonics in the Spread Eagle across the road from the house, but it didn't help him sleep much. He was the worst sleeper in the world. One night he climbed into bed with our Nicholas, who was about fourteen at the time. Bobby had done the same on England tours with me.

Not long before we flew out to Budapest to do the film I'd been with Bobby at a charity match on the island of Gotland off the coast of Sweden. I only had a short journey from Manchester but Bobby was coming all the way from a coaching school he'd set up in the townships of Soweto in South Africa. To get to Gotland you had to take a ferry from the mainland and I always remember waiting for a few hours for Bobby's arrival. When he came he was immaculate as ever, and you'd think he'd just come out of the window display at Burton's Menswear.

We were talking and I said: 'You look a bit bouncy; what's the matter with you?'

'I tell you what, Miguel,' he said. 'I've just fallen in love.'

'What do you mean?'

'I've just met a girl on this flight. She was an air hostess but she wasn't working, she was on standby. I've been with her for eight hours on this plane and we talked the whole way. It's totally different. I feel I'm in love. I've just met someone special.'

That was the day he met his second wife, Stephanie. We played the game, flew back to London, and it was on my mind all the time. Bobby had this spring in his step. I kept it to myself. I knew Tina Moore and the children very well, and I had never known anything at all like that with Bobby. He was still like a schoolboy all through the filming, and I'm sure he was in contact with Stephanie then. He really had fallen deeply in love and the split with Tina came soon afterwards.

Bobby had a close circle of friends, and I was privileged to be one of them. That's how I came to be friends with Jimmy Tarbuck and Kenny Lynch. They would stay at the house if they were doing a show in Manchester. Jimmy has never changed in all the years I've known him and he is the ultimate professional in everything he does. Every year I played football there was always a telegram from Jimmy before the first match saying, 'Have a good season.'

One time Jimmy was working at the Palace Theatre. I had been out of action with a broken leg and had only just come out of plaster. I was still limping a little but I hadn't been out of the house socially for six weeks so I decided to go and see Jimmy's show. We had some champagne in the dressing room afterwards and we went on to the Brown Bull in Salford where George Best and I used to drink. It was about half past twelve and I was stood at the bar having one drink. The fella at the bar said: 'Can you pass this drink over?' and as I did it a man put a white label on the drink. It had number 1 on it.

'What's that?' I asked.

'It's exhibit one. You're being done for drinking after time,' said the policeman.

'This isn't even my drink, and I've only had one,' I said.

Jimmy was beside himself laughing as he watched all this. It was a police raid and I was the only one with a glass in my hand. I hadn't touched a drink for six weeks, but the headlines were all about football star Mike Summerbee being caught drinking after hours. I was fined and had a criminal record for that. Thanks, Jimmy.

I first met Kenny Lynch when we played a testimonial match at Crystal Palace that had been organised by the comedian Bob 'The Cat' Bevan. Alan Ball and Bobby Moore were playing, too, and we were getting paid £40 to turn out. I wasn't married at the time and I said to Lynchy: 'Why can't you get me one of these blonde model girls to go out with, like the ones you see in the magazines?'

'Leave it to me,' he said,

After the game Bobby had somewhere else to go and Kenny drove him and me to the King's Road in his little black Mini. He was going out with Pat Booth at the time, who was a very famous model. She was the love of his life, and we met up with her and another stunning model whose stage name was Diago. They were so attractive, wearing very short miniskirts, and I was gobsmacked. We went to Danny La Rue's club and he was on with Ronnie Corbett. They were doing a double act. We walked in with these two models, and Johnny Haynes and the Fulham lads were there and they clocked me, which was absolutely fine by me. It was a super night out, but nothing happened. There was no aftermath.

I suppose football and showbiz have always collided because the stars of both are paid entertainers. You're up on a stage showing off, and you know the critics will knock you down if you don't perform well. I have always believed in the words of American President Theodore Roosevelt: 'The credit belongs to the man who is actually in the arena, whose face is marred by dust and sweat and blood.'

There was certainly a lot of dust when Bobby Moore and I went off to be film stars. But first of all, curiously, there was a football conversation. The night before we flew out to Hungary, we had a few drinks at a club in Berkeley Square in London. The Irish midfielder Liam Brady was there, too, and he was in the throes of leaving Arsenal for Juventus. He said he wasn't sure whether to go to Juventus or not, and he sat with us asking what we thought. Both of us encouraged him to go. Liam was a fantastic player and we thought the Italian style of football would suit him. We'd all had a few drinks, and he went ahead and signed and his career continued to flourish.

We flew out on a Hungarian Airlines flight to Budapest and we sat at the very back of the plane. We thought we'd try out the Hungarian wine, and it was like drinking Domestos. We'd had a few when the plane landed, and outside we could see a real hubbub with lots of camera crews there.

'We're going to be movie stars,' said Bobby, 'so let's start out in the right way.' We had a few drinks inside us.

By the time we got off the plane, of course, everyone had gone. We found out that Pelé, one of our co-stars, had been in first class on the same plane and they had all come to film the arrival of the Brazilian football legend, the greatest player in the history of the game.

There was nobody there to meet us. We had to buy visas just to get into Hungary – twenty dollars each. We found a taxi and were introduced to the world of Hungarian F1 drivers. Every cabbie was completely mad in Budapest; every journey was a race, even if it was only a hundred yards. The view was great at the hotel, where they put the pair of us on the top floor in adjoining suites. This was more like being a film star.

The weather was fantastic; it was blazing hot and Bobby said languidly: 'Gin and tonic?'

'I think so.'

We called down for gin and tonics, ice and lemon, and we slurped them back, and then some more. The gentleman who brought the gin and tonics had to wear a glove on his hand by the time we left because he had frostbite from all the ice he delivered to us.

And then we threw ourselves into a new world. I was playing

the part of Syd Harmer, an outside right in the POW team. There were no acting lessons; you just had to look and learn. At six o'clock the next morning they took us out to the set where the POW camp had been mocked up, thirty miles out of the city. They cut our hair short and gave us our uniforms and a script. We went into one of the POW huts that doubled as a cafeteria for the movie in the mornings. Michael Caine was there. He already knew Bobby. The German actor Max von Sydow was there, and Stallone and Pelé. They had no idea who I was at the start, and I wondered if I would be out of my depth.

I think the director, John Huston, who had made classic films like *The Maltese Falcon*, *Key Largo* and *The African Queen*, was also wondering about the footballers. I had the impression he thought we would be temperamental because we were well known in England, that we'd behave like the film stars we weren't. But that wasn't the case. We always turned up on time and we threw ourselves into the film-making process. We enjoyed John's company and he enjoyed ours. He was a wonderful man, and nobody minded that his beautiful eighteen-year-old daughter Allegra was with him.

The greatest influence on me during the film, though, was Michael Caine. He is such a normal person; there is no side at all to him. He helped us all, and I think the actors appreciated that we had no side with them. A key part of the movie is the challenge to play a football match between the Germans and the POWs. Once that challenge had been accepted by Michael's character, we all had to do individual things to prove we should be in the team. My character, Syd, had to dive into the goalmouth and head a cross into the goal.

Michael came into the compound and I had to say a few words to him. He told me he would turn a certain way so that it kept us both on camera, and the tricks of the trade were wonderful to see. We used to go and watch him when he was filming and see how easily he did it, stepping the right way as the camera rolled past and not looking at the camera.

Michael socialised with us as well. One night we went out for a meal with him and Pelé. My wife Tina and Tina Moore had also come out for a week and we had a lovely night out in a restaurant. I always remember that Sylvester Stallone had kept himself to himself before that, and he was sitting in a corner with his agent that evening. He wasn't aloof but maybe he found it difficult coming into the football world that he knew nothing about. Michael called him over and he sat next to Tina, and suddenly Stallone was a part of the group.

Another night we were out was at the end of election day in Hungary – one of those elections where there is only one man to vote for. You weren't allowed to drink on that particular day and the table was full of Coca-Cola and orange juice. Michael Caine had gone to Paris but was flying back and had been told about this. He walked into the restaurant that evening wearing a combat jacket and trousers, and it looked as if he'd put on three stone. Of course, his pockets were full of miniatures, and so we spirited them under the table and were able to get pissed again. There was a lot of camaraderie; in many ways it was just like a sports dressing room with all kinds of team-mates.

One thing I noticed was that all the actors wanted to be footballers – and all the footballers wanted to be actors. We used to have a match every morning, just messing around, and the actors would join in. But I think we learned more from them, because anyone can kick a football. Some great friendships developed, too. A few months after we came back Tim Piggott-Smith was doing a play in Manchester with Helen Mirren and

Bob Hoskins. I went to see him and we ended up talking sport all night because Bob loved football.

For the locals in Hungary, however, there was only one real star of *Escape to Victory*. And that wasn't Stallone or Michael Caine. It was Pelé. So many people came just to see him, and he is one of the nicest people you will ever meet. The respect that Pelé and Bobby Moore had for each other was unbelievable, and their friendship spread through the rest of the camp, to myself and the Ipswich lads and Ossie Ardiles. We didn't call him Pelé, though. To us he was Eddie, because that's the name he likes. His real name is Edison Arantes do Nascimento.

The greatest difficulty in making *Escape to Victory* was trying to make the football action seem authentic. The secret of this was that they put great actors in and then great footballers to make it look a proper game. There were three phases: the build-up to the game, the game itself, and the escape. In the build-up the actors were teaching us how to make it look as if we were acting. Michael Caine insisted we all had some words to say, and that pleased us.

Critics laughed at the idea of it making the football look credible; they thought it couldn't be done. Our job was to make it believable, and the football scenes did take a long time. John Huston came up and said he needed help with the football action, so Bobby and me helped with the choreography of the game. For the tackling you will see that it's just the bottom part of the body on film. Then the physical contact is the top part. Then we worked on the scoring of the goals.

People always ask about the Pelé overhead-kick goal. But he only did it once. That was all he needed – one go.

There were cameras all round the stadium. If you were picking your nose it would be caught on film somewhere. There seemed to be more cameras than you get at the Olympic Games. So, when the Pelé goal was scored every camera picked it up. In the film it comes in three incidents. The first is where Ossie Ardiles flicks the ball up and you can see his eye on the ball all the way. Next there is Russell Osman, who takes the move on and again you see his eye on the ball the whole way. Finally, there is Pelé's overhead kick, with his eye completely on the ball.

Eye on the ball is what makes the football work. And it's a lesson to any young kids who want to play the game. The footballers don't come over as pieces of plastic, and it has become a favourite film for many people.

The filming was fun, and at the end Bobby and I threw a party in our hotel suites. John Huston came with his secretary and Allegra and we filled the bath with ice and put beer and wine in it to chill. John hadn't mixed during the six weeks of production, but now he was fascinating to talk to. He gave us directors' chairs with our names on to take home.

It had been a wonderful summer being Syd Harmer the POW, but it wasn't the real world and, subconsciously, I did get a bit carried away with the idea of being a film star. I came home full of myself and Tina has told me it was the nearest she ever came to wanting a divorce. She soon brought me down to earth when I was home, and reminded me we had two young children who hadn't seen their father for six weeks and needed some attention.

As a footballer I had never been bothered about newspaper reports. I knew the sportswriters and I knew what they thought before it was in the paper. But I was apprehensive about the reviews for *Escape to Victory*. I wanted them to be good. Some critics who didn't know football didn't give it particularly good reviews. But it did brilliantly at the box office and the general public loved it. It was a proper film, an adventure story with proper football. Nearly three decades on it is still being shown on television here in Britain and all over the world. I remember one day I was walking on a beach in Portugal and people started shouting to me: 'Hey, Syd, how are you, Syd?' I knew then it was a cult film.

Some lovely friendships developed from the movie. We still see Russell Osman quite often, and Tina and I went to see Michael Caine and his wife, Shakira, in Los Angeles. I have made a lot of shirts for Michael since, and not long ago there was a magazine article in which he mentioned that he wears Summerbee shirts.

I've seen Pelé a few times since as well. A couple of years ago he was in Manchester signing photos at a shop in the city. I went to see him and the place was packed with people, among them Manchester United and England full-back Gary Neville. I saw Pelé and shouted 'Eddie' and he turned round and it was just as if we were still on the set of *Escape to Victory*.

Another person I saw again was Allegra Huston. She came over for a function in London connected with the film, and Tina and I invited her to stay with us for a couple of days because she had some other business in the north. When she arrived there was some music playing in the house and she said: 'Come on, Mike, dance like you did in Budapest.' That was it. The axe fell straight away and Tina sent her packing.

We laugh about that now, and Bobby Moore found the story especially funny. I had so much in my life to thank Bobby for, and being a film star for a summer was just a small part of that. It wasn't long after the film was made that he was divorced from Tina and Stephanie became his second wife. They were so much in love and she was with Bobby right through to the end when he died so tragically young in 1993.

I always remember the last time I saw Bobby. He was working for radio, doing football commentaries, and he was up in Manchester staying at the Copthorne Hotel. I hadn't seen him for a little while and he rang to say that we should meet for lunch. We went to an Italian on Deansgate and I couldn't believe how he looked. He was so gaunt and emaciated. It was Bobby, but it wasn't Bobby. The Italian waiters there were football daft but they didn't recognise Bobby Moore. I saw a little bit of blood come down his nostril and I wiped it off. It brings tears to my eyes now thinking about it.

I walked with Bobby back to his car. Stephanie was driving and they followed me out of Manchester to the Copthorne, and I always remember she pulled the car up beside mine as they turned into the hotel and Bobby waved weakly. It was the last time I saw him.

It was obvious then that Bobby didn't have long to live but it was still a huge shock when he died. Tina and I went to the memorial service at Westminster Abbey and Jimmy Tarbuck spoke movingly. I looked up to the top of the Abbey and I'm sure I saw a white dove flying around high above us. I said to Tina: 'It's probably Mooro checking up that we're all dressed right and proper.'

I think of that when I think of Bobby. I think of the famous picture that Harry Redknapp has on the wall of his office, the photo of Pelé and Bobby exchanging shirts after the England vs Brazil match in the 1970 World Cup in Mexico. It is one of the great moments of sport.

And I think about when we were on tour with England in the summer of 1968 in Italy. We roomed together in Florence before that battle of a match against Yugoslavia in the European Nations Cup semi-final. Then we drove down to Rome, with Bobby at the wheel. Before we started he pulled out a portable record player and said: 'Right, you, hold this, and we'll put Sinatra on.' I spent four hours holding this thing and listening to Frank Sinatra while Bobby was in seventh heaven driving in the sunshine.

You won't get anyone like Bobby Moore again. He was a wonderful man. He was a proper fella.

18

FULL CIRCLE

Among all the mementos of a life in football – the faded telegrams, the England international call-up letters, the photos, the caps and the Christmas card from Sir Alf Ramsey – I found a newspaper article from forty years ago. I told the interviewer: 'One day I will write a book about my life in football. I'll warn youngsters not to get carried away. I'll tell them that football is not all glamour.'

There was no glamour in my final football match. There was a little glory maybe, but definitely no glamour.

My professional career had been over for eighteen months when I agreed to help out an old friend and shirt customer, Bob Murphy, who was the manager of non-League club Mossley. A couple of months earlier Bob had said he was short of players: would I turn out in an emergency if required? I said I would, not thinking he would ever be that desperate. Well, Mossley reached the first round of the FA Cup, and there was Bob on the phone asking me to play against Crewe Alexandra. He registered me as an official footballer once more – and I had to find some boots again.

Michael Crawford was staying with us at the time and he took Tina along to watch the game; I told him not to start laughing or anything. I had to do the best I could. I got to the ground at about half past twelve, far earlier than I ever used to in my career, but I knew I had to warm up gradually. When you haven't played for a long while you only have to stop and you won't be able to move again. I was out on the pitch, gently preparing for more than an hour, and then came into the changing room.

'I'm going to make you the substitute, Mike,' said Murphy as I went in.

'You can't do that,' I said, and it wasn't ego talking. 'You have to put me on now, otherwise I won't be able to play at all. It's taken me an hour to warm up on the pitch. Put me on from the start.'

As he was doing the team talk I kept walking round all the time, kept moving. I couldn't afford to stand still for a moment. Then it was out for the game and a fella in the crowd shouted: 'What are you doing out on the pitch, you bastard, Summerbee?'

'How does five hundred quid sound?' I said to shut him up. Actually, I was playing for nothing. For the first time in my life I was an amateur.

Tony Waddington was the manager of Crewe, and I had been a thorn in his side for years when he was famously the boss of Stoke City. I had always played well against them. He saw me coming out in a Mossley strip. 'Oh no,' he said, and he put his head in his hands. 'I thought I'd got rid of you.'

The Mossley pitch had a slope and we played downhill in the

first half. I stayed out on the wing and just clipped a few balls in when I had the chance and jogged back to help keep the team shape. At half-time it was 0-0 and I had to keep moving through the break. I could already feel that stiffness creeping into my body. In the second half we were going up the slope and to me it felt like climbing Mount Kilimanjaro. Behind me at full-back was a young lad who kept overtaking me and I was really struggling, sucking air up my rear end. I could hardly move, but I kept going. A minute from time there was a corner on the left-hand side. I went over and took it, and the centre forward, who was a big fella, rose up and, boom, the ball was in the back of the net. 1-0. We'd won the game and there were all the wide-eyed celebrations you get when a minnow wins an FA Cup tie against a League side.

The Mossley chairman came in afterwards and looked straight over at me and said: 'You'll be playing in the next round.'

'No I won't,' was my instant reply. 'I can't. It will take me three weeks just to walk properly again.'

And I'll tell you how stiff I was. I dropped the soap in the shower and I couldn't even bend down to get it. One of the young lads had to pick it up for me. Outside, I found Tina and Michael and they were laughing their heads off. That was it. Finished. Job done. It was the very last match I played. The boots went in the skip again.

By that time my son Nicholas was beginning to develop as a young footballer, and it was my turn to start watching. He never really saw me play, certainly not in my prime at Manchester City. He came once with a friend to watch me play for Stockport, but his love of the game sprang, I suppose, from playing in the garden at home and listening to me talking about what I did for a living – and how I did it. He loved playing in the garden with his mates from the estate across the road. Looking back, I wish Nicholas had gone to the state comprehensive with them rather than the private school we thought would be good for him. It turned out to be a waste of money. All he wanted to do was play football.

The man who got Nicholas playing in teams was George Batey, who had been a prisoner of war and who was our gardener at that time. He was a lovely man and became a great friend. George would take Nicholas to his matches for Poynton Boys on a Saturday because I was away with football. He used to watch him play and said how well Nicholas was doing. I could see he had ability when he was playing on the back lawn, bending balls round trees and different things, and eventually I had an opportunity to watch my son.

All the parents were there and he did play very well. I was quiet to start with, but soon joined in shouting 'advice' from the touchlines, as parents are so keen to do. I was trying to help him, but actually it was hindering him, and I'm absolutely certain today that parents should not interfere in any way when they are watching their children play junior football. It does no good, and can be very harmful. A few times referees came over and told me to shut up, and they were right to do so.

Nicholas definitely had talent and he went for a trial at Manchester City, but they didn't think he was any good. Then there was another week's trial at Norwich City, but they didn't sign him either, and he was crying when he rang through to say he'd been rejected. My heart was torn because I hated my son being upset and disappointed. But I also knew this was the tough reality of professional football that hits thousands and thousands of youngsters each year who are lured by the glamorous image of the game.

What Nicholas needed, as all lads do, was a break. And his opportunity came, just like mine, from Cecil Green, the director of Swindon who had turned up on my doorstep a quarter of a century earlier. He was still at the club and had heard about Nicholas and invited him down for a trial match. Lou Macari was the manager of Swindon then, and when Nicholas played exceptionally well that day Lou decided to take him on YTS terms. The last time I'd seen Lou he was chasing me round the field in that League Cup match with Stockport, and he wasn't a man doing sentimental favours for an old buddy.

The reality of a young player's life shocked Tina when the day arrived to take Nicholas to Swindon. He was staying in digs with some of the other lads and she cried all the way home, having seen the spartan accommodation he would be living in. I thought it was just fine. The thing was, I don't think Tina expected to have a son who would be a footballer. She hadn't encouraged it, and neither had I.

I was open-minded when Nicholas set his heart on being a player, but I knew how difficult the game was and I was apprehensive. Looking back, I do wonder whether he became a footballer because he thought it was something he had to do, and I wonder what my father would have said if he'd been alive. He had endured a career in the reserves and the game had broken his heart.

It was a feeling of going full circle to have three generations of Summerbees become professional footballers, and the thought made me feel proud. There may be some other families who have done that, but I don't know of them.

Of course I went to watch Nicholas as often as I could. He did well in the youth side and eventually broke into the first team under Lou's guidance. He had seen something in Nicholas and encouraged it, and it was the same with his successor, Ossie Ardiles, my old pal from *Escape to Victory*. The best manager for Nicholas, though, was Glenn Hoddle, who picked him regularly as he inspired the Swindon side to play some fantastic passing football. I loved watching the Swindon team when Glenn was in charge, and he was the one who really opened a career up for Nicholas.

Fate had another twist in store when Nicholas followed my path again with a transfer to Manchester City. He wasn't as aggressive as me, but he was reasonably quick, long-striding like myself, and he was as good a crosser of the ball as you will see. That's not just a father's opinion. People in football will tell you that.

The transfer was nothing to do with me. Francis Lee had taken over as City chairman and Brian Horton was the manager. He was the one who wanted Nicholas to come to Maine Road. At the time I was so chuffed, but it didn't take long for me to realise it was a difficult route to take for everyone concerned. I certainly found it hard to watch, particularly as I had rejoined the club in a meet and greet role on match days.

That gave me access to everywhere in the ground, and one day I was stood in the tunnel behind Brian Horton and I was shouting to my son, 'C'mon, Nick, c'mon, Nick' and such like.

Brian turned round and the look on his face said he was not best pleased. I didn't understand that I wasn't in a position to do that. If I'd been sat in the stand it would still have been foolish, but it wouldn't have been so bad. From the tunnel it wasn't too good at all. Francis pulled me in on the Monday and said that Horton wanted to see me. I went in and the manager of Manchester City gave me a proper bollocking – just like the old days.

'You don't do that,' said Brian. 'I don't want to see you down there in any situation. Let your son get on with the game.' He was totally right. The bollocking was well deserved and it has stuck in my mind to this day.

I am quite a volatile person and I remember one situation when I was walking round Maine Road talking to people in the corporate boxes.

This fella said to me: 'Your son's crap. He is the worst player on the field.'

I walked past him without a word, but a little later I passed by again and he said: 'You heard what I said? Your son's crap.'

So I grabbed him by the scruff of the neck and put him against the wall. 'You can have whatever opinion you want,' I told him, 'but just keep it to yourself. Or pull me aside quietly and tell me one to one. But don't say it out loud in front of people. It's not the easiest thing in the world, you know. It's not easy for me. It's even less easy for Nicholas. It's a difficult thing.'

Of course, he wrote to Francis Lee complaining about my behaviour. Francis called me in and showed me the letter and said: 'That sounds like you, Mike.'

'It was me,' I said.

'Well, be careful what you say and do,' said Francis, delivering another mild bollocking to Summerbee.

There is always a minority in football who are stupid, and one of the problems was the general expectancy that Nicholas would be just like me. But every player is different, and he wasn't another aggressive Summerbee. I thought Nicholas did very well at two clubs where I had played before, but the comparison was always there to be dealt with. I never really knew what went through his mind, but I was glad when Nicholas was transferred to Sunderland. I don't like to say it, but I felt a huge sigh of relief when that happened.

A couple of months later he was back at Maine Road, playing for Sunderland against City. When I'd come back to the club as a Burnley player the crowd had given me a standing ovation. That day they treated Nicholas as the world's biggest villain, and it was a day I'll never forget. I had arranged a box at the back of the Kippax where my mother, Dulcie, could watch the game with Tina and our daughter, Rachel. My mum only saw me play once, and this was the only time she watched Nicholas. It did nothing to alter her negative view of the world of professional football, the world that had crushed her husband, my father, George.

Nicholas was given some real stick that day by the City fans. I told him to play up to it, tap his pocket to show he was being well paid at Sunderland, and to put the ball outside the quadrant at corner kicks, which is always a provocation. It was the kind of trick I got up to in matches where the crowd was all against me, like the derby clashes at Old Trafford. It wasn't in Nick's character so much, but he played well that day and, of course, he made the only goal of the game, crossing for Kevin Phillips to score. The abuse he received was unbelievable and it shook Tina and me up badly. My mother was boiling with anger at the way her grandson had been treated. I would have picked a fight with every one of the fans abusing my son, but what good would it have done?

I've never had a rose-tinted view of football, for all the charms of the game. That day was maybe the bleakest of all.

The move to Sunderland was good for Nicholas to begin with. He was playing as a winger with two top strikers in the centre to find, Phillips and Niall Quinn, and for a couple of seasons he had a really good time and won an England B international cap. But when Peter Reid wanted to transfer him out to Bradford, and Nicholas refused the move, his love for the game soured. He was hurt badly when he was effectively pushed out of Sunderland, and these days he's running a car company and doesn't have much to do with the game.

I was very proud of the way he played and the success he had, but I also know it was very difficult for him to follow a famous father. I never had the problem of being compared to my father, who'd been a player but not so well known and who had died by the time I became a professional.

Nicholas was always the sensitive one of our children, and Rachel the tough one. Her love was horses from the moment I took her next door to see a foal that was for sale. It was called Nancy and, of course, I had to buy it. Horses became a huge part of her life, and she still rides now. Rachel has also given us four lovely grandchildren, including young Samuel Summerbee, a lively ten-year-old with a natural love of sport. He is daft for football and cricket and golf, and has ability at all three.

Sometimes I go to watch him play, and when referees don't turn up I end up being the ref. In those games there are no free-kicks. All the kids are diving around today in youth matches because they imitate the professionals they see on television. So, I just say get on with the game when I'm the ref. You get parents screaming from the touchlines and I go over and tell them to be quiet or I'll send them away from the ground. That's a strange position for me to be in, but it has to be done.

Samuel likes cricket, too, and we went to watch the England Under-19s playing Sri Lanka. When it rained I went to see my very good friend Paul Beck, who has a box at Old Trafford, and we found Andrew Flintoff and Steve Harmison there, too. Samuel was chuffed to bits, and then went out to watch them practise in the nets.

Who knows if Samuel will grow up to be the fourth generation of Summerbees to play professional football? But it is wonderful fun to share his boyish enthusiasm for games like football and cricket.

Cricket has always been a passion of mine. There are photos in the scrapbook of George Best and myself going out to bat together in some match or other in the mid-1960s. And I'm privileged now to count Andrew Flintoff as a good friend after getting to know him through helping with his benefit year run by Paul Beck. He's a Preston lad, just like me. Andrew calls me 'Leg' (pronounced 'Ledge'), short for Legend, which is very nice.

His attitude to life reminds me so much of another dear friend from the past, Colin Milburn, the dynamic England Test batsman, who often stayed at our house and was virtually in residence some of the time. We met just after the car accident in which he lost an eye and which ended his cricketing career. Our friendship grew very strong. He was very close to Nicholas as well, and the kids found it fascinating when he took his glass eye out and put it on the kitchen table. He was the greatest company and a wonderful man.

When Colin was staying I used to go to work and he'd come down late wearing my dressing gown. He'd be having breakfast with Tina and the window cleaner looked in and thought, 'Aye, aye what's going on here?' The same day Colin took Tina up for lunch in the hills and the same chap was cleaning the windows there and he came to warn me about what he'd seen. I've never laughed so much in my life.

Sadly, Colin Milburn died far too young. He had a heart attack on the stairs at a hotel and his life couldn't be saved. I went to the funeral in Burnopfield, in his native North East, and we walked through the village alongside the casket. Then I helped to carry it into the church along with Ian Botham, Matty Roseberry from Durham County Cricket Club and his son Michael. His death affected me very deeply and I was appalled that only one person from the Lord's Taverners cricket charity came up for the funeral service. That was Sir Colin Cowdrey. I had become a Taverner through Colin Milburn, who did so much work all round the country raising money for the charity. The next day I sent my resignation to them because I thought their poor turnout was a disgrace.

I have been lucky with friendships in my life but the older you become the more services you attend to remember people who have gone too soon. I recall going to the memorial service for John Thaw, who had become a pal after I made the shirts for *The Sweeney*. He was a Manchester man from Longsight, and he would look me up whenever he was in town and we'd have a bit of fun together. Instead of leaving flowers, the guests at John's service were asked to leave something for his grand-children. I left the words of Theodore Roosevelt printed at the front of this book. They apply equally, I think, to sportsmen and actors, and I hope it meant something to them.

I have always admired people who are prepared to put themselves in the firing line to try to get things done – and especially the right thing. Aside from our close friendship, that's why I was so keen to be involved when Francis Lee fought his takeover battle to rescue the fortunes of Manchester City in the 1990s. I supported him, as others did, and Francis did a great job in stabilising the club and controlling the debts. He built a new stand at Maine Road in place of the Kippax and, as I've said, was instrumental in the club eventually moving to the City of Manchester Stadium. It was a huge legacy to the club, never mind the legacy he left as one of the club's greatest players.

He also gave me the opportunity to return to City in a hospitality role that I enjoy very much. It gives me, in a small way, a chance to put something back into the club and the game I love. As well as working on match days I also run the City Luncheon Club, which seems to work quite well. I make a contribution where I can, visiting a supporter who's in hospital or speaking for the club on television.

It gives me a chance to have a rapport with the fans just as I used to as a player. I was particularly honoured when I was inducted into the Manchester City Hall of Fame, alongside players like Billy Meredith and Bert Trautmann and many of the trophy-winning team I played with. So many supporters were at the ceremony and I thought that when they put me in the Hall of Fame they were putting in all the fans as well – because it was the supporters' encouragement that did so much to make me a success. It is the supporters who make a football club. Chairmen come and go. Players come and go. But the club and the supporters are always there whatever the fortunes of the team on the field. Yes, it can be difficult being in the same town as Manchester United but there have been times when City have been the premier club in Manchester, and I know that will be the case again.

I think the Hall of Fame is a wonderful idea because it's vital to celebrate the past as well as the present. I'm an avid reader of history books; it's my main hobby along with gardening these days. I neglected my school life as a boy, and as a footballer you just concentrate on the game. My education has come from reading and I believe you never stop learning. I love my gardening, too. It's quiet and peaceful and it gives me time to think. I suppose it's age coming on.

The friend I think about most of all is George Best. Never a day goes by that he doesn't come into mind. Our friendship remained so strong through all the years, even when I saw him only intermittently when he went to live in London. Whenever we met the old rapport was instantly there. I remember one day when Tina and I were invited to Michael Caine's party at Langham's in London. Many people were there, Bobby Moore, Michael Douglas, Jimmy Tarbuck among them. I walked in and George was waiting for me at the bar. He was on his own and he was out of it; he'd had too much to drink. We spoke a little and I knew he was in trouble. None of us wanted George to be seen staggering around, and the photographers were all lined up outside looking for a humiliating picture. So I called a taxi and then a group of us, including Bobby Moore, Michael Caine and the sportswriter Hugh McIllvanney, stood round him in a circle and walked George out to the cab and avoided an embarrassing situation.

It was a long way from the Kardomah coffee shop. And yet in a way it seemed like no time at all that I was talking quietly at the bar with George.

There was another time, too, when I was in London with Tina and the word was that George had gone missing. We decided to go to Tramps nightclub, because I had a funny feeling he'd be there. It was early evening and George was sat there at the bar on his own. He looked so lonely, and he was a lonely man. It was a sad evening and we talked together for a long time. It's all right people going on about all the girls and women in his life. There were always people around but they drifted away. George Best was essentially a lonely man. He spent more time on his own than he did with other people.

The last time I was with George we were doing a Sky TV documentary before a City vs United derby game. They filmed us talking at a restaurant and then we went to Maine Road. The gates were closed and we spoke outside and when they had finished filming he was taken home in a car. I never saw him again.

No, I didn't go to the hospital in the final few days of his life when he was in intensive care and the whole world seemed to be watching. Bobby Charlton and Denis Law did go, but I didn't want to see George that way. I couldn't bear that.

When he died – and I know this may sound strange – I felt a sense of relief. I was relieved he wasn't going to suffer any more, that he wouldn't have the problems, and that people wouldn't be hanging on to him. George Best was the first superstar of football, and so much of his trouble was in not being able to handle the situation he was in. I felt that when he left Manchester United he was a lost soul.

I went to the funeral in Belfast, and it showed to me the greatness of George. The most amazing thing was to see hundreds of thousands of people on the streets in the pouring rain, people from both Protestant and Catholic communities. He brought his divided country together, and no other person could have done that. What also sticks in my mind is the magnificence of the Stormont building and sitting inside for an hour waiting for the service. I could hear the piper playing outside in the distance and the most poignant moment for me was the coffin being brought inside as the piper played. It did me in. I was in a daze from then on. I had my private thoughts, but really I was just overwhelmed with sadness.

I have been back three times to Belfast since and each time I have been out to the cemetery to lay some flowers. There are always people paying their respects, and always flowers. It cheers my heart, because I know what a great man George Best was and how much I have to thank him for.

He helped me at a vital time in my young life, and I have so many others to thank as well. My mother and brother were so important in the way they encouraged me, and so was my father in the short time I knew him. I wouldn't have gone anywhere in football if it weren't for the sharp eye of Cecil Green and the belief of Bert Head in playing young lads at Swindon. I have to thank Joe Mercer for picking up the phone, and Malcolm Allison for being the greatest coach there ever was, and Johnny Crossan for helping me settle in Manchester, and all the team-mates who made City a champion football club, and so many people like Bobby Moore for their unwavering friendship and support. I can't name them all but they know who they are.

And, of course, I have to thank Tina. She's been my rock, and she's the one who encouraged me to ransack my memories for this book. She knows better than anyone that the life of a professional footballer is not all about glamour, but she has seen the joy and fun it can bring, too.

I threw my heart and soul into the game and was lucky enough to enjoy years of success with Manchester City. Football is hard-wired into my brain, and I discovered a little while ago just how true that is. I was in the garden weeding one Saturday afternoon in May 2008 when I suddenly thought to myself: 'I've just scored.' It was the strangest feeling, and I looked at my watch and the time was ten past three.

The day was the fortieth anniversary of the match when we

became League champions in 1968 by winning at Newcastle. And I scored the first goal at exactly ten past three that Saturday afternoon.

INDEX